BEHIND THE BENCH

Behind the Bench

Coaches Talk About
Life in the NHL

Dick Irvin

M&S

Canadian Cataloguing in Publication Data

Irvin, Dick, 1932-

Behind the bench: coaches talk about life in the NHL

Includes index.
ISBN 0-7710-4359-7 bd.
ISBN 0-7710-4360-0 pbk.

1. Hockey – Coaches – Anecdotes. 2. Hockey – Canada –
History. 3. National Hockey League – Anecdotes. I. Title.

GV848.5.A1I7 1993   796.962'092'2   C93-094393-7

The publishers acknowledge the support of the Canada
Council and the Ontario Arts Council
for their publishing program.

Typesetting by M&S

The support of the Government of Ontario through the Ministry of
Culture, Tourism and Recreation is acknowledged.

Printed and bound in Canada on acid-free paper

McClelland & Stewart Inc.
The Canadian Publishers
481 University Avenue
Toronto, Ontario
M5G 2E9

2 3 4 5   98 97 96 95 94

This book is dedicated to the memory of my father,
who coached in the National Hockey League
for twenty-six years
and loved every minute of it.

To get men to do what they don't want to do in order to achieve what they want to achieve. That's what coaching is all about.

TOM LANDRY

Being behind the bench is the best job in hockey.

PUNCH IMLACH

CONTENTS

Introduction

Early in the 1992–93 National Hockey League season Mike Keenan parted company with the Chicago Blackhawks. Keenan had been the team's coach and general manager for the previous four seasons, and had coached the Philadelphia Flyers for four years before moving to Chicago. Shortly after coaching the Blackhawks to the 1992 Stanley Cup finals, Keenan relinquished the coaching part of his duties. A few months later, he was fired.

In announcing that Mike Keenan was no longer with his organization, Blackhawks owner Bill Wirtz said, "Mike continued to express second thoughts about giving up coaching, which is a very difficult thing . . . a terrible transition." Keenan readily admitted that was true.

This is a book about hockey coaches, written mainly in their words. Most of the men I interviewed have coached or are still coaching in the NHL. Those who are currently behind the bench are exactly where they want to be. Most of those who are not there any more wish they still were. Like Mike Keenan, they have at times had difficulty coming to terms with a life in which they are not coaching a hockey team.

The financial rewards for NHL coaches are rapidly improving while, at the same time, the average length of time any one coach stays in any one job is rapidly shrinking. The "coaches are hired to be fired" cliché has never been more accurate. There were twenty-two teams in the NHL when the 1991–92 season began. A season and a half later, twelve of them had changed coaches. Yet most hockey coaches can't think of anything they'd rather do. Roger Neilson has been the head coach of five NHL teams, a record if you want to call it that. I talked with Roger ten days after he had been fired by his fifth team, the New York Rangers, and asked him, "Do you still want to coach?" His immediate reply was, "Of course I do."

This is not a book of X's and O's. You won't learn how Pat Quinn plans a power play, or how Brian Sutter studies opposing teams on video. But you will learn much about the life of a coach in the NHL, the highs, the lows, the hirings and the firings. You will read some very candid recollections of personal moments between coaches and players that took place behind the closed doors of dressing rooms and coaches' offices. Scotty Bowman and Glen Sather described to me what it's like to coach superstars and super teams. Pat Burns, Al MacNeil, and Jacques Demers talked about the pitfalls facing men who dare to take on the precarious task of coaching the Canadiens in the hockey-mad city of Montreal. I chatted with Al Arbour shortly before he coached his fifteen-hundredth game in the NHL, and to Dave King shortly before he coached his seventeenth. Storytellers like Harry Neale and Emile Francis told me stories. Milt Schmidt and Howie

Meeker took me back to the six-team NHL. Don Cherry regaled me with tales about Don Cherry.

During the time I was researching and writing this book I was working as a member of the radio and television broadcast team covering the Montreal Canadiens. This enabled me to conduct interviews from one end of the ever-expanding NHL map to the other. I sat with Bob Gainey at 8:30 in the morning in his office at the Sports Center in Bloomington, Minnesota, where his team, once called the North Stars, used to play. Thanks to the NHL's continuing urge to expand, there were interviews in Tampa, Florida, and San Francisco, California. No matter where I was, the message came through very clearly that the life of a coach isn't an easy one, yet they all love to coach. I had a great time listening to them tell me why. Now, it's your turn.

Happy New Year, Harry

HARRY NEALE

Early in the 1992–93 NHL season, Hockey Night in Canada *was telecasting a Montreal–Philadelphia game at the Philadelphia Spectrum. The broadcast crew of Bob Cole, Harry Neale, and myself was idly watching the pre-game warm-up when Harry turned to me and said, "Why don't you write another book? Write one about coaches. You'll get lots of stories, like the one about how I got fired in Detroit."*

Harry then told me of a drive he took through the tunnel connecting Windsor, Ontario, to Detroit, Michigan. When Harry drove into the tunnel in the early hours of December 30, 1985, he was the coach of the Detroit Red Wings. By the time he came out of the tunnel, he was pretty sure he wasn't.

HARRY NEALE

I had been hired by Detroit the previous summer. Jimmy Devellano [Jimmy D.] was the general manager. We had a terrible start and now that I think back I should have recognized some signs there. By Christmas we had won only eight games. Before we left on a trip to New York, Jimmy D. talked to me during a practice at the Joe Louis Arena and said, "Harry, we need a miracle." I thought he was referring to the game against the Rangers but it turned out he had got the word from the owner, Mike Ilitch. He meant a miracle to turn things around right away or I was gone.

We went to New York and lost real bad, 10–2 or 10–3, something like that. We chartered a plane home and landed in Windsor about 1:30 in the morning. Danny Belisle, my assistant coach, lived near me in Troy, Michigan, and I was giving him a ride home. We hadn't heard any of the other scores that night so we turned on the car radio. We were still waiting for the scores when we got to customs. We cleared customs and were heading for the tunnel when the scores came on.

After the guy gave the scores he announced, "The Red Wings are holding a press conference tomorrow morning at 10:00, at which time it is expected that Harry Neale, coach of the team –" Then we went into the tunnel, and the radio faded right away. We couldn't hear it in the tunnel. The tunnel is about a mile long, and I'm stepping on it to try and catch the end of the story. But by the time we come out the other end the sports is finished and they're playing music. I'm thinking, oh my God, it must be all over.

My wife's mum and dad and sister were staying with us for Christmas and New Year's and I figured there would be bedlam when I got home. So I got home and there are no lights on, no messages, everybody is asleep. I figured I wouldn't wake anyone up and tell them what I think is going on, but at the same time I couldn't believe nobody from the Red Wings had called my home.

I went to bed, tried to sleep, and woke up around 7:30. I asked my wife if anyone had called and she said no. But it wasn't long before the phone rang. It was Varton Kupelian, one of the beat writers. He said he had the information that I was going to be let go. I told him I didn't know anything about it. That was the only call I took.

Then I phoned Jimmy D. He's a guy who goes to bed at 2:00 or 3:00 and gets up at 10:00 or 11:00. After a lot of years of scouting that's the timetable he was on. So I got him out of bed and I said, "What in hell is going on?" He said, "Harry, I was going to tell you when I got to work today."

I said, "Jimmy, let me get this straight. You were going to let me come down to the Joe Louis Arena for practice, get out of my car, come into the rink, and have five cameras and ten radio stations and every newspaper within fifty miles waiting for me, and you were going to tell me in front of them? What in hell kind of an operation is this? If I'm fired, I'm fired."

He says, "Well, Mr. Ilitch is going to make a change."

I said, "I'm a big boy, Jimmy. I can take the news, but I don't like getting it this way. And my contract, I want you to know, says in the last line that I get all my money if I get fired before this contract ends, whether or not I take another job, and I'm free to look for one."

He started to stutter and I told him I didn't want to argue about it. So he said, "Okay, that's the way it is."

I must say Detroit was very nice to me and paid me right to the end. They paid my pension and let me keep the company car. If you can be nice to someone after you've fired him, the Ilitches were.

Don Wallace was the executive producer of *Hockey Night*

in Canada, who I had got to know over the years. I had always told him I would call him for a job when I got fired and that's what I did.

There was a game the next night in Montreal between the Canadiens and the Russians and he told me to go to Montreal and they would use me on the show. When I got there, there wasn't a spot for me in the booth during the game but Wallace told me I would be used during the intermissions. You interviewed me right in the seats at the Forum, and I guess you could say that was my start as a television commentator. Later that season I did some games for TSN, and then in the playoffs I worked with you for the seven-game Montreal–Hartford series. I've been in the booth ever since.

When I interviewed Harry so soon after his harrowing ride through the Windsor–Detroit tunnel he looked, felt, and sounded just awful. But that was to be expected. The lopsided loss he suffered in New York was likely the last game he would ever coach. It was the end to a career behind the bench that had taken Harry Neale to a lot of places and provided him with a lot of stories.

HARRY NEALE

When I was ten years old, my father, who worked for Imperial Oil, was transferred from Sarnia to Toronto. I was devastated when he told us we were leaving Sarnia. I said I would go if we could get a house next to Maple Leaf Gardens. I thought that would solve the problem, but of course that wasn't exactly the spot he wanted us to live in.

When I was playing bantam or midget hockey I went down to the Gardens with a couple of buddies to see about getting a job selling programs at Leafs games. We figured that way we could get in for nothing. My dad was dead against it so he was happy when I didn't take the job, although I could have. But when we found out we had to do the selling in the hallways and couldn't watch the games – well, I never took the job.

A few years later I played for the Marlboro Juniors and we won the Memorial Cup. I played with some real good players . . . Al MacNeil, Bobby Baun, Carl Brewer, Bob Pulford.

The Leafs wanted to sign me so I went to their training camp at Sudbury. I couldn't make the team, which didn't surprise me, and they sent me to Rochester, which was co-sponsored by Toronto and Montreal.

They were training at the Montreal Forum and I sat in the dressing room beside Fred Shero. He was a career minor-leaguer, about thirty-five years old, but he looked like two hundred to a nineteen-year-old kid. He asked me a few questions and when I told him I had a year to go at the University of Toronto to get a degree, he dropped his skate. True story. He dropped his skate and says, "You have two years of college, only one to go to get a degree, and you're here at this fucking training camp? Are you out of your mind trying to play minor-league hockey?" And he turned away from me, picked up his skate, and put it on. What he said hit home.

We were staying at the Queen's Hotel and I was rooming with a guy named Wally Clune. We were getting $3.50 a day and they gave us a free breakfast. Clune was trying to save money because he had to leave his job while the training camp was on. And I'm thinking, what the hell is this all about anyway? Here's a guy trying to save money on $3.50 a day and I want to have the same kind of a life?

So I went back to Toronto and, when I was taking a bus to the airport, they had my bag on top of the bus and the strap broke and my suitcase fell off and my stuff was all over the highway. There I was trying to get my clothes out of a ditch, still not sure I was doing the right thing, but I went back and finished school. And my folks were sure happy to see that.

After college I got a teaching job in Hamilton and started coaching high-school hockey. I was going to summer school so I could keep moving up to another pay category, and as far as I was concerned I was going to be a high-school teacher the rest of my life. A friend of mine, Glen Sonmor, went to coach at Ohio State and after a year there he took a job at the University of Minnesota. He called me and said I should apply for the Ohio State job, which I did, and I got it. I thought it would be great to go to a place where you practise every day on your own rink and where I could get my Master's if I wanted to come back and keep teaching high school. I never did get it, but I came within a course or two. I coached at Ohio State four years. That was when Woody Hayes was the famous football coach there. He was completely autocratic, a hugely powerful guy. I knew him, but he would never have much to do with a lowly hockey coach.

I went back to Hamilton to coach junior hockey and that's when Sonmor came into the picture again. He was hired by the Minnesota Fighting Saints of the WHA to be coach and general manager and he called me to come down as his assistant. So I went there. Glen found out he couldn't do everything because he was travelling a lot trying to recruit NHL players. So I took over as coach about thirty games into the season.

I was there three and a half years. We folded about halfway through the fourth year. We had some good players – Dave Keon, Johnny McKenzie, Paul Holmgren, John Garrett, Mike Walton. But the last season we were there was tough. We went eight weeks only getting paid once. We kept playing, but when the next pay period came up and we didn't get paid, the team folded. During that time we had the best record in the league, and the guys were playing for nothing. The only time the team went bad was on the 1st and the 15th of the month. If we were playing on those dates and realized we weren't getting paid, we lost.

We had to make sure the players had their meal money. We figured they might play without their salary but there was no chance they would play without meal money. One time we're set to go on a trip to Houston and Baltimore and we needed $300 per man for the trip, about $6,000 total. Sonmor and I are in the airport and the plane is due to take off and we didn't have the money and we're scared. The players were all on the plane and just when they're getting ready to close the gate here comes the owner of the team, Wayne Belisle, running through the airport like O.J. Simpson in those commercials. When he gets about twenty feet from us he throws a bag at me, I catch it, and we get on the plane. He had been to see all his friends and into bars around St. Paul getting the money and there was $6,000 cash in the bag.

Now we're sitting on the plane sorting it all out. We've got twenty envelopes and twenty piles of money. The pilot comes back and asks us what we're doing. A lady had spoken to the stewardess and told her she thought two bankrobbers were on the plane counting their money. Luckily the pilot knew something about hockey. If he didn't we would have been getting off in Houston and getting arrested.

A couple of weeks after the Fighting Saints folded I got a call from Ron Ryan, who owned the New England Whalers. He said he was going to make a coaching change and would I take the job. I said I would and flew into Hartford the next day. The coach they fired was Don Blackburn, a good friend of mine and very popular with the players. So I go into the dressing room for my first talk with the team and the guys are looking at me as if to say, "What the fuck are you doing here anyway?" I remember thinking, what am I going to say? It was one of those times when you know your first comments could kill you if you are wrong. So I said, "Gentlemen, I did not cause Don Blackburn to lose his job. You did. I'm just the guy they hired to pick up the pieces. I'm no miracle man, but I'll tell you this: If you're gonna sulk and pout and be pissed off at me because Blackburn lost his job because you guys didn't play well, then we're going nowhere. You guys who haven't been playing now have a hell of a chance to play. You guys who have played should start feeling good about yourselves. We're going to practise today and we're going to start trials. It's your decision, not mine. I'm here for the rest of the year. That much I know."

So we go out to practise and I drove the shit out of those guys until they could hardly stand up. We made the playoffs with a game to go in the season. We played Cleveland in the first round. They had Gerry Cheevers in goal, and we beat them. Then we played Indianapolis. They had picked up Keon and a couple of others who had played for Minnesota. The series went seven games and we won the final game 6–0 and now the players think I'm really something. I mean, they're thanking me for coming in and coaching. A month before, they were ready to kill me for taking Blackie's job. We played Houston in the next round and that series went seven. We lost the final game 2–0, with an empty-net goal. But they're so excited in Hartford, even though we lost, they had a parade for us. I was embarrassed about the parade but I told the players we all had to go. Overall they had a terrible season, but it was very dramatic at the finish.

The next season we lost in the first round to Quebec. That was the last year for the WHA team in Houston where the Howes had been playing, Gordie and his two sons. By then we had some good players, including Keon and McKenzie who had played for me in Minnesota. In the summer I got a call from Jack Kelly, our general manager, who tells me we got the Howes. I'm thrilled about Gordie Howe. He's been my idol and here I am about to coach the guy and I can't believe it. But I'm thinking all summer, Gordie is fifty years old so don't tell me I'm gonna be the guy to have to tell him he can't play any more. I mean, it could happen. Well, thank God it wasn't me. It was Blackie, who had his job back two years later, after the Hartford team joined the NHL.

So now I'm coaching Gordie and his two sons, Mark and Marty. When it came to handling the boys Gordie never said a thing. I didn't play Marty much, and one night after a game Colleen Howe was waiting for me. When I came out she said, "When I come to a game I come to see my *three* boys play."

I had to give Gordie shit one night. We had played Cincinnati New Year's Eve and Robbie Ftorek had hit Marty Howe and broken his jaw. Now we were playing Cincinnati the last weekend of the season and we had our spot all clinched. Our goalies were going for the award for least goals against and we're leading 3–2 when Gordie goes after Ftorek and gives him the stick right in the mouth and gets five minutes. We hung on to win, but when the game was over I waited for Gordie to come off the ice. I told Gordie, "You can't take a penalty like that under these circumstances." Gordie listened, and then looked at me and said, "You're right, Harry. But I can't let Ftorek get away with what he did to Marty New Year's Eve." This is three months later. He got my message, and I got his.

There was one time when I put a curfew on the team on the road and I went around checking all the hotel rooms. Gordie roomed by himself. That was the one concession he asked for. When I got to his room I see the light under the door and hear the TV on and I think, how can I check the room of a fifty-year-old guy who's the greatest hockey player that ever lived? So I didn't.

Gordie is an early riser like I am, so the next morning when I come down he's already sitting in the lobby doing his crossword puzzle. He called me over and said, "Didn't we have a curfew last night?" I told him yes, so he said, "Well, nobody checked my room. I usually go to sleep right after the news but I stayed up last night until midnight. Aren't I on this team?" He was offended because I hadn't treated him like the other players.

While I was coaching him he was going for his 1,000th professional goal. All kinds of media showed up, *Sports Illustrated* included, and they had to follow us around for a while because it took him eight or nine games to get from 999 to 1,000. During that time we're in Edmonton. The game before he had been hit on the right hand. His left one had arthritis and he used to keep it in a bucket of warm water on the bench between shifts. In Edmonton he asked me to give him a little extra warning before his line was due on the ice. I look down and he's sitting like this: he's got his gloves on his lap, he's got his left hand in a bucket of warm water because of his arthritis, and he's got his right hand in a big bucket of ice because it's been injured. He thought the right hand was broken, but he wanted to keep playing, and he did, for five or six more games before he got the goal. He scored it in Birmingham against John Garrett. It was a crime to see him get a milestone goal like that in Birmingham, Alabama. After he got the goal he had his hand X-rayed and, sure enough, there was a small crack in there. If Mark or Marty had a hangnail Gordie would tell them they shouldn't be playing. But when he had a broken hand he wouldn't stop playing, or practising, until he got the goal.

There was one moment in a game in Quebec I'll never forget. A beautiful story. Gordie was on right wing and Mark on left wing. Gordie got the puck on the far side and Mark is heading up the ice, right in front of our bench. Both Mark and Marty always called him "Gordie" when they were around the team. I don't know if they had an agreement, but that's what they called him, always Gordie. Anyway, on this rush, when Gordie's got the puck, one of their defencemen fell down. Mark yelled for the puck. I guess he was excited because he yelled "Dad!" instead of "Gordie" and some of the guys on the bench could hear it. Gordie looks up and hits him with a perfect pass, right on the tape. Mark goes in and scores, puts it right over the goalie's shoulder into the top corner. Keon and McKenzie were sitting on the bench. They heard it, and maybe only a few others in the rink heard it, and they saw "Dad" put the pass right onto his son's stick. I never thought guys like Keon and McKenzie were all that sentimental but they had a look on their faces that showed they knew they had seen a moment that very few people experience. They talked about it and it was lovely, just lovely.

The Vancouver Canucks hired Harry away from Hartford during the summer of 1978 and he was with them for seven years as coach and/or general manager. The highlight during that time was when they reached the Stanley Cup finals against the New York Islanders in 1982. Harry was coach that season with Roger Neilson as his assistant. But when the Canucks made their surprising surge in the playoffs, Roger, not Harry, was behind the bench.

HARRY NEALE

It was late in the season and we were on a road trip and playing very well. We won in Boston, Philly, Montreal, and Quebec. It was the most amazing road trip we had ever made. Feelings were pretty high when we played in Montreal and Quebec because Tiger Williams made some awful comments about the French.

In Quebec there was no glass or anything around the bench. There was this loud-mouthed guy who was there when I was in the WHA and still there when they got in the NHL, and I used to think I'd like to walk up and paste that mouthy son of a bitch. He was about eight seats and one aisle away from our bench.

Wilf Paiement and Tiger collided along the glass down from our bench. Paiement had Tiger pinned and wouldn't let him get away and they were yappin' it up pretty good. This fan I'm talking about came down from his seat, reached over the glass, which was quite low, and swings at Tiger. So I raced off the bench, climbed over two or three people, and I was going to drill this guy. I threw the punch but it stopped about a foot short of him. I had miscalculated and I nearly threw my shoulder out. Some of our guys came off the bench with me, Curt Fraser and Doug Halward are two I remember, and while nothing much happened it could have been a real nasty scene.

Naturally I'm called on the carpet and John Zeigler comes out to Vancouver for the hearing. We look at the tape and it shows that my punch didn't land. But it also shows that the guy didn't hit Tiger like I thought he did. He missed him and grabbed the glass. So Zeigler says, "Harry, I'm going to suspend you. You'll find out tomorrow for how long. But you can tell your buddies who have the same job that the next time a coach leaves his bench he'll get twice as many games as you're going to get."

There's five games left in the season and we're hot as a pistol. So I thought that he would give me three games, or maybe four. So what happens? He suspends me for eight games! That means I won't even be able to start the playoffs. So Roger goes behind the bench, and he only loses one of the last five league games and then we beat Calgary in the first round best-of-five, three straight. I'm at every practice and I go through all the planning with Roger, but I can't go on the ice or behind the bench.

Now with the team doing so good I'm thinking, why the hell would I want to go behind the bench? I knew that on June 1st I was going to become general manager because Jake Milford was retiring. If I hadn't known that, I would have gone back as coach. So Roger stayed on as coach and the rest is history. He always tells me that if he hadn't been coaching we never would have made the finals. I tell him if I had been coaching we would have won the finals. That's something nobody knows, but that's how it happened.

The sad part of that story is that I had to fire Roger a year and a half later. That was a real gut-wrencher. In that season and a half we were twenty-five games under .500 and of course we're trying to live up to when we made the finals. But that year, 1982, we didn't play anyone in the playoffs with more points than we had, until the Islanders. That will never happen again.

We were in Edmonton and played a helluva game but lost 7–5. That was as good as we could do against the Oilers most nights. Our owner, Mr. Griffiths, had spoken to me, and I was supposed to fire Roger if we lost that game. I get back to my hotel room and the message light is on and I know who it is. So I phoned Mr. Griffiths, who is in Hawaii, and he says, "Have you told Roger yet?" I said I hadn't and explained to him that we had played really well that night. "Harry," he said, "there is no need for two people to lose their jobs over this one decision." So I hung up, went next door, and fired Roger. It was awful.

Looking back I have to say Tiger Williams was the most unforgettable character I ever coached. In one way he was my most coachable player and in another he was absolutely incorrigible.

One night a rookie defenceman, and I can't remember exactly who it was, had made the same bad mistake two or three times in the first period. Between periods I came down on him pretty hard, telling him that if you want to play in this league you can't make the same mistake three times in one period. As I walked away the guy mumbled something. I turned around and Tiger was grabbing him by the sweater-front and yelling at the guy, "That's his job. He has to give you shit when you make a mistake. Don't get mad at him. Get mad at yourself." And I thought, here's a guy who's solving a problem for his coach.

But then there were other times, like when he would refuse to come off the ice during a power play, things like that. Three or four times a year I used to have to say to Tiger in front of all the players, "Tiger, if you want to coach this team that's fine by me. But you'll have to clear it with Mr. Griffiths because he owns us. Go on upstairs and get the job if you can, but right now you're having a helluva time playing on this team, never mind coaching it." But you know what Tiger could do? He could forget that and be your most determined, faithful player. I really admired that quality. There are some guys that if you bruise them they're bruised for the rest of the time you coach them, and that's a dangerous thing.

Scotty Bowman was the toughest coach to go up against once the game started. I often wondered what it would be like to coach a team that had three lines that could score, like he had in his big years in Montreal.

One night in Vancouver it was obvious early in the game that he wanted to play Guy Lafleur against one of our left defencemen, Dave Logan. Dave was a tough kid but a little slow afoot. So all night the chess game went on. Every time he put Lafleur on I took Logan off. I didn't want to tell Dave Logan that. I mean, you don't tell a kid you can't put him on the ice when the best player in hockey is against him. So it got late in the game and it's 2–2. Either I forgot, or else Scotty made a quick change on the fly, and what do you think happens? Lafleur gets a one-on-one rush against Logan, flies by him like he's going ninety miles an hour, and scores, and they win the game. I thought, that son of a bitch Bowman, he waited fifty-five minutes to get what he wanted. He used to do things like that all the time.

When it came time for me to get fired in Vancouver it was quite a story. I go to the office about two weeks before the draft. It's early in the morning and the phone rings and it's Al Eagleson calling from Toronto. He says, "Is anyone else there?" I told him I was alone. He says, "Hang up, go home, and call me. You're gone."

I lived about ten minutes away and it's around 9:00 when I get home. My wife looks at me and says, "You're gone." I say, "Yep," and phone Eagleson. He says, "They're bringing Dave King in tomorrow to announce him as the new general manager and coach of the Canucks. The reason I know is because I'm the head of Hockey Canada and that's who King has been working for. But my board doesn't want to release him. The Canucks will pay you twenty-five per cent of what's left on your contract." I had two years left so I said, "Come on, Al. Tell them if I don't get another job I want all of it. If I do I want sixty per cent." And that's what I got. King never did get permission to go to Vancouver and I ended up in Detroit to start the next season.

And that's where Harry worked, for a little while, until he took that fateful early morning ride through the tunnel between Windsor and Detroit and turned on his car radio to get the hockey scores.

2

Some Old-Timers

Who was the first hockey coach?

Who was the first to stand in the middle of a dressing room, in civilian clothes, surrounded by a group of men wearing hockey uniforms, and give a pre-game pep talk?

"All right, boys. Remember that big Jones on their defence is pretty slow. Use your speed on him. Go to the outside. Billy, I want you to forecheck deep when you're killing a penalty. Rush the puck carrier. Don't let them get started. Joe, I want you to play the point on the power play, right side. And don't be afraid to yell if you're open and they're not getting the puck to you. Okay, guys. Everyone up . . . have a good warm-up . . . let's go!"

Or words to that effect.

In the earliest days of competition for the Stanley Cup, teams almost always had a playing-coach or playing-manager. Only twice in the first twenty-five years of com-

petition, 1902 and 1912, was the winning coach a non-play-
ing member of the team.

In 1902 the winning team was from the Montreal Amateur Athletic Association. The team picture includes eighteen men: ten players and eight civilians. In the latter group
is C. McKerron, identified as "coach."

The photo of the 1912 champion Quebec Bulldogs is
much more crowded with twenty-four people, but only
nine are players. Included in the hefty group of civilian
hangers-on is coach C. Nolan.

The last playing-coach of a Stanley Cup-winning team
was Frank Patrick, with the Vancouver Millionaires, in
1915. The next year, when the Montreal Canadiens won
their first Stanley Cup, the team was owned, managed, and
coached by George Kennedy.

Through the years many teams in amateur and minor-pro
hockey have employed playing-coaches. There were a few in
the NHL, the last being Charlie Burns, who worked forty-
four games as the playing-coach of the Minnesota North
Stars in the 1969–70 season. Today the league does not
allow playing-coaches.

In 1917, shortly after the National Hockey League came
into being, the Toronto Arenas appointed Charlie Querrie as
their coach. Querrie posted a set of rules on his team's
dressing-room wall which showed that, even then, coaches
meant business. The rules read, in part:

1. First and foremost, do not forget that I am running this
   club.
2. You are being paid to give your best services to the club.
   Condition depends a lot on how you behave off the ice.
3. It does not require bravery to hit another man over the
   head with a stick. If you want to fight, go over to France.

4. *You will not be fined for doing the best you can. You will be punished for indifferent work or carelessness.*

5. *Do not think you are putting something over on the manager when you do anything you should not. You are being paid to play hockey and be a good fellow.*

6. *I am an easy boss if you do your share. If you do not want to be on the square and play hockey, turn in your uniform and go do some other work.*

Charlie Querrie was no doubt a character, as were several other coaches who are in the category of "old-timers." If you consider those who earned reputations for winning, and for longevity, in the period up to the 1967 expansion of the NHL, a few names stand out. The list includes Lester Patrick, Art Ross, Jack Adams, Hap Day, my father, Dick Irvin, Sr., and Toe Blake.

Lester Patrick and Art Ross were true pioneers of the game. Patrick played hockey for McGill University at the turn of the century and was on the Montreal Wanderers team that won the Stanley Cup in 1906. Forty years later he was still trying to win the Stanley Cup as general manager of the New York Rangers. The Wanderers won again in 1907. Patrick wasn't on that team but Art Ross was. Forty-seven years later Ross was in the last of his thirty years as general manager of the Boston Bruins.

The longevity recorded by some of the old-timers baffles those who have similar jobs today. Jack Adams was hired by Detroit starting in 1927–28, the second year of the franchise. He was general manager of the team for the next thirty-six years, as well as coach through the first twenty-one.

Art Ross was general manager of the Boston Bruins from the time they began play, in 1924, until 1945. He also coached at various times, for a total of sixteen years.

Lester Patrick was coach and general manager of the New York Rangers when they joined the NHL in 1926. He held both jobs for thirteen years, and was general manager for an additional six, to 1946.

Adams, Ross, and Patrick served as general managers of their teams for an accumulated total of eighty-five years. My father, Dick Irvin, Sr., (I'll drop the "Sr." from now on) was a coach in the NHL for twenty-six consecutive seasons, beginning in 1930–31. Al Arbour has broken his record for games coached and Scotty Bowman for career wins. But I think it's safe to say nobody will ever again coach for that many uninterrupted seasons.

One result of their being in the same jobs for so long was that they often didn't get along too well. Add Major Conn Smythe, the belligerent owner and overall boss of the Toronto Maple Leafs, and you had a small group of unique and stubborn individuals, each of whom would battle tooth and nail to get whatever edge he could for his team. They clashed during games as coaches and, in the cases of Patrick, Ross, and Adams, clashed in the boardrooms too, as general managers. Feuds were legendary, and real.

Conn Smythe described Art Ross as the most devious man he had ever met. After a particularly acrimonious meeting of league general managers, Ross and Red Dutton, then the GM of the New York Americans, got into a fistfight. Ross came out second-best with a broken nose, a broken cheekbone, and a few lost teeth. Smythe was quick to tell the press what happened, adding that "it couldn't have happened to a more deserving recipient."

Ross, however, could give as good as he got. Following a Maple Leafs visit to the Boston Garden in the late 1930s, the Bruins received a complaint from a Catholic priest about the bad language he had been subjected to from Smythe, who had been watching the game from a nearby seat. Ross

seized the opportunity to make a big case out of it, bombard-
ing NHL President Frank Calder with letters insisting that
Smythe was ruining the image of hockey with such
behaviour and should be thrown out of the game. The bot-
tom line was, Ross meant it.

In Smythe's words, "Every place Ross and I met, we
fought." That pretty well told the story of their stormy rela-
tionship, until Smythe, a military man to the core, learned
that Ross's two sons had joined the RCAF during World War
Two. A short time later the two men happened to meet when
Ross was accompanied by one of his boys. Smythe had a
picture taken with them and the Smythe–Ross relationship
was much warmer from then on.

Lester Patrick and my father had a violent argument
behind the players' benches during a game in Toronto in the
late 1930s, going nose to nose and nearly coming to blows.
At that time there were several hockey pictures hanging on
the walls at Madison Square Garden, the Rangers' home
rink, and my father was in a few of them. When Patrick
returned home after the confrontation in Toronto, he had all
the pictures of my father taken down.

For almost twenty years, the two men barely spoke to
each other, until, after Patrick had retired, they ran into
each other in the early 1950s at a baseball game in Montreal
and spent the afternoon swapping stories and memories. By
the time the last batter was retired they were the best of
friends. When my father died in 1957, one of the first tele-
grams of condolence my mother received was a beautiful
one from Lester Patrick. In it he suggested various passages
in the Bible from which she could gain strength.

Lester Patrick was the man who sold New York on the
game of hockey. Conn Smythe had originally been hired to
run the fledgling Rangers but was fired shortly before the
season began. Patrick took his place, and his flamboyant

personality was exactly what the game needed to make inroads into that very tough market. He was great copy for the New York press and soon celebrities from Broadway and the movies were showing up at Rangers games. Their presence gave hockey a much-needed boost. The same thing started happening in Los Angeles when Wayne Gretzky arrived on the Hollywood scene.

In only their second season the Rangers won the Stanley Cup. The Rangers played the Montreal Maroons in the final series. In the second game the New York goaltender, Lorne Chabot, was hit in the eye with the puck and had to stop playing. With no substitute on hand the players persuaded their forty-four-year-old coach to don the pads. After some mild protesting, and with his usual flair for the dramatic, Patrick turned to the team's trainer, Harry Westerby, and said, "Harry, I'm going in goal."

To prove all of this is the stuff legends are made of, Patrick allowed the Maroons just one goal, the Rangers won the game, and then went on to win the Stanley Cup. Another sidelight is that after Patrick became the Rangers' goaltender, Odie Cleghorn became their coach behind the bench. Cleghorn, who had been coaching in Pittsburgh, was a spectator at the game and was pressed into service. Yes, things were much different then.

In Eric Whitehead's book **The Patricks: Hockey's Royal Family,** *Frank Boucher, a star centre for the Rangers who took over from Patrick as the team's coach in 1939, gave this description of Lester behind the bench during a game: "He struck dramatic poses and was in turn kind, sarcastic, pompous, vain, callous, and contrite, depending on the circumstances. He had both a compelling arrogance and a winning humility."*

(Fast forward to the present as you read that. Do the names Scotty Bowman and Mike Keenan come to mind?)

Lester Patrick himself once offered this as his philosophy of coaching:

> *It's very simple. I look for the leaders, and let them lead. I give my last instructions in the dressing room just before the game, then I sit and let them think about whatever they like. I see some of the players just sitting there placidly, thinking about nothing much and worrying about less. Then I look at Bill Cook, one of my stars, who has already made his mark. Is he at ease? Not on your life. He's a bundle of nerves, just aching for the game to start to break the tension.*
>
> *The placid player can be depended upon for a safe, dependable game, but not for the inspired kind of hockey needed to win championships. I need the Bill Cooks. The other players, when it comes right down to the crunch, will follow the Bill Cooks. Then I just tag along, and enjoy it.*

The name "Patrick" is linked with the phrase "Hockey's Royal Family." Counting that one appearance as a goalie in a Ranger uniform, Lester played for, managed, and coached the team. His two sons, Muzz and Lynn, did exactly the same thing.

In the next generation of Patricks, Craig Patrick, Lynn's son, played for five NHL teams, though never for the Rangers. However, he joined the team in later years as both coach and general manager. In 1991 Craig Patrick was general manager of the Stanley Cup-winning Pittsburgh Penguins. That was the first time since 1940, when Lester was general manager of the champion Rangers and his sons Lynn and Muzz were players, that the name Patrick was inscribed on the Stanley Cup.

Since 1966, the Lester Patrick Trophy has been awarded annually to a man who has contributed to the advancement of hockey in the United States. And of course for the past several years the NHL had a Patrick Division, also named in honour of Lester.

In addition to running their teams from behind the bench, many coaches have also held the role of general manager. This entails watching the team's purse-strings – and the old-timers were masters at that task.

Lynn Patrick once told me how he tried to get a raise out of his father. In the previous season Lynn had been the highest scoring left-winger in the league and had been voted to the first All-Star team. Nonetheless, when it came time to talk contract for the next season, Lester firmly refused to give his son any more money. When Lynn pleaded his case, using his point total and All-Star status as ammunition, Lester gruffly told him, "Yeah. But I made sure you had good linemates." A disgruntled son finally had to sign for what his stubborn, cost-conscious father offered, which meant no raise in pay.

Through the thirty years he ran the Boston Bruins, Art Ross had no greater centre-ice player than Milt Schmidt. Along with Eddie Shore, Schmidt was a major reason hockey became big in Boston. He spent sixteen seasons as a player in Boston, won the Hart Trophy, the scoring championship, two Stanley Cups, and was a four-time All-Star. But when he first joined the Bruins in 1936 as an eighteen-year-old rookie out of Kitchener, the future Hall of Famer quickly learned that dealing with Art Ross, the general manager, was no easy task.

MILT SCHMIDT

Ross ran everything. He negotiated all the contracts. I can tell you a story about my first contract. I wanted $500 more and he said the team couldn't afford it. I said, "C'mon. I know you can afford it. I know that you played to sell-out houses last season and your overhead isn't all that bad."

We argued for a while and then I told him I was gonna go back home to Kitchener and play junior hockey. With the money I could get there under the table I would make just about as much as he was offering, and besides, I would be able to be home with my mother.

Ross said, "Sit tight for a minute. I'll go to see our owner, Mr. Adams, and see what he says." So he went out of his office for about five minutes and then came back and told me that Mr. Adams said he couldn't see fit to give me the extra $500. So I grabbed the pen and signed the contract, then got up and started walking out the door. I didn't say anything.

Ross called me back and told me he was going to take $1,500 out of my contract. My contract was for $3,500. This was in 1936. He said he would send the $1,500 home to my parents and that I would be able to live on what was left. He knew that we were a poor family and didn't have very much. He also knew that I probably would have spent it on a new car, or new clothes because what I had on my back was likely all I had. But that was that.

Anyway, on the way out I went by Mr. Adams's office. I can remember it as though it were yesterday. I thought that I would go in there and introduce myself because I had just signed a contract to play for the Boston Bruins, and I would ask him why he wouldn't give me $500 more. His secretary was sitting just inside the door. I introduced myself to her and said, "I've just signed a contract with Mr. Ross and now I would like to meet Mr. Adams." And she said, "I'm sorry. He hasn't come in yet today." That was my first experience with Art Ross. [Laughs]

When it came to coaching the hockey team he was a man of few words. If he ever wanted to say something to somebody between periods, if a guy had done something bad, a real bonehead play, he would give him a look with what he called his "bad eye." He'd come into the dressing room and he'd get out a cigarette. He was a very heavy smoker. He wouldn't say anything for a while, then he would start looking around the room. He'd catch each guy's eye and the players would just sink. They weren't sure who he was looking for, but then he would stop at the player he was after, he'd focus on him for about five or ten seconds, and very slowly bring his hand up and point to the guy's head. "Use it." That's what he meant.

He was a fantastic guy behind the bench during a game, arranging and matching lines. He always had a puck in his hand, and then in later years he got a small part of a hockey stick and wrapped a large piece of tape around it. He always sat down at the end of the bench, and he'd be rapping the boards in front of him with the puck or the stick. Today he would have got a penalty for it. But that's what he would do when he wanted a line change, and brother, you had better be ready once you heard that. If you didn't you were in deep trouble.

He had a good sense of humour. I remember one practice when he was trying to help me with my shot. I guess he thought I should have a harder shot, and he was right. I couldn't break a pane of glass with the puck when I shot it. I fired a few. He watched me for a while then started to laugh. He said, "You're hopeless. I'm going to go work with some-one I can help." [Laughs]

His greatest asset was the fact that he could spot right away where a player should play, with what linemates and against what players on the other team. He knew when a player was getting to the end of his career and how to handle that, when to get rid of him in a trade if possible.

Getting back to salaries again. We didn't make much money and we had to work in the off-season. I worked one summer for Bell Telephone. On my job I would be out on country roads trimming tree branches away from power lines. Ross heard about it and wrote me a letter notifying me that he wasn't paying me a salary to climb trees and get close to power lines, and he wanted me to quit that job immediately. I wasn't capable of writing a decent letter back to him so I got my sister to write one for me. So she did, telling him that if he paid me a half-decent salary for playing hockey I wouldn't have to work in the off-season.

I didn't hear anything more about it until I got to training camp and he got on me right away, told me he didn't want any smart or sarcastic letters again. I told him what was in the letter was the truth. There were very few hockey players in those days spending the summer showing off their muscles on the beach. We had to do something. We had to find work after the season was over.

The men I am putting in the "old-timers" category were great innovators. Art Ross devised a new puck and a new net that became standard in the NHL. He was the first coach to pull his goalie, when he replaced "Tiny" Thompson with an extra attacker in a game against Chicago in the 1931 playoffs. Ross came up with the idea of a guard on the back of skate boots to protect against injury to the Achilles tendon.

Lester Patrick and his brother Frank were similarly involved in changes to the game. In the early 1900s Lester became the first rushing defenceman. He also talked officials into changing the rules to allow goaltenders to fall to the ice to block a shot. The Patricks were at a soccer game in England where the players had numbers on their uniforms, something that hadn't arrived yet in North America. They introduced that idea into hockey, and other sports followed suit. They were the first to propose that blue lines be painted on the ice and were instrumental in the introduction of the basic post-season playoff system, another idea that was to be copied by other sports.

Jack Adams has never been thought of as an innovator in the style of Art Ross and Lester Patrick, but he too made a significant contribution to changing the game. In the spring of 1938 the Red Wings and the Montreal Canadiens played exhibition games in France. Adams saw a demonstration of curling as part of a nightclub act (which means he was likely at a different nightclub in Gay Paree than his players). When the act was finished they flooded the ice for the next show. Adams brought the idea back to the NHL owners, and in a few years between-period ice-flooding was part of the rules of hockey.

Adams ran the Red Wings his way, which to him was the only way, for an amazing stretch of thirty-six years. He was both general manager and coach for the first twenty-one of those years, in which time the Red Wings won three Stanley Cups. The Wings of the Adams era won the Cup four more times after he gave up the coaching job. He was called Jolly Jawn, and he could be that when things were going his way. But he was also a tight-fisted battler from the old school, who crushed most of the ideas about running the team that weren't his. He also played a big part in crushing the first attempts by NHL players to form an association that could air grievances to the owners. In Adams's eyes, if you were lucky enough to play in the NHL you didn't have any griev-ances. Almost all of his players meekly accepted that point of view.

During the ongoing dispute between the NHL, its current players, and some NHL alumni over pension monies, Gordie Howe has often been a spokesman. During the 1992 players' strike Howe recounted some Jack Adams stories to show how he and others of his time were treated. Gordie recalled *asking Adams for a $500 raise when he learned his wife was pregnant with their first child and, as he put it, "almost being thrown out of the Olympia." The Howes later learned that when the baby was born Adams had called to tell Colleen's doctor to keep her and the baby in hospital as long as possible, because he didn't want any distractions at home affecting Gordie's game.*

Max McNab has been involved in pro hockey as a player, coach, and executive for almost fifty years. He played for the Red Wings in the late 1940s, joining the team just after Adams had replaced himself as coach with Tommy Ivan. But there was no doubt in anyone's mind who was really in charge of the Red Wings.

Max McNab

One year when I went to training camp in Sault Ste. Marie with Detroit they had a very good hockey club. Players like Ted Lindsay and Sid Abel were stars and everyone knew that Red Kelly and Gordie Howe were going to be stars. Adams had a meeting with all the players and said, "Every spot on this team is open." [Laughs] I mean, there were six or seven guys in the room who were going to be Hall of Famers. I sort of wondered about that statement.

He wanted everyone in the organization to think they were the best. He worked on the theme, "the sweater, the sweater, the sweater." We played Toronto one year in the playoffs and Jack kept telling us that there wasn't anybody on the Toronto team who deserved to be in the NHL. I was a centre and I knew I wouldn't get to play very much. But if I did I would be up against either Ted Kennedy, Syl Apps, or Max Bentley. But Adams used to do that, he used to stretch the truth a bit too far sometimes.

When I got to Detroit the players used to talk about the

"train tickets" story. Jack was always sending third- and fourth-line players back and forth between Detroit and the farm team in Omaha. He'd come into the room before a game and walk around making small talk. But he'd have train tickets to Omaha sticking out of his pocket so that everyone could see them. It was his way of telling them that they were one bad game away from getting a ticket to the minors.

When I got there Tommy Ivan had taken over as coach, but Jack would be in on every meeting. He used to come into the dressing room and say to nobody in particular, but of course it was meant for guys like me who didn't play very much, "Well, I see where those kids in Omaha won again last night. That's four or five in a row. Somebody down there must be doing something right."

He always kept you thinking. He'd walk up to you all of a sudden and ask, "Who are we playing in our next five games?" And you knew he wanted the right answer. He wanted you to be thinking about hockey all the time.

Adams himself wasn't thinking very clearly during the 1942 Stanley Cup finals, pulling a stunt that very likely cost his team the Stanley Cup. The Red Wings were playing Toronto in the finals and won the first three games. When the fourth game was played in Detroit, everyone thought the Wings would be celebrating when it was over. But Toronto won 4-3. It had been a night when Adams had constantly argued the calls of referee Mel Harwood. When the game ended Adams and several of his players accosted Harwood as he was leaving the ice.

The melee was a wild one. Harwood claimed Adams punched him. NHL President Frank Calder was at the game, agreed with his referee, and promptly suspended Adams for the balance of the series. The Red Wings, playing without their coach, fell victim to what is still the biggest comeback in final-series history as the Maple Leafs swept the next three games to win the Stanley Cup.

The Jack Adams era in Detroit lasted another twenty years. It ended with him suffering the fate that awaits so many in sport who devote their life to one team. He was fired. He died in 1968. Six years later the Red Wings donated the Jack Adams Trophy to the NHL. It is awarded annually to the "Coach of the Year."

The coach whose Toronto Maple Leafs defeated the Adams-less Red Wings in that historic 1942 final was Clarence "Happy" Day, who, a few years later, would become the first man to coach three-straight Stanley Cup winners in the "modern era" of the NHL.

Hap Day had been an excellent defenceman and was captain of the Maple Leafs when they won their first Stanley Cup in 1932. After retiring as a player in 1938, Day did some work as a linesman at Maple Leafs home games and was permanently employed by Conn Smythe at his sand-and-gravel company. ("C. Smythe For Sand" was painted on the side of the company's trucks.) In 1940 Smythe engineered a deal whereby my father, who had been coaching the Maple Leafs for nine years, joined the Montreal Canadiens, making way for Day to become coach of the Maple Leafs. Today's coaches should be so lucky to have their employer line them up with another job before letting them go.

Day was coach in Toronto for nine years. His teams won five Stanley Cups. The 1942 miracle comeback was followed by three straight starting in 1947. Day tried to be his own man but it wasn't easy with Smythe running the show, even during games. Veteran sports-writer Milt Dunnell told me that Smythe installed a phone line between the bench and his seat in the first row of the old green section at Maple Leaf Gardens. On nights when his boss would be particularly busy on the line during a game, Day would dis-connect the phone at his end. After that happened a couple of times Smythe employed kids as runners to carry written messages to his coach.

Day's Leafs staged their miracle comeback in 1942 when Major Smythe was on military service. Smythe was sta-tioned at the Petawawa base, which wasn't that far away from Maple Leaf Gardens. To Smythe's credit, at that time the war effort was his top priority, as much as he loved his Leafs. Although Smythe kept in touch with Day by phone, and obtained leave to attend the deciding seventh game, it was Day's show. After the Leafs' third-straight loss he benched regulars Gordie Drillon (the last Maple Leaf to win the scoring championship) and defenceman Bucko McDonald, replacing them with Don Metz and Ernie Dick-ens. Before the fourth game in Detroit, Day read his team a letter he'd received from a fourteen-year-old fan. In it she insisted she still had faith in the Leafs and was sure they could come back and win the Cup. As the story goes, Day read the letter with such conviction that even the team's hard-boiled veterans were inspired. Whatever, Hap Day's coaching played a major role in what is still hockey's most amazing Stanley Cup comeback.

When Day left coaching he was Smythe's right-hand man in the front office for another eight years. In 1958 he too was eased out by the Major to make room for another hand-picked replacement, in this case Smythe's son Stafford. Smythe didn't have another job waiting for his long-time faithful employee as he had for my father, and Day left the organization a bitter man. He was never involved in hockey again.

Hap Day was the first coach to gain a measure of fame by emphasizing defensive hockey. Opponents would rant and rave over the so-called "clutch and grab hockey" that Day's

*teams employed. But it worked, as the record shows. Howie
Meeker joined the Maple Leafs for the 1946–47 season and
won the Calder Trophy as rookie of the year. Howie remains
a firm admirer of Hap Day, the person and the coach.*

HOWIE MEEKER

He kept me in the league when I first came up, I'll tell you
that. I was twenty-one and had never played any real quality
hockey at all. My strength was handling the puck and there
was no SOB going to put me out of a job. Hap put me with Ted
Kennedy and Vic Lynn and in two weeks he taught me how
to play the game without the puck. He was a very strong disciplinarian, and if you worked for him and gave an honest
effort you knew you were gonna get your next shift.

He knew exactly where every player was every minute of
the day, I swear. I woke up one morning around 9:00 and the
phone was ringing. It was Hap on the phone and he said,
"Where were you last night?" I think I had gone to a movie.
He said, "No you weren't. You were out." Well, I don't drink,
and I hadn't been out. I might have been chasing girls but in
any case my car had been stolen. He had found out where my
car was. He knew about it before I did.

With the schedule the way it was the Monday was usually
our day off. We'd always have a party somewhere and he
knew the drinkers. At the Tuesday morning practice the
five guys that drank the most the night before had to stay out
longer than anyone else. He knew exactly who they were,
every time. [Thirty years later the players on the Montreal
Canadiens were saying the same thing about Scotty
Bowman.]

His main area of discipline, though, was on the ice, especially behind our blue line. He was in total control of the
team when we didn't have the puck. Once we got over the

blue line he was no longer in control. You were. If you did what he wanted, knew what to do behind your own blue line, then you were always in the hockey game. I just think it was the greatest system to play under because he didn't put any pressure on you to score goals. He put pressure on you to keep the puck out of your net.

In my early years there Day was the boss. But after that Smythe was the boss. When he had been away at the war the team became financially successful, and successful on the ice. The first thing Smythe did to re-establish his authority when he got back was to get rid of Frank Selke, who had been running the business side, and Selke ended up with all those great teams in Montreal.

A few years later I think Smythe deliberately set out to get rid of Day. I coached there in '56–57 and Day was supposed to be my boss. But he wasn't the boss. Smythe was there second-guessing him and calling the shots. After that year I was gone, and a year later Hap Day was gone too.

Families of men who have become coaches after having been players will tell you that their man "brings the game home with him" to a far greater degree as a coach. The game is then a full-time obsession. It is especially hard on the families of coaches who are known in the trade as "hard losers." I speak from personal experience here. The two men who coached the Montreal Canadiens in the twenty-eight years between 1940 and 1968, Dick Irvin and Toe Blake, must rank at or near the top when it comes to being a hard loser.

When my father was coaching the Canadiens and they would return home the morning after losing a game on the road, we would wish he'd go directly to the office instead of coming home. But he seldom did and we used to wonder why, because he never spoke to us when he did come home.

Sometimes his brooding silence would last through lunch and dinner to bedtime. He would start to acknowledge our presence the next day, if we were lucky. Car rides home after a loss at the Forum were brutal. Just silence, nothing but silence.

Toe Blake was cut from the same cloth. During five or six of Blake's thirteen years as coach in Montreal, I was the official scorer at games played at the Forum. When the games were over I would deliver the official statistical sheet to both coaches. Visiting coaches who had lost never seemed to be all that upset. Mind you, this was in an era when losing to the Canadiens at the Forum wasn't exactly a rarity. But if the Canadiens lost, I would dread the trip into their dressing room. This was in the era before a horde of TV cameras, radio tape-recorders, and reporters of both sexes filled the room. After a loss on home ice things were quiet. Very quiet.

Blake would be sitting on the edge of a table in the middle of the room, fedora tilted back, eyes blazing and staring at the floor. Everything being said was in whispers. I would thrust the stats sheet at Blake, he'd grab it without a word, and I would take my leave as quickly as possible. There were no thank-yous. Come to think of it, there were few, if any, when his team had won.

Toe's last season as coach was the first of the expanded NHL, 1967–68. At one point the Canadiens were on the West Coast for games in Oakland and Los Angeles. The team lost in Oakland, then took a midnight flight to L.A. The flight was terribly bumpy from start to finish. Several of the passengers, including a few players, became ill. When it was mercifully over and everyone was on the ground waiting for their luggage at the L.A. airport, Blake was standing off by himself, very much into his losing-game personality. Pat Curran of the Montreal Gazette *was covering the team.*

Pat, who isn't a good flyer, bravely decided to engage the coach in some small talk and opened with, "Rough flight, eh, coach?" Blake, eyes riveted on the floor, snarled back, "I wish the fuckin' thing had crashed!"

Toe Blake was one of the NHL's top left-wingers in the 1930's and 1940's. He coached the Canadiens for thirteen years from 1955–56. His team won the Stanley Cup the first five years he was behind the bench, a record that likely will last forever, and three more times after that. Blake's presence was dominant on a team that featured a galaxy of superstars. Veteran hockey writer Red Fisher covered the Canadiens through all of Blake's regime. In my last book, The Habs, *Red described Blake as "a kindly old coach, a gentleman, and a son of a bitch, all in the same sentence."*

Gilles Tremblay played left wing for the Montreal Canadiens for nine seasons. Toe Blake was his coach for the first eight. Today Gilles is a highly respected colour commentator on La Soiree du Hockey, *the French-language counterpart of* Hockey Night in Canada.

GILLES TREMBLAY

When I first came up in 1960 Toe said, "Gilles, I know you can be a good defensive player for me. But if you want to stay in this league you're gonna have to balance your game. You'll have to score some goals. I was a left-winger when I played so you'll have the same job I had. You'll have to believe me and follow my instructions. I'll get on you during practices, I'll give you the whip." He did, but it was for my own good. In my second year I scored thirty-two goals.

He might work on individual players but overall he was fairly easy at practice. He didn't want to burn anyone out. It was a long season and he knew it. He'd been through it as a player, and as a coach. He knew exactly what to do to get the maximum out of each player. Nobody could say he was ever burned out by Toe at the practices.

He couldn't stand to lose. I never saw anything like it. He used to sit there after we lost and the newspapermen would be afraid to ask him questions because he was so stressed, so mad.

The first year of expansion we were in last place at Christmas. The guys were mad that year because so many players who had gone to the new teams were making two or three times what we were making. A guy like Jimmy Roberts, for instance. So we weren't playing very well and Toe was talking about us finishing in first place. Big Jean [Béliveau] said at a meeting one day, "I just hope we're going to make the playoffs." Toe was the only one talking about first place. That's the way he was. That's all he thought about. As it turned out we did finish first, and we won the Stanley Cup.

After their record streak of five straight Stanley Cups, Blake's Canadiens went through the next four years without even getting to the finals. One reason seemed to be a lack of toughness, a problem that was solved to a large degree when John Ferguson arrived in 1963. He was Blake's kind of player, tough, intense, competitive, in many ways a clone of the coach. Fergie went on to become one of the most popular players in Canadiens' history.

JOHN FERGUSON

Toe Blake never forgot a thing. He never forgot who missed an important face-off or a wide-open net. He had a memory like an elephant.

He used to have three or four whipping boys. I mean, he couldn't give Béliveau hell, or Henri Richard. So he'd find somebody in the room to use that way. When I first came up it was usually me, Ralph Backstrom, and Jean-Guy Talbot. He knew he could bounce things off me and I wouldn't get upset or do anything. But it used to get to Backstrom and it used to get to Talbot.

One morning he came into the room for the meeting on the day of a game and he really gave it to Backstrom. He absolutely tore him apart. When he had finished he went out the door. That was before they had protectors on the sharp edge on the back of a skate blade. Backstrom picked up a skate and fired it at the door just after Toe had gone through it. The skate hit the door backwards and the heel of the skate drilled right into the plywood and stuck there, right in the door. The guys almost killed themselves, they were laughing so hard at poor Ralph. [Laughs]

One of his favourite things to do at the meetings was to talk about the other team. He'd say, "I'm not gonna mention Hull," or "I'm not going to mention Mahovlich . . . Howe . . . Mikita." He'd say, "I'm not gonna mention any names because it will backfire. But Fergie, you're gonna check Ronnie Ellis . . . or Howe." He'd say he didn't want to mention names, but he always did.

When we played Rangers I always had to check Rod Gilbert. One night Gilbert ran wild against us at the Forum and Toe really gave it to me. The worst ever. That night I had a lot of penalties, so with all the time I was spending in the box I wasn't able to check Gilbert very much. Anyway, Gilbert gets four goals that night and has sixteen shots, which is a record. So Toe really gave it to me and it didn't matter to him that I had all those penalties. To him it was all my fault. I'll tell you, whenever we played Rangers after that I never took my eye off Gilbert, never gave him two inches of room.

We were afraid of Toe but there were times when he would lighten things up, make us laugh. All the years I played for the Montreal Canadiens, we never had a curfew. We were a team that always liked to have a good time. But we policed ourselves the nights before a game and I always respected the Canadiens for that.

In the thirteen years Toe Blake coached the Montreal Canadiens his team played 914 regular-season games and another 119 in the playoffs. Blake was behind the bench for the opening face-off every time. Only once was he not there when the game ended. On December 13, 1967, Blake was thrown out of a game in Boston by the referee. With Blake gone Jean Béliveau, the team captain, took over. Béliveau was one of the greatest players ever to play for the Montreal Canadiens. He is also the only man whose coaching career with the team lasted just two periods.

JEAN BÉLIVEAU

We played in New York the night before and I had got a little knee injury. We went to Boston and Toe told me to rest my injury and not play. I was sitting in the press box. Just after the end of the first period one of our trainers motioned for me to come down to the dressing room. So I went down and Toe said to me, "You're gonna coach. I've been thrown out of the game." I don't really know what happened. I guess he said something to the referee when the period was over.

I remember Boston was leading 1–0. I always thought that Jacques Lemaire, who had a low hard shot, should play the point on the power play. Well, we got a power play and I said that I was going to satisfy myself now that I was the coach. So that's what I did and, boom, Lemaire scored from the point. I will always remember that. We ended up winning the game 5–2.

After the game we got on the bus and the boys started to

yell out, "Hey, Jean, when do we practise tomorrow? Can we do this? Can we do that?" Toe was sitting in his usual spot at the back of the bus and he didn't say a word. That was my career as a coach.

One of Toe's main strengths was knowing the capacity of his players. I remember one night in Detroit when Doug Harvey was having a bad game, fooling around with the puck and losing it to them. On the bench Toe said, "Look at that. I'll bet you in twenty-five seconds he's gonna get a penalty. He's gonna have to trip somebody when they take the puck off him." And sure enough, right after that Doug got a penalty. He seemed to know after the first shift or two if a player was going to have a good night or a bad night.

It's very hard to coach a great team and keep it winning. Toe was able to do that. Other teams, I've seen them with a lot of All-Stars and never win anything. Today, when I see defencemen passing the puck across in front of their net, I know that would drive Toe crazy. He used to say, "Hockey is very simple. Just two V's. One away from your net, the other toward their net."

I remember Toe Blake crying after winning and crying after losing. He made some of the players mad but we all recognized that the guy had put everything he had into what he was doing. Today, with millionaires in the dressing room, well, I don't know how he would handle things. I know how some of today's players react, how they want to comment on everything that happens. I think he could coach, but it would be difficult for him. I don't think he would enjoy it like he did in the past. The game of hockey was his life.

Jack Adams wasn't the only coach to swing at a referee during the playoffs. In 1961 after his team had lost a game in Chicago when Murray Balfour scored a power-play goal in the third overtime period, Blake rushed onto the ice and *threw an overhand right at referee Dalton MacArthur. Blake claimed the punch hadn't landed. The league thought otherwise and fined him $2,000, but didn't suspend him. Afterwards Blake would say, "Imagine how much they'd have fined me if I'd hit him."*

Toe wasn't the only tough competitor in the Blake family. The night of Jean Béliveau's two-period coaching career I was doing the late the sports on CFCF-TV. The newsman, the weatherman, and the sportscaster used to come on at the beginning of the program and give their "headlines." That night I said, "Toe Blake was thrown out of the game tonight in Boston and guess what? The Canadiens won."

The next night I ran into Toe and his wife at a charity sports dinner in Montreal. Mrs. Blake lit into me immediately, accusing me of making fun of her husband with my remark. She said her piece (with Toe laughing in the background), and never spoke to me again the rest of her life.

During the 1992–93 NHL season, the New York Rangers fired Roger Neilson and replaced him with Ron Smith. When he took over Smith was asked if he was the Rangers' interim coach. His reply was, "Every coach is an interim coach." It's the old hired-to-be-fired routine. A cliché, but, like many clichés, true. However, the two men who coached the Montreal Canadiens during the twenty-eight years starting in 1940 stretched that theory to the limit.

When Toe Blake quit coaching it was his decision. Blake simply didn't want the pressure any more. But after staying on the job thirteen years Blake was hardly interim. Likewise his predecessor, Dick Irvin, who had been behind the Canadiens bench fifteen years before that. In Montreal, as was the case in Toronto, where he had coached the Maple Leafs for nine years, my father wasn't fired. But the message was pretty clear. He went from Toronto to Montreal, then *from Montreal to Chicago. Both times they didn't open the door for him to leave, but it was left ajar.*

Dick Irvin's coaching career was covered in detail in my first book, Now Back to You Dick. *But, as we say in television, for those of you who have just tuned in here's a brief recap. He started and ended his career with one-year stints with the Chicago Blackhawks. In between came the twenty-four years in Toronto and Montreal. His teams ended the season in first place eight times, won the Stanley Cup four times, and finished out of the playoffs only twice. He coached in the Stanley Cup finals fifteen times in twenty-six years.*

Many of the greatest players in the histories of the Toronto Maple Leafs and the Montreal Canadiens played their first NHL games with my father as their coach. They include Syl Apps, Gordie Drillon, Turk Broda, Elmer Lach, Maurice Richard, Ken Reardon, Jacques Plante, Doug Harvey, Dickie Moore, Bernie Geoffrion, and Jean Béliveau.

Dick Irvin was nearing the end of his playing career in Chicago when he first got the idea he might like to become a coach. The Blackhawks trained at Notre Dame University, in South Bend, Indiana. It was there he watched the legendary coach Knute Rockne put the school's football team through its paces in practice. Rockne caught Dick's attention right away and he started thinking about a coaching career when his playing days were over.

When I hear, or ask, the question, "How has coaching changed?" I often think of something that happened in the 1930s that I know wouldn't happen today. The Irvin household was based in Regina while my father was coaching the Toronto Maple Leafs. The hockey season was much shorter then, so players and coaches would return home for the summer. A few Toronto players also lived in Saskatchewan. When it came time to head east for training camp they would assemble at our home on Angus Street, pile into Dad's 1932 Buick, and set off on the long drive to Toronto. When the season ended they'd get back into the Buick and head back home again. Nick Metz, Ken Doraty, and Murray Armstrong were some of the Toronto players who accompanied their coach on these trips. Don't even ask if that sort of thing would happen today.

During his last season in Montreal, 1954–55, and the following year in Chicago, my father began to suffer from the inroads of the bone cancer that would take his life May 16, 1957. He went to the Blackhawks' training camp in 1956 but was very ill and retired after spending just a few days there.

During the playoffs in 1992, in Boston, I ran into Forbes Kennedy, who told me a Dick Irvin story I had never heard. Forbes played eleven years in the NHL with five teams. His rookie season was with the Blackhawks in 1956–57.

FORBES KENNEDY

Dick had seen me play junior hockey in Montreal and helped arrange for me to have a tryout with Chicago. At the training camp you could see he was pretty sick. We'd be working out and he'd be sitting in the stands, huddled in a blanket, while minor-league coaches ran the workouts.

We were getting ready for a morning practice when Dick came into the room. "Fellows," he said, "you know I've always told you if you didn't give me 100 per cent you couldn't play on this team. Well, now I can't give you 100 per cent so I'm leaving. I can't coach any more. I have to go home. Good luck."

I'm telling you, you could have heard a pin drop in the room. Most of us just sat there looking at the floor. Some of the veteran players got up and shook his hand. There were a few guys in the room, including Dick, with some tears in their eyes. What with the record he had I figured I was in on some hockey history, sad as it was. I'll never forget it.

When my father became coach of the Blackhawks in 1955, the owner, Jim Norris, gave him a contract for $20,000 a year, making him the highest paid man on the payroll. I'm not certain he was the first NHL coach to earn more than any player on his team, but I'm pretty sure he was the last.

3

The Many Lives of
Emile "The Cat"

EMILE FRANCIS

I go back a long way with Emile Francis, but I knew about him long before he knew about me. When I was fourteen and fifteen years old I would go to Queen City Gardens, in Regina, to watch the home-town Caps play in the Western Senior League. Their goalie was a fiesty kid from North Battleford, Emile Francis. We called him "The Cat," a nickname given him by Dave Dryburgh, a sports-writer for the **Regina Leader Post.** *When Francis was playing junior hockey for the Moose Jaw Canucks Dryburgh had written: "The Moose Jaw goalie, Francis, is as quick as a cat." The nickname quickly caught on, and when you mention "The Cat" now, some forty-five years later, everyone in hockey knows who you mean.*

Francis played in the NHL for the Chicago Blackhawks and the New York Rangers, with several minor-league stops along the way. After retiring as a player in 1960, he joined the Rangers organization as coach of their junior team in

Guelph, Ontario. He moved up to the parent club in 1962, where he was coach and/or general manager for the next fourteen years.

Francis coached 654 regular-season games with the Rangers, a team record. In 1976 he joined the St. Louis Blues, where he performed both functions as well. He joined the Hartford Whalers in 1983 and is still with that organization as its president.

The Cat is now sixty-seven years old and still as fiesty as when he was the cocky kid goalie for the Regina Caps. When I sat in his office in Hartford to record some of his memories it had been forty-five years since we were first in the same hockey arena at the same time.

EMILE FRANCIS

It's a funny thing, Dick, but it seems maybe I was born to lead. I can go back to during the war when I was going to a Catholic public school run by a nun. Her name was Sister Berschmans and we remained friends for many years. I was about eleven or twelve. There weren't many men around because they had all gone off to fight the war so she put me in charge of the baseball and hockey teams. My job was to issue out the equipment, which was mainly the sweaters, and get them all back. I'd have to haul them back after every game because if you lost a sweater you'd never get it back.

We won our first championship in hockey when I was running the team. We were in an open-air rink and the game was played in the morning. It started at 8:00 and ended at 9:00. Three twenty-minute periods, no stop-time. We've got a 1–0 lead and it's into the third period. I could shoot the puck pretty good and even then I was smart enough to realize you had to slow the game down when you're leading and there's no stop-time. We only had one puck, so I would shoot it over the boards into a snowbank. So they had to go and look for the puck and that would kill off a couple of minutes. A few minutes later I'd do the same thing again. So we struggled along like that and we won the game 1–0. The coach of the other team, which was from Connaught School, was one of their teachers and he wouldn't give us the trophy, which they had won the year before. I said, "Why not? It's our trophy. We won it!" He said, "It's because you cheated by shooting the puck into the snowbank all the time."

We get back to our school and Sister Berschmans is waiting for me and she says, "Who won?" I said "We did, 1–0, but they wouldn't give us the trophy." She asked why and I told her. She went right to the phone and called a taxi. A taxi ride then cost twenty-five cents and then twenty-five cents was a lot of money. She says, "You and I are going over to Connaught School and get our trophy." So we went there and as soon as we're in the door she asks someone, "Where's Mr. Jones teaching?" They told her so we went to his room and she knocked on the door and says, "Mr. Jones, we've come for our championship hockey trophy." He went into a closet, gave us the trophy, we got back in the taxi and went back to our school. She called all the kids together and showed them the trophy. Then she gave everybody the afternoon off. That's when I found out rather early that it pays to win.

When you talk about me learning a leadership role, I started early. I went into the Reserve Army when I was sixteen and at seventeen I was a sergeant-major. Just as the war ended I entered non-commissioned officers school. I was offered a chance to join the full-time army and go to the Military College, in Kingston. But there was no war so I didn't think it would be too much fun being in the army with nobody to fight against. So I turned that down and ended up going to Moose Jaw to play hockey.

When I was playing hockey, first junior and then senior, I was also hired to play baseball. I played a couple of years for the Bentley brothers, Max and Doug, in Delisle, Saskatchewan. They were big stars then in the NHL, and for the ball team they brought in me and Bert Olmstread and some black players, imports from the States. Then North Battleford wanted me to come back home to play ball there. My uncle had been running the team. Baseball was getting very big there at that time and they told me they wanted me to play shortstop and also be the playing-manager. I thought, who would want to do that when he's only twenty-two years old? Then I thought that sometime down the road I wouldn't be playing hockey any more. The job would give me more experience as far as handling people went, and all that. So I took it.

In those days we were importing players, black and white players from all over the United States, and Cuban players too. I ran the team for the next ten years and we won seven championships. I kind of think that some people in hockey were watching me and thinking that if this guy can handle the kind of people he's handling, maybe he'd be a candidate someday for coaching in hockey, and that is what it came to.

Tiny Thompson had been a great NHL goalie and in those days was working for the Chicago Blackhawks. He signed me to play junior in Moose Jaw and he was the one who signed me when I turned pro in Chicago. All the years I was playing he kept telling me that when I was through playing hockey I would have to come and work for Chicago. He told me that eventually I would be coach of the Blackhawks. So when I decided to quit playing he tried to line me up to coach the junior team in Moose Jaw. In those days, and I'm talking about 1960, you could retire from hockey but you couldn't continue to work in hockey unless the last team you belonged to released you or they received some form of indemnification.

I had finished with the Spokane Flyers of the Western League but still belonged to the Blackhawks. Roy McBride, who owned the junior team, was having a tough time making a deal with Tommy Ivan in Chicago. I had already done some recruiting for Moose Jaw and Tiny called me to come down there for a press conference to announce that I was the new coach. I asked him when they were going to complete the deal and he said he would talk to Ivan again the next day.

So I pack my bags and the next day start driving from North Battleford to Moose Jaw, 280 miles. I get to Davidson, about halfway, and all of a sudden I pulled the car over and got out and started walking up and down the road. I'm telling myself that with no deal yet I could be working there for two or three months and then if they still can't make a deal I'd be out of work. So I got back in the car, turned around, and drove back to North Battleford. When I walked into the house my wife couldn't figure out what was going on. I never did work for the Blackhawks.

Prior to all this, I had run into Muzz Patrick. He was running the New York Rangers and I met him in Los Angeles when I was there for the Western League finals. He asked me what I was going to do the next season and I told him I thought I might pack it in. I was having a bad time with a shoulder injury. He told me there were a couple of coaching openings in his organization but I said Tiny Thompson had been talking to me about Chicago, so that was that.

A week after I decided not to go to Moose Jaw they announced that Metro Prystai was the Canucks' new coach. I bet you it wasn't an hour later I get a call from Muzz Patrick in New York. I told him what had happened between me and the Moose Jaw team and he asked if I would be willing to go with the Rangers if they could make a deal. That was about 1:00 in the afternoon. About three hours later he called again, said the deal was done, and told me what he'd pay me to coach in the Rangers organization.

There were two jobs open, one with their senior team in Trois Rivières and the other with the junior team in Guelph, which they had just bought. I told him that I had been a pro hockey player for fourteen years and I was going to an organization where I'd just as soon start at the bottom. I said I'd like to work with the kids for a while so I would go to Guelph. He told me they needed me there right away so that's where we went, lock, stock, and barrel. My wife and I packed up the two kids and we went to Guelph and we were there for two years.

It turned out to be a very good move for me. We had a good team and I brought in some players who became National Leaguers. Rod Gilbert, Jean Ratelle, Mike McMahon, Al Lebrun. That was the start of a new career for me as far as coaching hockey, and it all began in Guelph.

Right from the start I wasn't a bit nervous. I think it was because of all the experience I had running ball teams. I mean, that was just like having ice cream for dessert with chocolate sauce on it. It was something that it seemed I'd been doing all my life. I had some very tough guys to handle in the ten years I spent running ball teams. I fired some and traded some. I'll admit that at first I did miss playing hockey. But there were so many things to do in Guelph working with kids sixteen, seventeen, eighteen years of age that I forgot about my playing days pretty quick. There was so much going on I didn't have time to think about it.

Coaching defencemen and forwards came pretty natural to me and I'll tell you why. I had been a goaltender all my life and first off you've got to know how to play goal. And from the first day I started as a kid until I hit the NHL, nobody ever told me how to play goal. Nobody. I learned on my own through trial and error.

Now, back in my days playing with Chicago, I got an example of why goaltenders have such a bond with each other. One night we're playing in Boston, and Frank Brimsek was their goalie, one of the greatest, but I had never met him and I was sure he didn't know me from a hole in the ground. I had been having trouble with shots to my catching hand, which normally was the strong point of my game. I was a little guy but I had that good hand, but I had been beaten badly two or three games in a row on my catching hand. I couldn't figure out why.

In those days it was an automatic fine if you were caught talking to a player from another team. They'd fine you a hundred bucks. That night in Boston, at the end of a period, we were skating past one another and, when I'm about ten feet in front of him, I said, without looking at him, "Can I meet you after the game?" He yelled back at me, without looking at me, "Meet me downstairs at the Iron Horse." That was a bar-restaurant in the Boston Garden.

So I go there and introduce myself, even though we had been playing against each other for a couple of years. I told him about my problem with shots to my glove side. Brimsek said, "I've read about you and I know you're a baseball player. I play ball too. I'll tell you what you're doing. You're coming out to meet the guy with the puck like you would be charging a ground ball. But you're coming out too quick and then you have to start backing up. Think about baseball. You end up backing off the ball. Instead of your hand leading you, it's behind you. That's where you're messing up. Just by a fraction of a second, but that's what you're doing."

Wouldn't you know it, the next day all I did was slow myself coming out on the angle to cut off the shooter and there it was, just like that. I started to play better. But it took another goalie to tell me.

Nobody works closer with the defencemen than the goalie. You've got to know what they should do on a two-on-one, and you've got to be the quarterback when the play is in the corner. The defenceman hasn't got eyes in the back of his head so you've got to let him know what's going on. You work hand in hand. So when I started to coach I could relate very well to the defencemen.

The forwards. Who knows them better than a goalie? When a forward isn't scoring, who do you think he'll go to? He won't talk to the coach. He'll come to his goalkeeper and ask him questions. Am I telegraphing my shots? or whatever. All the years I played goal I'd stay out after practice and work with the defence and forwards. We'd talk about the game. That way you learned all facets of hockey, and you had to.

When I left Guelph it was to go to New York to work with the big team. Muzz Patrick brought me in as the assistant general manager and my job was to set up a whole farm system. That was in 1962 when NHL teams had sponsored clubs. [A sponsored team was owned by an NHL club which then owned the professional rights to all its players.] The Canadiens had sixteen and the Rangers had four. So that's what I did the next two years, going all over the map setting up teams, and hiring scouts. I think I wore out five suitcases with all the travelling.

In 1964–65 I became the general manager of the Rangers, and then during the following season I removed Red Sullivan as coach and took over myself. I knew that in doing so I was going to have to sacrifice a year or two but I was going to go with young players. In fact, when I took over, Jean Ratelle wasn't even there. He was back in Montreal and not even playing hockey. So one of the first things I did was get him back to playing hockey and I put him in Baltimore.

My first game as a coach in the NHL was against the Montreal Canadiens. We were down 3–1 with fifty seconds to go in the game so I pulled the goalkeeper. The players were looking at me as if to say, is this guy out of his head? To me there was no sense trying to protect a 3–1 loss but I guess they were surprised because the Rangers likely had never scored two goals in the last fifty seconds. They didn't that night either.

Now we go to Detroit for my second game and they beat us 7–1. We had a 10:00 flight home the next morning. As soon as the game was over I went looking for the fellow looking after the Olympia and said, "Can I have the ice at 6:30 tomorrow morning?" He says, "You'll have to pay overtime because we don't come to work that early. But if you're willing to pay, we'll be here."

I said I'd pay the overtime. Then I went into the dressing room and announced, "Bus leaves the hotel tomorrow morning at 5:30!" The players thought I had changed the flight so I said, "The bus isn't leaving for the airport. It's leaving for the rink." So we were on the ice at 6:30 the next morning and they didn't see a puck for ninety minutes, and even then it was just to look at because I had it in my pocket. I said, "You guys didn't touch this thing last night and you're not gonna touch it today." And they didn't. All they did was skate, and I mean skate. Before I was through with them they were hanging over the boards.

After the practice I said, "You don't know me too well because you haven't played for me. But one thing I'll guarantee, you're not going to give me ulcers. If anyone gets them it'll be you, not me. So we might as well work together and have some fun. Otherwise, it's going to be a long year."

That first year I coached, hockey wasn't much of an issue in New York. The Rangers were averaging 8,300 people a game and fighting for their lives. We were trying to put it all together as fast as we could, when an incident happened that put us on all the front pages. We were still playing in the old Madison Square Garden and it was early in my second season as coach. We were leading Detroit 2–1 with about three minutes to go in the game. The puck is passed out from the corner in our zone and Norm Ullman takes a quick wrist-shot. You know if you score, or think you score, the stick automatically goes right up. So that's what he does, but this time the puck comes right back past him and the play is heading up the other way. But the goal judge had turned the light on and the referee, Art Skov, blows his whistle and stops the play.

Now I see him go to talk to the goal judge, and then he goes over to the P.A. announcer and tells him it's a goal for Detroit and they put the score up on the board, 2–2. With that I took off and ran down to the end of the rink and I had to squeeze in because the boards were so close to the front-row seats.

I battled my way through the fans and start yelling at the goal judge, "What are you doing putting the light on?!" There was a guy sitting right beside him and he says to me, "Why don't you get out of here?" And I said, "I'm not talking to you."

I turned to the goal judge again but before I could say anything else I see this guy standing up and I figure I better get in one punch, real quick. So I nailed him. Little did I realize that two of his buddies were sitting on the other side of the goal judge. All of a sudden all three of them are coming at me. The goal judges used to sit on a little stool so this one grabs his stool and takes off. One of my players, Vic Hadfield, came back to see what was going on and when he saw it was me he yelled at the rest of the guys and all of a sudden they were climbing over the screen, and jumping down into the seats like commandos scaling the rocks on D-Day.

Now remember, we're playing at home and these are our own fans. I had taken my coat off so my arms would be loose and as the players kept jumping over the screen their skates cut my suit coat to ribbons. It lasted about twenty minutes. I was cut under both eyes and they took me to the clinic to stitch me up. Then they bring in the three guys and they were cut up pretty good too.

The Garden police were there and when it had all quieted down they told me the three guys wanted to apologize. The League fined twelve of our players a total of $1,800 and I got fined $250, and we figured that was that.

Two days later a guy comes to my office and hands me a piece of paper and tells me that I'm being sued for a million bucks! Bill Jennings was president of the Rangers and when he came by that afternoon I showed him the paper and asked him what it all meant. He was a lawyer. He reads it over, then gets a copy of the *New York Post*, opens it to page three, and shows me a story about Bruce Norris, who owned the Detroit Red Wings. Norris was being sued for a million by some guy for alienation of his wife's affections. Jennings says to me, "You're being sued for a million too. Now you're in the big leagues." And I said, "Yeah, but take a look at me. I'm all stitched up. At least Norris had some fun."

We ended up in court seven years later on that one. There were the three guys and I was put on the stand for a long time. The insurance people had coached me how to handle myself, don't say this, don't say that, don't get mad. Their lawyer starts right in on me by asking, "How much do you weigh?" I replied, "154 pounds, soaking wet." People in the court started to laugh and the judge banged down his gavel and told me to just answer the questions.

Now the guy gets going with questions about the night of the fight, like, "Do you remember who wore number 11? . . . Who wore number 9? . . . What is known in hockey as a goon? . . . An enforcer?" Number 11 and number 9 were Vic

Hadfield and Reggie Fleming and they were the first two guys over the fence that night. But I let on I didn't remember any of this and finally he puts his face about one inch from mine and tells me that for a general manager of a hockey team I don't have a very good memory. I told him right back that as a lawyer he'd make a good hockey announcer. The people in the room were going crazy.

The trial lasted three weeks and the evidence finished on a Friday. The judge told the jury they had to come back Monday with a verdict. So the jury marches out and, because of renovations being done to the courtroom, instead of going out the back way as was normal they had to walk right in front of me and everyone else. The last guy who walks by puts out his hand to me and says, "Good luck." Right away the judge calls them all back and asked him, "What did you just say to Mr. Francis?" The guy answered, "I'm a Rangers fan and just wanted to wish his team good luck." The judge bangs down his gavel and yells out, "Mistrial!" So we had to go back and do it all over again two years later. They had a new judge and that trial lasted only five days and this time the jury did walk out the back way, not in front of me. They finally awarded those three guys $90,000 and you know what they did when it was all over? They walked up to me and asked me for my autograph.

Well, that's New York.

There are many people who have been watching hockey for a long time, myself included, who feel that, at the peak of his career, Terry Sawchuk may have been the greatest goaltender in the history of the game. Sawchuk was at that peak with the great Detroit teams of the early 1950s. When the Red Wings won the Stanley Cup in the minimum eight games in 1952, Sawchuk allowed the opposition just five goals. His record of 103 career shutouts will probably stand forever.

Sawchuk's star dimmed after the Red Wings traded him to Boston in 1955. Beset by personal problems, he changed teams frequently, even going back to Detroit for a while. In 1967 he briefly brought back memories of his greatness when he combined with Johnny Bower to backstop the Toronto Maple Leafs to a Stanley Cup championship.

His last season was 1969–70 when he appeared in eight games for the Rangers as back-up to Ed Giacomin. His last game appearance was in Boston in the 1970 playoffs. He made two or three brief appearances in one game when the Rangers coach, Emile Francis, tried to stall for time by changing goalies. (Time-outs were not permitted then.)

The Rangers were eliminated by the Bruins. Exactly one month later, Terry Sawchuk was dead. With the exception of medical personnel at the hospital where he died, the last person to see Terry Sawchuk alive was Emile Francis.

EMILE FRANCIS

When our season ended I went to Quebec City to scout some junior playoff games and the guy I was watching was Guy Lafleur. I'm at a game and over the P.A. system comes an urgent message: "Emile Francis is wanted at the office."

I went to the office and there was a long-distance call waiting for me and the fellow introduced himself as a doctor from Long Beach, New York. That's where I lived. He said, "I have one of your hockey players here in serious condition and I have to tell you he might not live through the night." I asked him who he was talking about and he said, "Terry Sawchuk."

I asked if he had been in a car accident or a fracas of some kind and the doctor said he couldn't tell me. He said, "When he came in here three weeks ago he made me promise I wouldn't tell you. But now he is in such serious condition I feel I must advise you of the situation."

I flew back to New York the next morning and went right to the hospital in Long Beach. I inquired at the desk where he was and they asked me if I was a relative. I told them no, but he works for me. They kept telling me I couldn't see him. So I left the desk and nobody stopped me when I went toward the emergency ward. I walked right in and, sure enough, I saw Terry right away, down at the end of the hall. When I got to him he said, "How did you know I was here?" I told him that wasn't important and asked him how he felt. He said, "Some days I'm good. Some days I'm not."

I asked him what happened and he said, "Well, I'm gonna tell you what happened but don't blame Ron Stewart. [Stewart was a teammate.] We got into a bit of an argument and I took a swing at him, lost my balance, and I fell over a barbecue pit. He came down on top of me and something pierced my stomach. So he brought me in here. I've been here about three weeks."

Right away I told him I was going to get him out of there and get him to New York. I called our team doctors and they came out. They looked at him and said that he should stay there for that night. He did, and we moved him by ambulance to New York first thing the next morning. They took him to the New York University Hospital. He was bleeding badly internally and they conducted about five hours of tests on him. When the tests were over they held a meeting. There were three doctors, Terry, and me. They told him he had a very serious problem and that they were going to have to operate as soon as possible.

Terry asked them to get a priest, and they did. About an hour later they wheeled him into the operating room. That was about 6:00 in the evening. I was in the hospital and when he went by me he took a ring off his finger and gave it to me. It was a Detroit Red Wing ring. He said, "Make me a promise. If anything happens to me, will you be sure my son gets a chance to play." [Sawchuk had lived apart from his wife and family for quite some time.]

I told him that nothing was going to happen, that he'd be okay. I stayed there until the doctors finished the operation, which was around 11:00. They told me the next forty-eight hours would be crucial but if he made it through that he should be all right. But he didn't make it. At 5:00 in the morning he died.

They called me right away and I had to go to the morgue on Second Avenue to identify the body. It was Memorial Day weekend but there were still people working in the morgue. They didn't know who I was and they didn't know who he was. A chap came out and said, "Is there anyone here named Francis?" I identified myself and he told me to follow him. We went down a couple of flights of stairs and he opened the door and there were about thirty bodies lying there and the first thing that hit me was that they were in bags just like the bags we use to carry hockey sticks in. And there he was, his head out of one end of the bag with a tag around his neck. They had "Terry Sawchuk" written on the tag.

I'll always remember that because he and I played against each other many times in the old United States Hockey League. If I were to pick the number-one goalkeeper I've ever seen it would be Terry Sawchuk. I thought to myself standing there in the morgue about what an awful way it was for him to finish up. He was only forty-one years old.

To end the story, we arranged for his son to play junior-B hockey in Kitchener and I think he could have been a good goalkeeper too. I don't know if the passing of his father influenced him or not, but after one year he said, "That's it."

As with almost all coaches, it seems, Emile Francis finally reached the end of the line in New York.

EMILE FRANCIS

What happened to me at the end in New York is very simple. I got fired. I ran the Rangers for fourteen years without any problems. Then all of a sudden Paramount came in as the owner and it was the first time I realized that a big outfit could come in on a takeover and that's what they did.

The first year went fine. But the people who ran the Knicks basketball team kept asking me if Alan M. Cohen had been talking to me about how I should be running the hockey team. Alan M. Cohen was the chairman of the board they put in at the Garden. He came from Gulf & Western, who owned Paramount. I told them no, and they said, "You're lucky."

My luck ran out the next year. That was 1975–76 and we were still fighting the WHA. I felt the work load was too heavy so I put Ron Stewart in as coach. December 28th I get a call from Bill Jennings and he says he's been talking to Alan M. Cohen and Mr. Jennings told me Mr. Cohen thought it would be a good idea if I put myself back as coach because the team wasn't going very well. I said, "Bill, let me tell you something. I've run this team now for fourteen years without any help, and I don't need any now."

The next Sunday I'm in Montreal at a general managers' meeting and about 10:00 at night I get a phone call. I'm sitting there with Steve Brklacich, my personnel director. I answer the phone and it's Bill Jennings. He says that there was a meeting held over the weekend and that Alan M. Cohen would like to meet with me the next afternoon at 4:00. So I hung up, turned to Steve, and said, "Well, that's it for me as far as being the general manager of the New York Rangers."

I flew back to New York the next morning, went straight to the office, closed the door, and started to pack my things. I had to go to Room 200 at 4:00. So I went up to Room 200 at 4:00 and Bill Jennings opens the door. I look around and say, "Where's Alan M. Cohen?" Jennings tells me that Mr. Cohen had another very important meeting and couldn't come to this one.

Mr. Jennings then told me that I had a choice of doing two things, resign or be fired. I said, "After being with me as long as you have you know I've never quit on anything in my life, and I'm not about to quit now. So if you want to fire me, go ahead."

He says, "You're fired. It will take about an hour to get a press release put together." I said, "Tell you what. You take that press release and shove it." And I left.

I had been with the New York Rangers as a player and in management twenty-five years. When I got home that night and told my wife what had happened she said I must feel bad. I said I didn't because any time you can be in one place as long as I was in New York it was quite an accomplishment. I won more games with the Rangers as manager and coach than anybody in their history, and coached more games than anyone in their history, and those are records nobody is going to beat.

By the time the next season began, the Cat was back, in yet another life, this one with the St. Louis Blues. After his New York experience he decided that the best way to avoid getting fired was to own part of the team. So Emile made a deal that paid him less money than he was making in New York but gave him ten per cent ownership in the hockey team. Unfortunately, there was a slight problem.

It was a ten per cent ownership in a team that was rapidly going broke.

EMILE FRANCIS

My first year in St. Louis, we ran out of money in December. By January 1st I was doing everything. I was the president, general manager, coach, and even the public-relations director. We had to let twenty-two people go, including the PR director, because we had no money. We had to stumble our way through the rest of the year without letting everyone know what rough shape we were in.

I told our accountant there were three things we had to make sure of. We had to keep paying the players because if we didn't their contracts would be null and void. We had to pay our electric bill because if they ever turned off the power we've got no ice and we can't play hockey. And we had to pay our insurance premiums on our assets, which were the players. All of this while we were playing pretty good and were in first place in our division.

Jimmy Connors is from that area. He came back and we ran a tennis tournament for three days and made $50,000. That really helped our payroll, meant another one or two paydays. He came out and played wearing a St. Louis Blues sweater, and I'll never forget him for that because he really got us out of a hole.

One night we were getting ready to play the New York Islanders and we've got a sellout going. About 6:00 the guy who ran the restaurant came running into my office and said that the lights just went out in his place. So I go out into the building and sure enough the lights are going out all over the place. I could see that the ice was starting to go soft. So I called our accountant and he told me he hadn't paid the electric bill in a while. So I told him to get hold of somebody, anybody, at the electric company and pay the bill or else we weren't going to have a game that night. And that's what he did. But they had sent a guy up to start turning off the power and he had about half of it turned off, and part of the half he turned off was the ice itself. But we got the game in.

For the last half of that season our credit was about a nickel. When we would go on the road we would have to pay the bus driver with cash and pay our hotel bills in advance. We could barely get enough hockey sticks because the equipment companies were cutting us off.

Through the last half of the season I had a standing rule that no player could take a hockey stick out of the dressing room. Anyone who got caught would get fined $200. We played the Montreal Canadiens in the playoffs and on the morning of one of the games I see Bernie Federko, large as life, walking out of the room with three sticks tucked under his arm. I asked him what he was doing with the three sticks and he told me his brother was in town from Saskatoon and he was giving him the sticks, autographed by the players, for a charity auction. I told him they had better get a lot of money at the auction because it was going to cost him $600. He turned around and took the sticks back into the room. That night there was a face-off in front of our bench and Federko was facing off against Pete Mahovlich. I look and he's got an autographed stick, one that he was taking out that day, and he's playing with it. I bet that's the only time in the history of the Stanley Cup playoffs that a guy was playing with an autographed stick. [Laughs]

But I survived all that. I guess if you can survive ten years of running a ball club like I did in North Battleford, you can survive anything.

The Cat's life in St. Louis lasted seven years. During that time the Blues won two division championships but hockey remained a tough sell. In 1982 he was awarded the Lester Patrick Trophy for his contributions to the game in the United States. Later that same year he was inducted into the Hockey Hall of Fame in the builders category.

The Hartford Whalers hired Francis away from St. Louis and he became their president and general manager at the start of the 1982–83 season. Under his guidance the Whalers, another franchise constantly living on the brink of financial disaster, enjoyed their best seasons. In 1989 the owners decided to replace him as general manager and the team has struggled ever since.

In close to thirty years in the National Hockey League the Cat has never been associated with a Stanley Cup-winning team. But he has loved the life, and has found his own rewards.

EMILE FRANCIS

The best thing about the game is playing, without a doubt. But the next best thing is coaching because it's like being in the trenches. The best thing about it is getting a player and seeing how he develops and improves, from the time he comes in until the time he leaves.

One of the finest persons I've ever met is Jean Ratelle. I first met him when he was seventeen years old and he could hardly speak English. You see him go along, meet a girl, get married, reach the National Hockey League, play for twenty years, and then get inducted into the Hockey Hall of Fame. It's like seeing him go up a ladder until he reaches the very top and you like to think that maybe you were a part of that.

I'll tell you how one of my proudest moments came about. Around 1964 I took a walk in New York on the day of a game. I see a bunch of kids go by me and half are wearing New York Rangers sweaters and half are wearing Montreal Canadiens sweaters and they're all carrying hockey sticks. I watch where they go and it's into a big hole in the ground, like a dugout basement, and they start playing hockey, and they're all on rollerskates. This is in the middle of New York City, around Ninth Avenue and Fiftieth Street. I stood and watched them for about twenty minutes. I checked into it and found out there were hundreds of kids around New York playing hockey this way.

I went to the people at Madison Square Garden and suggested we give kids in the area a chance to play real hockey, let them have the ice. I said maybe in ten years or so we could develop a player good enough for the Rangers. I talked them into letting me have the ice in the afternoons on days when the Rangers played, especially on Sundays.

John Muckler was coaching the Long Island Ducks and I brought him in as commissioner of the league. We started with a six-team league and had teams in New Jersey and Long Island. The first guy to come out of that league and play in the NHL was Nick Fotiu. He made it nine years after we started and he was playing for the Rangers, so we beat my target by one year.

A few years ago the All-Star game was played in Edmonton and the Mullen brothers were both in it and they had played in that little league we started in New York. Their father had worked as an ice-maker at the Garden, and he was there. Joey Mullen was the first American to score fifty goals in one season and he's been on three Stanley Cup-winning teams. I sat there that night and said to myself, all those years in New York were well worth it. The one thing I missed was winning the Stanley Cup. But that night I was thinking about those kids I saw in New York playing on their rollerskates, and I was watching Joey and Brian Mullen play in the NHL All-Star game, and for me, that was like my Stanley Cup.

4

Behind the Bench in Boston

MILT SCHMIDT   GERRY CHEEVERS

MIKE MILBURY

Nine men who at one time played for the Boston Bruins have also coached the team. Dit Clapper, Cooney Weiland, Milt Schmidt, Tom Johnson, Bep Guidolin, Gerry Cheevers, Terry O'Reilly, and Mike Milbury were all well-known once-Bruins who went on to coach in Boston. A chap named Don Cherry played just one game for the Bruins. As you may have heard, he too coached in Boston. For the purposes of this book he is a chapter unto his ownself.

One of the greatest of the many greats to wear a Bruins sweater, Milt Schmidt, retired as a player midway through the 1954–55 season. Schmidt immediately took over as coach from Lynn Patrick, who then became general manager. Art Ross, the man who ran the team when Milt broke in as a rookie in 1936, was still the top man in the front office.

MILT SCHMIDT

When I was still playing Ross had told me I would have a job with the team when I retired. But who was to say I would still be in Boston? So I asked him to put it in writing. He wouldn't do that, but he kept his word and gave me the coaching job.

My knees were bad, so halfway through the '54–55 season I retired and went immediately into coaching. The next season I had to sign a new contract. So I went to see Ross in his office and he hands me a contract for $2,000 less than what I got when I was playing. I reminded him he had told me I would get more money when I became an executive, but he said, "That was last year. It's no longer in effect." So I had to sign for $2,000 less than I had been getting. But it kept me in the league and I got a salary out of it. What was I going to do? I wasn't going to go back to Kitchener and work in a twine factory or an ice house or a shoe factory like I did before.

Lynn Patrick was my last coach when I played and in my estimation he was the best of all my coaches when it came to teaching the game. The best by a country mile. When I started to coach he used to remind me that I could not look down the line on the bench and find a Milt Schmidt there. He said I wouldn't have that privilege, which he had had. I was flattered, but I understood what he meant.

Lynn was the one who got me thinking about being a coach. In that last season I knew my career was coming to an end. I was thirty-six years of age and my knees were so bad I had to have them taped up before every game. In those days the tape they used, well, when you would take it off afterwards you dragged the skin right along with it. My knees would be bleeding and raw all the time. I remember Lynn saying to me that when I retired he would recommend that I take over as coach of the team. I had never really thought about coaching before that. Then it started hitting home and

I figured, gee, that might not be such a bad idea. I wouldn't be taking the bumps out there, the lickings that I had been taking, and giving a few too. That's the time I started thinking about taking a run at it, and I did.

I had to adjust my thinking when I started to coach but it didn't take me very long. At first I did think that, hey, these guys aren't giving. They're not backchecking, they're not hitting, they're not doing this and that. Then I said to myself that everybody isn't alike and I couldn't expect others to play the game the way I did. They all had their own skills, skating, stickhandling, and all that. You had to find that out and get them to use those skills to the best of their ability.

Overall I found that the greatest asset you can have as a coach is the ability to motivate your players, to make them play hard and not just go through the motions. That was the tough part for me, to see them loafing. That irritated me something terrible because I don't think I was one to loaf when I played and when I was coach I tried to get rid of the ones who did. I think I was a pretty good taskmaster. Some of the boys used to tell me I gave great pep talks.

At first I really enjoyed it. We got to the finals in my second and third full seasons and I figured it wasn't such a bad job after all. Then all of a sudden the material I had to work with went down and down. Our replacements weren't as good as they should have been. A few trades didn't work out and it got tougher and tougher. Then you'd be hearing the wisecracks from the fans and I had never had to go through that as a player. It was starting to get to me. I found myself saying, "Who needs this?" So when they told me they were making a change to Phil Watson, to be honest with you I was the happiest guy in the world.

Before I was completely retired from the game I had had all the jobs. I was a player, a coach, and a manager. Playing was the best job and coaching was the toughest job. If you don't have the players you're not gonna be able to do well. That's all there is to it.

I think that in my day asking for discipline from the players was much easier than it is now. Then you had fewer teams and everybody was hungry. The salaries weren't all that great and there was always somebody looking over your shoulder trying to get your job. Today you've got so many teams, a player can tell a team that if they don't want him he can go across the street and play for someone else. I admire any coach who can get it out of the present players.

Milt Schmidt had five productive years as the Bruins general manager. In his first season, 1967–68, he engineered the deal with the Chicago Blackhawks that brought Phil Esposito to Boston. That was a big step towards the Bruins' Stanley Cup victories in 1970 and 1972. Having Bobby Orr on defence didn't hurt either.

In goal for the Bruins in those two Cup-clinching games was Gerry Cheevers. An easygoing, storytelling kind of guy who loves going to racetracks and owning racehorses, Cheevers had a Hall of Fame professional career that began in Boston in 1965 and ended there in 1980. Along the way there was a three-and-a-half-season side trip to the World Hockey Association.

Gerry coached the Bruins for close to five years, starting in 1980. However, his debut behind the bench had come two years earlier when he became the first man to coach in an NHL game while wearing goal pads.

GERRY CHEEVERS

Don Cherry was our coach and we were playing a Saturday afternoon game in Minnesota. I was the back-up that day. Our goalie was a kid named Jim Pettie. He'd just been called up and he was a great guy. They called him "Seaweed." He started to hang around with me right away and I loved him. The game was going good for us but then Grapes got involved in something with the referee and got kicked out with about fifteen minutes left in the third period. The Bruins were winning 4–0. Don walks by me on his way to the dressing room and says, "You take over." Just like that, and he kept walkin'.

As soon as I started to coach we went from a Cherry style to a defensive style because I really wanted Seaweed to get the shutout. I played all the defensive guys from then on. Our best defensive forward, Donnie Marcotte, must have been on the ice the rest of the game. We got another goal and won 5–0. When it was over I went into Cherry's office with the pads on, put my feet up on the desk, you know, playing the part of Joe Coach, which was comical at the time, I suppose.

We flew from Minny to Chicago for a game the next afternoon. Pettie was a real character and from the time we take off he's buying all the guys drinks to celebrate his first NHL shutout. It was quite a party, then and afterwards. The next day I'm the goalie in Chicago so I inherit a team that's in pretty tough shape. We got killed. I'm in the net and they must have had fifty shots. So I helped the kid get his shutout and then I paid the price.

I really loved playing for Don Cherry. It was the greatest time, and I just wish we could have won a Stanley Cup because it would have been the icing on the cake. You looked forward to going to work. There was never a dull moment. He read everything right. I'm not so sure about the X's and O's part of it. But he got everything out of every guy. It's a long season and there are days when it drags. He recognized that, made it fun. He had a good feel for the game.

Now, about my coaching career. It was immediate. What happened was, one day I had to go see our team doctor about my future as a player. He said he thought I could play another year but they would have to operate on my knee, clean it out. I was tired of all that so I decided to pack it in.

I hadn't thought about coaching and I had no idea what the Bruins were thinking about me. I went to see Harry Sinden and told him I wasn't going to play any more. I told him I'd had enough, twenty-one years of it, and I was packin' it in. Going south. He said, okay, but I want you to think about coaching. I mean, Holy Christmas. But I decided I'd do it.

So there I was, head coach right away, and at the beginning I was awful. I had no idea. First of all, what I thought was going to be the hardest part was coaching the guys I had been playing with, like Cashman, Doak, Marcotte. I was 100 per cent wrong because they were all in my corner. My problem was that I forgot about the younger guys. I worried about the guys I'd played with and I didn't have to. The younger guys were the ones who needed the help, needed the coaching, and I wasn't very good at that.

We got off to a terrible start. One win in our first ten, something like that, and we kept struggling. Then I got what I think was my biggest break as a coach. My appendix burst and I had to spend six or seven days in hospital. It was around Christmas and it was the kind of a chance I don't think too many first-year coaches get. I spent all that time in the hospital analyzing what I was doing wrong, thinking about it. That's when I realized that even though the young players were in the NHL they still needed coaching, needed somebody to tell them what to do. I was worrying too much that I would lose my relationships with the older guys, lose the camaraderie. I was a much better coach after that and in the second half of that season we had the best record in the league. So that was a great break for me getting my appendix out that first year or I might never have figured it out.

I never had a problem with the guys I played with. But as the years went by and their careers were coming to an end, problems crept up. A lot of them were having private problems. Hopefully they all worked out. But hockey is different from anything. There's so much pride in the individual. It's tough to quit this game without a gun to your head.

To me, Wayne Cashman was the finest competitor I ever played with. I think you could ask any of the Bruins who were on those two Cup-winning teams and it would be unanimous that Cash was the fiercest competitor. So as an ex-teammate, and a friend, it was very tough for me to have to ease him out.

Management kept asking, "Can Cashman play another year?" And I kept saying that I wanted him to keep playing. I told him what was going on, that I wanted him to keep playing, but if a young kid comes along who can do the job, then he wasn't going to play as much. Simple as that. We had some good ones like Barry Pederson, Tom Fergus, Normand Leveille. But to tell a guy who competed like Cashman did that he might not play because a kid might be taking his job, that's tough. If the job was getting done that was all right. But if it wasn't, that really ate him up and he thought he should have been playing. As far as me being a coach went, that was the toughest.

I sat Cash out in the playoffs one year. Here we are, we played together, we went through the wars together, and after a team dinner we ended up hitting each other over the head with chairs. Then we finished the night polishing off twenty-four beers. There was still mutual respect. It was always there.

The Normand Leveille story was a very sad time for

everybody. He was still a teenager and had a good rookie season. Early the next season we were playing in Vancouver and
he got hit. It was an innocent hit, or maybe just a bump, not a
hit. More like a brush, at least that's how it must have
seemed because nobody really could tell exactly what had
taken place.

It happened right at the end of a period. Normand came
into the room and looked like he was completely spaced out.
There's a little trainer's room in Vancouver and that's
usually the first stop for the coach between periods. They
brought him into the room and I looked into his eyes and our
trainer looked into his eyes. The trainer told someone to get a
doctor, real quick. That was it. He had already begun to have
a stroke. He was never able to play again, of course, and that
was a very difficult time for everybody, especially the
younger players on the team. It was very sad.

I never spent much time coaching the goalies. If an
ex-goalie becomes a head coach I think he should hire a
goalie coach. Jim Craig came to play in Boston. He was the
big hero of the U.S. Olympic thing in '80. He was okay but he
needed some maturing before he could become a good NHL
goaltender. Let's put it this way, I didn't do much with him.
And when he didn't make it he said that Cheevers never
spent any time with him. If I had been the goalie coach I
would have. But I was the head coach. I had twenty-four guys
to worry about. If people think that just because a head coach
has been a goalie then his goalie is going to have a big edge,
that's entirely wrong.

I enjoyed the competitive part of coaching. You remain
competitive, you still like the challenge. I remember being in
an exhibition game against Mike Keenan. It was his first year
in Philly. Here comes a guy with a great rep and in an exhibition game he's matching lines. It looked like the game was
going to last three and a half hours. Finally, in the second

intermission, I yelled at him, "Hey, Mike. For chrissake, just tell me who you want me to put on and we'll get this thing over with!" But he kept matching, kept pulling guys off when I'd put certain guys on. I had never seen that before in an exhibition game.

We had good teams. In '83 we played the Islanders in the semis and they beat us in six games. That's when they were winning four Cups in a row. But if you switched the goalies in that series we would have won four straight. We had Pete Peeters and he just couldn't play against the Islanders.

They used to call me a "fun-loving player" and I was. But did I have any fun coaching? I won a lot more games than I lost and because I had fun when we won as a player I approached it the same way as a coach. Unfortunately, you have to lose occasionally and I had no fun that way. You can't have fun when you lose, you just can't. Strangely, I slept better as a coach when we lost. When we won I would enjoy it, go for a sandwich and a couple of beers, yap, be talkative, go home, watch a late movie. If we lost I was in bed by 11:30 and asleep like a baby, right away. [Dick Irvin reacted the same way, only with him it was a cup of tea, not a couple of beers.]

I had a good record. I still can't believe I got fired. When it happened we were just above .500 and I could feel it coming, see the writing on the wall. There was speculation at the time that I had resigned but that's not true. I was fired. I wasn't enjoying the situation we were in and when Harry told me, I said, "Thank goodness."

It's tough to coach a team these days more than three years, certainly during the fourth and fifth years if you don't win the championship. We came close. I was there almost five years. I can't complain. Their next coach was Butch Goring and they got him out of there after one year. Then there was O'Reilly, then Milbury. Rick Bowness lasted only one year. Boston goes through a lot of coaches. I don't know why.

For a while after they let me go I still thought I could coach. The shock wore off by the summer and I had an interview with the Rangers. The meeting was for 2:30. I got there early and I was ready. There's a great bookstore right across the street from the Garden, the Bowery Bookstore. I hung around there for a while, then went for the meeting. I met Craig Patrick, a nice guy, and his assistant was Anders Hedberg. By the time the formalities and small talk were over it was about 2:30. Then we talked for an hour about my ideas about hockey, checking and systems and all that shit. Then I left. It was 3:30 and I had to go back to the airport to get the shuttle.

The traffic was murder at that time of the day. I sat in a cab for an hour and a half getting to the airport. When I finally got home I just sat there for a while and then said, "I could never do it. I could never do it in New York. I really don't want to do this any more." And that was it. That was the last thought I ever had about coaching again.

So, when it came to my coaching career in the NHL, I only gave them one chance to fire me. When it happened we were in Los Angeles. If you're going to get fired you might as well get fired there. You had Hollywood Park next door, Santa Anita not that far away, and you could stop in Vegas on the way home. That was better than getting fired in Detroit.

Mike Milbury is a native of the Boston area who played on defence for the Bruins from 1976 to 1987. He was head coach for two years starting with the 1989–90 season. That year the Bruins lost to Edmonton in the Stanley Cup finals. In 1991 the team reached the Wales Conference final series, losing to Pittsburgh. Milbury then moved into the Bruins' front office as the assistant to general manager Harry Sinden.

MIKE MILBURY

When I started to coach Harry talked to me about the three things a coach is responsible for: discipline, motivation, and conditioning.

These days people are much more in tune to what they have to do to get in good condition. But it's still a critical part of the game. Discipline is getting them to do what you want them to do without programming. I guess included here is some kind of a, quote-unquote, system they now talk about. But the overwhelming consideration from his viewpoint is to have a coach who can motivate a team. Especially now, more than ever. It was much easier during the days when people respected authority more than they do now.

Motivation is a critical factor in a player's success and our game lends itself to that. If you have five basketball players against five basketball players you can't do anything unless you've got a seven-foot centre. But in hockey, for whatever reason or combination of reasons, guys who are motivated, who show a lot of effort and desire, can overcome a lot of the obstacles there are in the game. Obviously, a player like Mario Lemieux is going to be tough to overcome. But if you can get your guys up for every game you can put on an entertaining show and be pretty successful in the win–loss column.

In the past people more or less did what they were told. Now you've got people who, from an early age, are taught to ask questions. We have guys now who want explanations for all kinds of things and it makes it difficult. There's no explanation. You just do it. I mean, that's how it's supposed to be. It's tough for a coach to come up with an explanation. The coach says it has to be done a certain way. If you can't get a coach operating under that premise you don't have a successful coach.

Today you hear that a coach can't last more than four years with any one team. But that's almost a generation. He's lasted a generation of hockey players. I believe that after a certain length of time you can't come up with enough new tricks to keep motivating a group of guys. I think that's one of the most intriguing and enjoyable parts of the job, but it's also very taxing on you.

Motivation can require confrontation with a player and sometimes it gets nasty. It requires creativity in terms of when to lighten up. Instead of taking them to practice, stop the bus and go to a pub. You don't just skate the guys around the block fifty-five times. You've got to do it with a purpose. Harry taught me that when you're really down on the team, skate them down and back, down and back. Then you tell them that from now on you dump the puck into the opposing zone when there's no play to be made at the blue line. Then you skate them down and back again, as many times as you can come up with a reason for doing it. It worked for me. But after a while you might get repetitive. The guys have figured out your approach and they've stopped listening. But that kind of thing is a challenge for a coach.

When I played I had my eye on an executive job in hockey but not necessarily one as a coach. Harry told me, in no uncertain terms, that if I was going to be a manager I had to know what was going on in a coach's mind. So he sent me to be coach and manager with our American League team in Portland, Maine. I spent two great years there and then I had the two years here coaching and being the assistant general manager. There have to be ways to get to the players as a manager. I don't think I would have had that insight had I not myself coached.

When I was in Portland we played in Fredericton and our next game was in Utica two nights later. The guys all had girlfriends lined up in Utica on their day off. I didn't say anything to them but after the game in Fredericton I had the bus driver take us to my old college, Colgate. When we pulled up to the Colgate Inn they all looked at me and said, "Where the hell are we? Why are we stopping here?"

What I wanted was a chance for this whole male-bonding thing. Get together for a few days with nobody else around, no pressure. After two days they just loved it, had a great time. They got together, formed friendships, had a couple of wild and crazy nights, and came out of it feeling better as a team. I think you've got to do that kind of stuff. You've got to continually look for ways to bring them together and get them to listen to you.

At this point in our conversation I said, "Mike, you might not like this but I think I saw you lose it a couple of times behind the bench." Suddenly the atmosphere in the room wasn't quite as warm as it had been. Mike's eyes pierced mine as he coolly and pointedly asked, "When?"

I gulped and replied, "Well, when you kept slamming a stick against the glass in Pittsburgh after Samuelsson hit Neely. I've seen you run back and forth behind your bench screaming at the players, especially after you'd just had a big goal against you. That kind of thing. You always struck me as being a very emotional coach and I used to wonder if sometimes your emotions got the better of you, that you were really mad. Was I right on that?"

MIKE MILBURY

No, you weren't. I mean, I allowed myself the luxury. I am emotional and you can allow yourself the luxury of venting that emotion but always in your mind you've got to have a purpose, a reason. I'll give you an example, and again I go back to the minor leagues.

The Canadiens used to have a farm team in Sherbrooke. We had a Japanese player on our team, Steve Tsujura. Every time he came on the ice the organist in Sherbrooke would play a Japanese song, a little Oriental ditty. It began to grate on me.

One night we're down 2–0 and Steve comes on the ice and the guy starts playing it again. It was annoying and the wrong thing to do. I knew I really couldn't affect whether he would do it or not but I thought maybe we could use it as sort of a rallying cry. So I said to Gordie Clark, my assistant coach, "Make sure the players don't follow me."

I left the bench and started running up the stairs in the direction of where the organist was sitting. It caused all kinds of havoc. I wasn't about to beat up the organist. I knew it was a wild and crazy thing to do but I was trying to get to my team. I was trying to make a point with the organist too, so I felt I could get away with it.

I don't remember ever getting a bench penalty for losing it when I didn't want to. I don't remember ever doing that. I once threw all the sticks on the ice, every water bottle, everything. My wife said, "I thought you were going to start throwing some of your lesser players on the ice too." They had to stop the game. But I knew exactly what I was doing at the time. I allowed myself the right to be stupid for a moment, to show some emotion. But I also hoped it had an effect, that I was making some point to some player, for whatever reason, at that time.

I thought coaching was great. I loved it and I miss it. But there are demands. I think the ideal coach is a guy who's about forty-five to fifty, whose family has grown up or maybe he's single with no responsibilities other than coaching, because it is all-consuming. My primary reason for passing the torch is because I've got four kids. When I was coaching I never saw them, never interacted with them. I was there but my mind was on the power play, or penalty-killing. Coaching is such a passionate profession, you are consumed by it. Maybe I'm wrong there. Maybe there are other guys who can drop it. But if there are, they are few and far between.

Don Cherry was a successful coach and he didn't drop it. The guys used to get mad because he'd pick me up on the way to the rink and he would practise on me what he was going to say to the team when we got there. First he would practise it on Rose before he left his house. Then he would practise it on me and then he would finally deliver the thing to the players in the room. He constantly rehearsed what he had in mind and it was very successful. I think he was a good motivating coach. But there was nothing else on Grapes's mind but hockey. Rose will tell you there was very little fun, very little time for her and the kids. At thirty-nine I just felt I had to spend some of this time with the kids. I have much more quality time with them now than I ever did.

5

Vintage Grapes

DON CHERRY

Now to Donald S. Cherry, the most famous ex-coach of the Boston Bruins. We talked over lunch, or perhaps I should say I listened over lunch. Once the waiter had our order Grapes took a piece of paper out of his pocket, then pointed to my tape-recorder lying on the table. "That thing going? Okay. I lay in bed last night thinking of stories for your book. The good stuff. This morning I put them on this list. Here they are, in no particular order."

So, here they are.

DON CHERRY

The first one I thought of, it was in Boston and we were going for first place overall with the Montreal Canadiens. Sammy Pollock was running the Canadiens and I had Harry Sinden. Pollock, it was unbelievable what he did. He felt what was good for Montreal was good for the rest of the league. He talked Washington into playing an afternoon game instead of a night game. This is no kidding. They played in the afternoon and then chartered into Boston. They were all in bed in their hotel watching us play Atlanta that night on TV.

Harry wouldn't hire a charter for us coming back. We had to get up at 5:00 in the morning and we're all half-dead. We fly back but we can't land in Boston because of a storm. The plane is really dippin' and divin' and we gotta land in Hartford. Some guys were scared so I holler, "Well, boys, if we go down, we're goin' down in first place." Know what Milbury said? He said, "Yeah, with a game in hand."

We finally get to the Garden about 5:00 [twelve hours later]. We go to the room and, this is the God's truth, I turn out all the lights and the guys go to sleep on the dressing-room floor. So now we're playin' the Canadiens and we're winning 2–1 in the third period. But we're exhausted and they score a couple in the last two minutes and they beat us.

The game ends and I'm talkin' to Red Fisher, who was covering the game for his paper in Montreal. I said, "Harry is so cheap he wouldn't hire a charter for us." A little while later I'm sittin' with Harry in my little office and Red comes sauntering in and says to Harry, "What's this Cherry tells me about you being too cheap to hire a charter last night?" I almost fainted right there, on the spot. That really started it, me gettin' fired in Boston.

Another story about Harry. I just thought of it. Harry got Czechoslovakian pucks at the start of one season. They had no emblem on them, or anythink. They were the cheapest pucks of all time. So after a game I said, as a joke, "Those pucks are so cheap, when they go in the stands the fans fire them back at us." Then I said, "No rookie wants to score his first goal in Boston because they don't want a cheap, Czechoslovakian puck on their mantel." A writer in Boston, Leo Monohan, put all that in the paper. Stuff like that just went on and on with me and Harry until it got to the point we didn't even talk. He'd send me notes and I'd send him notes. I wouldn't say nothin'.

When I first got to Boston they had a great team and I was going to be coaching great players. But it didn't really hit me, you know, when I first walked in there, because I was pretty good in the dressing room. When it did hit me was the first time I walked out behind the bench. I always came in after the national anthem. So there I am and, wait a minute, there's Phil Esposito, Wayne Cashman, and Bobby Orr. Bobby Orr? What am I doing here? It was just like, hey, this can't be! Three years before, I was an unemployed labourer. I could not get a job in a factory. I remember I put in an application at a place called St. Joseph's Paper, in Rochester, and I couldn't get a job working in their factory. Three years later I was coaching the Boston Bruins.

I'd tried to get a job in hockey. I'd phoned everybody. I went down to Charlotte for an interview and some southerner says, "What is your philosophy on hockey?" What the fuck was I doin' sittin' there trying to talk philosophy with some guy from Charlotte?

I phoned Bud Poile with the Vancouver Canucks and you know what he said? He said, "If you were your brother, I'd hire you." If I was my brother? What was he doin', tryin' to make me feel good? I couldn't get a job.

So then what happened was, I made a comeback as a player at thirty-six years of age. In Rochester. Doug Adams was the name of the guy runnin' the team. The players hated him and the fans hated him. They had a rule that you could only play six guys over twenty-six, so halfway through the season they made me the coach. We were eighteen points out of the play-offs when I took over but we almost made it. Tied 3–3 our last game when we needed a win against Cincinnati. We outshot them 14–1 in the third period. I kid you not when I say that when I took over I knew I wasn't going to have a job when the season finished. I honestly believe that I would have killed to win. I really would have.

So the season ends and I got fired. This is a great story. Adams calls me into his office. He didn't like me, the PR person didn't like me, and the secretary didn't like me. Nobody liked me, and I'll tell you why. Because I wanted to win and they didn't want to win. They had argued with me that we had to play Serge Aubry over Lynn Zimmerman because it was in Aubry's contract that if he didn't play in a certain number of games they had to pay him another $5,000. They didn't care about making the playoffs. They just wanted to screw Serge Aubry out of five grand. That's hard to believe, but it's true. So there I was again, fightin' management.

After the season Adams calls me in and I can still see him sittin' there with his little cigar. He says, "We're making a change in your department." I was the whole department. So anyway, I left, I was gone. They all laughed at me. I called the secretary "Dragon Lady" and she was laughin' and so was the PR guy, Mike Sullivan was his name. I said, "You know, it's funny to you guys but you shouldn't laugh at me. I'm like a bad penny. I'll be back."

And three months later I was hired back.

What happened was, the team had eight owners and they got together and asked me to coach. Adams was gone so Rose says, "Why don't you be the general manager too?" I called up the chief owner and he said that was okay, but the money would stay the same. So there I was, a coach and general manager in pro hockey, for fifteen grand [in 1973].

I had a good friend playing for me there, Darryl Sly. He got in a fight with a guy named Gord Labossiere, who was big and tough. Darryl didn't fight but Labossiere forced him to fight and gave him a bad time. There was a guy on our team, Red Armstrong, and after the period he was kidding

Darryl and I could see it was really hurting Darryl. So I said to Armstrong, "Okay, you got a big mouth. Why don't you fight him? Go ahead and we'll all watch what happens when you fight him." He never did, and from then on he kept his mouth shut.

The guys saw me do that and I got more respect in the room. A coach's job is to get a good atmosphere in the room. I always liked to have a player that I called a "straw boss," like they call guys on construction. A labourer who somehow becomes a leader. If the foreman wants the guys to work overtime he goes to the straw boss and gets him to start it. Know what I mean? Coaches have to have guys do that too. For me in Boston it was Bobby Schmautz. He wasn't the captain or anythink but somehow he seemed to be able to get the guys to do things. I don't know what it was, but I found my man.

I'm not saying Scotty Bowman has a guy like that on his team. He did it in a different way. But Fred Shero did. Like me, he played. You have to know who to go to and who to lay off of. Like Terry O'Reilly. You couldn't criticize Terry O'Reilly in the dressing room. You just couldn't. You'd destroy him. You could give him shit on the bench, but not in the dressing room. He told me after he retired that sometimes, even on the bench, he would have to grab the front of his pants just so he wouldn't get up and smack me. But if I'd ever done it in the dressing room I would have lost him.

Then there were guys like Stan Jonathan. You had to stroke guys like him. I did it with Jonathan all the time and everyone knew he was my pet. I used to kid him about the pet stuff and it made him feel good. You have to find out how each player is going to react when you get mad at him.

The first year I coached in Boston I was like Mickey Mouse behind the bench. I get there, I see all those guys, they'd won two Stanley Cups and been to the finals the year before when they ran into a hot goaltender, Bernie Parent, or they would have won again. And I'm gonna come in and change the whole thing? They kept sayin' to me, "Don't worry, Grapes. We'll be there when the bell rings." The bell rang in the play-offs and nobody was there. Chicago beat us in the first round. One of the players said they weren't mentally prepared and it was my job to do that. So, next fuckin' year, Attila the Hun.

The next year Ken Hodge didn't like me. Hated me. Espo couldn't understand why he wasn't getting as much ice time. I would take him off and he'd look up at the clock. Dallas Smith, he was so much smarter than me and he's lookin' at me like, who is this dum-dum? I was the only guy in the world who didn't like Dallas Smith.

I was mean in the room. When I talked in the dressing room nobody did nothin'. Nobody taped their sticks, did up their skates, nothin'. Even Cash wouldn't tape his stick. Everybody paid attention, they had to look at me. I didn't want any of them doing this and that when I was talkin'.

Then, along comes Dick Redmond. We got him in a trade and it's training camp. I used to let the guys have fun then as long as it didn't go too far. One night somebody broke the glass door at the front of the motel. Now Harry's after my ass. So the next day I'm talkin' in the room. I was absolutely supreme in my tirades and this one was a beauty. I'm walkin' around the room as I'm talkin' and here's Dick Redmond, lying on the floor with his feet up on a chair. I can tell the players are thinkin', wait till Grapes sees this. So I come to him and yell, "What do you think you're doin'?" He says, "Well, I'm just . . ." and before he says anything else I kick him, like I literally kick him. And I said, "Get up when I'm talkin' to you." What I'm tryin' to say is that I started to act like Attila the Hun.

That summer I'd be washin' my car and I'd play that song, "Won't Get Fooled Again." I think it was by the Stones [actually, it was the Who]. And that was my theme song when I went to training camp. You know, ninety per cent of them liked it. They wanted it, and we went on from there to four first-place finishes.

I was in my second year in Boston when Harry made the big trade and Espo went to the Rangers. We were in Vancouver. Phil came in and shook hands with everybody and he was crying. That's the only time a coach ever had a revolt on the ice. I blew the whistle for a skating drill and nobody speeded up. They were all heartbroken. I got mad and called them over to the corner and said, "I'm gonna blow this whistle and you guys are gonna start skatin'. If Phil Esposito can be traded and also my best friend on the team, Carol Vadnais, then the rest of you can go too. The first guy that doesn't skate, doesn't break his ass, he's gone too." From then on there was no real problem.

Orr was with us but he'd been hurt and wasn't playing. He was really pissed off. He came up to me and said, "Did you have anything to do with this trade?" I said, yep. He says, "I'm not bragging, but couldn't you have waited until I got back?"

We lose in Vancouver so now Harry phones. He says, "You can't believe the heat I'm getting back here. I'm getting crucified for trading the greatest goal-scorer of all time and a good defenceman for a fat old defenceman, Brad Park, and a broken-down old centreman, Jean Ratelle. You should see the cartoons about me." I told him not to worry, that I had seen some good things against Vancouver. It was true, I just had a feeling.

Now we go to Oakland and we're winning 5–2 in the third period. We just had to win that game and I'm thinking it's probably the most important game I've ever coached. Orr was back. Oakland gets a goal and seems to be coming on and I'm panicking and yelling at the guys. I'll never forget this one. Bobby gets the puck behind our net and he starts making moves with his head, telling this winger to go there, that winger to go there. He starts skating up towards our bench and he takes a look at me like, come on, shut up, just settle down, don't start going nuts. All the time he's got the puck and they can't take it away from him. He was toying with them. We all settled down and we won. But Bobby only played ten games for me that year. His knee went and that was it. Imagine, 135 points one year, ten games the next.

I'll tell you another story about Orr. The first year I was there he won the scoring and Phil was second. The season is going along and then I start seeing times when Bobby has an open net but he won't shoot. He'd pass to somebody else. Then he'd blast one from the point, through everybody into the net, and he'd run over to the referee and start pointing at someone else to tell the ref the other guy's scored the goal. I can't figure this out so one night I said to Carol Vadnais, "What's going on here?" and Vad says, "He doesn't want to get too far ahead of Phil in the race."

That same year we're in Atlanta. This is a funny one. I'm really conscious of Bobby because he's like Secretariat to me. Remember Hilliard Graves? Remember how he used to try to go for the other guy's knees? He looks like he's trying to get Bobby in the knee and I was really steamin'. During the play I grabbed one of my guys, Hank Nowak, and I threw him, literally physically threw him, over the boards and yelled, "Go get him!" Nowak skates out about ten feet, then turns back to me and says, "Who?"

A lot of people ask me what the players thought of playing for a guy like me. Brad Park said it best. He'd say that when we would arrive some place for a road game they wouldn't say "The Boston Bruins" were in town. They'd say, "Don Cherry and the Boston Bruins." He said the players loved it because they were never bothered. They hated to give interviews, and with everybody rushing to interview me, it took the heat off them.

Coaches usually like to have what we call "whipping boys." I used that phrase in fun but it's what we call them. You have to have someone you can give shit to. With me it was Peter McNab and Bob Miller. McNab was a college guy. He was big but he wasn't rough and I know he knew that deep down I liked him. One night against Philadelphia, in the playoffs, I benched Peter for the last ten minutes. I put Stan Jonathan in his place because I thought we needed a tough guy to help protect our lead. We won the game and afterwards I'm walkin' along, like you know how I walk, and that night I was pretty cocky, and Diane McNab [Peter's wife] was there. She's really a nice person and she says, "Nice game, Grapes." And I said, "Yep. Outcoached them again." And she says, "You son of a bitch." [Laughs]

Bobby Miller, he was an American and he always called me "coach." All the American players call you "coach." It bugged me a bit so, one day, after he says, "Coach, can I ask you a question?", I said, "Yes, player." So he never called me "coach" again. I always thought the players should be lean and bony and have pale skin so the blue veins would stick out. One time, just before the playoffs, Miller went out fishing on a boat and got a suntan. We're on a plane and Cash says to me, "Wait till you see Miller." So I go to the back of the plane and they're all there. Miller was just a rookie then. I lit into him. I said, "What's this all about? Where were you, on a vacation? Go to Hawaii or somethin' while the rest of us got colds?" I'm really rippin' him for his tan, right? Then he says, "What do you want me to do?" And I said, "Get rid of it!" All the players laughed about that one.

Here's a story. A reporter came up to me and said that the Bruins reminded him of Vikings or barbarians. Barbarians, that was it. He said we swaggered. We'd show up for the morning skate and we'd be swaggering. We'd go into a bar, all together, swaggering, like we owned it. That was one thing. When I went to Colorado, my friend Whitey Smith, a construction foreman, said the difference between Boston and Colorado was that in Boston I'd swagger into a bar; in Colorado I'd sneak in. Schultz, the Hammer, in Philadelphia, he used to say he couldn't sleep for a week before he played the Bruins. He said his team had tough guys and we had tough guys, but four of them on the Bruins were nuts. Put that in the book.

So now, the reporter, it was in Washington, he said we were barbarians and I said, "Yeah. We like to drop in, drink your beer, rape your women, and grab two points." The guy put it in the paper. Rose went nuts. Zeigler got on the phone. Harry's mad. So the next time we're there we tie the game. You know what's comin', eh? The reporter's there again and he says, "You got in a lot of trouble because of what you said to me. Any regrets?" And I says, "Yeah, I'm wrong sometimes. Sometimes we do come in and drink your beer and rape your women. But sometimes we only get one point."

Rose didn't like the way I acted as a coach and she doesn't like the way I act on television on "Coach's Corner." She likes the *Grapevine* but she can't stand "Coach's Corner." I act the same – it's coming to me as we talk – I act the same on "Coach's Corner" as I did when I was coaching. Know what I mean? If you don't like it, too bad. Get rid of me. Fire me. Rose just can't stand "Coach's Corner." She's always so happy when it's over.

Once, in my second year in Boston, we got hammered in Atlanta 8–1. The Boston Bruins were never supposed to be hammered 8–1. At the end of the second period I didn't go into the dressing room. I went to a phone, called the hotel, and told them I wanted a two-room suite for after the game, cheese and crackers, sandwiches, and lots of beer. After the game I tell everyone I want them back at the hotel, in the suite. Now they're scared because we had just got rid of a couple of guys and after losing 8–1 a lot of them are figurin' they've had it. After I told them about the hotel I left and slammed the door, real hard. I didn't even talk to the reporters. I just let on that I was really pissed.

I get to the suite and I'm sittin' there pourin' myself a beer. Then they all come in together, not just two or three at a time, so they must have waited for everybody in the lobby. They come in and stand there and I get up, walk into the other room, and say, "Beer's in here, guys." They walk in and see the spread, beer, all kinds of food, there was shrimp. It must have cost about three grand. You know what Ken Hodge said? He's got free beer, free food, and he says, "Do I have to stay?" I knew right then Ken Hodge was finished. I said, "You don't have to stay one minute. Fuck off." He was gone, as good as not being a Boston Bruin from that day on.

Here's one for you. My son, Timothy, had to have a kidney transplant. It was during the exhibition season and I was such a coward I made all the road-trips and let Rose take care of the whole thing. Our daughter, Cindy, was donating a kidney for Timothy. In the United States if you can't get people to give blood you pay for it. It's not like Canada, our socialist country. Know what I mean? I go down and I give blood for Timothy. The nurse says, "Your team was just in here." Every guy had gone down and given blood. I didn't know about it and would never have known about it if I hadn't gone there myself.

. . . So now Harry finally fires me in Boston and I go to coach the Colorado Rockies. Imagine me, going from a tough first-place club to a not-tough club. After I signed we were looking at some pictures of the Rockies and I asked Rose what she thought of the team. She says, "They look like nice boys." So I bring out some pictures of the Bruins. They didn't look like nice boys. What an ugly bunch. Anyway, there I was, in Colorado. We played our first exhibition game at Colorado Springs, against Winnipeg. Timothy, my son, was there as our stick boy. After the game I'm sitting with him on the bus and I said, "Tim, the Rochester Americans were a better team than this one."

By the time the season was half-over I was devastated. I tried every trick in the book and nothing worked. I remember being in my car, going home after a game, and thinking I'd rather be working as a labourer. But I couldn't bail out on the players because a lot of guys on that team gave it their all: Rene Robert, Lanny McDonald, Schmautzie, Mike Christie. We had a few jerks, like Mike McEwan. Put that in the book. But most of them were good guys and gave me every ounce they had. You talk to Lanny today. He told me the most enjoyable time he ever had as a player was with Colorado. The players had just as much fun in Colorado as they did in Boston. I'm proud of that because it was tough.

The great thing was the fans. We'd lose and I'd be embarrassed and I'd walk across the ice after the game and they'd be yellin', "Don't worry, Grapes. We'll get 'em next time, Grapes." They never booed once. When we played our last game of the season there was a big snowstorm in Denver, the worst in ten years. Everyone said we'd be lucky to get 3,000 at the game. We had 12,500 and we were playing a shit team, Pittsburgh. We were long-gone out of the playoffs but the fans just wanted to be there.

I knew I was gone after that season in Colorado but I think I quit coaching two years too soon. I was pretty burnt out because I'd gone through all that went with coaching the Boston Bruins and losing to the Canadiens all the time in the playoffs. Then I went through hell in Colorado with Ray Miron, the general manager. He thought I wanted his job. Here's the strangest thing of all. They wanted to fire Ray

Miron and I told them no, keep him on, and we'll work together. It didn't work out that way. He was against me right from that first exhibition game in Colorado Springs because an agent he was drinkin' with after that game told me and that's how I know.

I put the final touch on the Colorado job when I went on TV with Dave Hodge two weeks after I was fired. He asked about what happened in Colorado and I said, "It's tough to fly like an eagle when you're surrounded by turkeys."

I think a coach has to pay his dues, has to start in a league like the American League. I did things my first year there that didn't work but I learned. I cost my team in Rochester some games because I tried things that weren't right. My first year in Boston, same thing. I had them look at the video of Philadelphia beating them in the finals the year before and it didn't work. I thought it would get them psyched up to play the Flyers but they didn't get mad at the Flyers. They got mad at me for showin' it. I remember Orr saying, "What did you have to do that for?" A coach has a tough job and you have to learn it.

Up until about three or four years ago there was a lot of bullshit about career coaches, tacticians they called them, men who had never played at a high level. I think that's changed now. I think of Pat Quinn, to me the best coach in the league today. I think of Teddy Green, John Paddock, the Sutters. Look at Bill Dineen and the job he's doing in Philadelphia, and he's sixty years old.

I'm not knocking the guys that never played the game, a guy like Pat Burns, although he did play a little hockey. Mike Keenan learned coaching at the university level and that's good hockey. But still, I mean it makes me think of the story about the person who says a baby doctor, whatever they're called, delivers a baby and he's a man. And someone says, think of how much better he'd be if he knew what the woman was goin' through.

When I was behind the bench I never carried a piece of paper and you know why? Because I played for a coach that had a piece of paper. We used to sit there and wonder, doesn't this guy know what lines we have? Doesn't he know the players? I'm not knocking Bob Johnson because he was a good friend of mine, but what can they be doing? They've got video replay now, the whole deal. It looks intelligent, it looks good. Oh boy, he's got something. He's caught something. You know what I mean? It impresses everybody.

What really kills me is when they have the goalie out. They gotta call the guys over and start drawing diagrams to tell them where to stand. You mean to tell me they never thought the situation would ever come when the goalie would be pulled? Think about it. They've got a board and a big black marker and they're drawin' plans. You go here. You go there.

Another thing that really kills me with these coaches, and this is good, they're up 5–1 and all of a sudden they start coaching. They're yelling at their guys, go here, go there. But if they're losing 5–1 they melt into the background with the trainer. You can't kid the players. I remember one coach we had. We were losing 4–1 and he just died, he quit. He never said a word. Then we come back and go up 5–4. Now he's back in business with the "You go here, you go there." I'm on the bench beside Gerry Ehman and Gerry says, "Take a look. He's back coachin' us again." But now some of these guys have to have a piece of paper. You never saw Punch Imlach with one. I played for him in Springfield. Did you ever see Dick Irvin with one? Toe Blake? They didn't even have assistants. I never had one either.

You know what I loved best about coaching? The morning

skates on the day of the game. I liked it behind the bench, but it's such pressure. I used to think I was Admiral Nelson. When we would go to training camp I used to tell the players we were taking off on a long voyage and I was their commander, Lord Nelson. I told them I would treat them like sailors on a ship. They knew I wasn't kiddin'. I'd say, "Some of you are gonna be here for the long voyage. But some of you, if you don't produce, it'll be like on a ship on a foggy night. You'll be dropped over the side and nobody will ever know you're gone. You know how everybody pulls their weight? That means the guys are on the line, pulling the sails, everybody pulls their weight. If you don't pull your weight on this club, you're gone, and I don't care who you are."

Oh, I just thought of something. A good one. In Boston one night, I came in after we won. I had made a few moves in the game, benched one guy, gave another one more ice time. Everything I did that night turned out to be the right move. It's a great feeling. So I said to Harry after the game, I said, "Harry, I was just like Admiral Nelson out there tonight. I really was. I was Admiral Nelson, right?" I knew I wasn't Admiral Nelson. I mean, fuck, but he went and told people the story. Now, it's a few years later and *Hockey Night in Canada* is going to hire me. Paul Mooney, Harry's boss, phoned them up and told them the Admiral Nelson story. He said they shouldn't hire me because I used to think I was a sea captain and was mentally unbalanced. The guy Mooney called was Ted Hough, the big boss, and he believed him. So he called in Ralph Mellanby, the producer who wanted to hire me, and told him the story. Mellanby said, "You don't have to worry about that any more because now Cherry thinks he's Ted Hough." [Laughs] So the Bruins tried to gas me off TV before I even started. Not only were they trying to ruin my hockey career, they were trying to ruin me on TV too.

I know coaches are cannon fodder these days. Guys you see coaching today, half of them will be gone pretty soon. I would have gone back if Hamilton had got a team. I was goin' back although Rose would've probably divorced me. Even today, if somebody came to me and I liked the idea and they said I'd be director of player personnel and coach I think I'd go back. Al Arbour's still coaching. So is Scotty, John Muckler, my contemporaries. The reason I won't get hired now is because I would take over the whole club. It would be just like it was in Boston, "Don Cherry and his so-and-so's are coming to town." The press would love me. The fans would love me. The players would love me. Know what I mean? Now say they want to get rid of me. How could they do it? How could they fire someone everybody loves?

6

Shenanigans in Chicago – From the Major to Iron Mike

BILL STEWART   MIKE KEENAN

Take a team originally named after a flower, transfer it to another city and name it after a restaurant, and you have the makings of some unusual stories. That's how the Chicago Blackhawks got started. In the 1920s the Pacific Coast Hockey League was on a par with the NHL. The champions of each league would play for the Stanley Cup. When the PCHL folded in 1926, one of its teams, the Portland Rosebuds, was purchased by a Chicago socialite, Major Frederic McLaughlin, who had made millions in the coffee trade. The Major owned a restaurant called "The Blackhawk," which he had named after the regiment he had commanded in World War One. Never shy about grabbing free plugs for his eatery, McLaughlin decided to give his hockey club the same name.

McLaughlin was a coach's nightmare. In the first ten years he owned the Blackhawks he hired and fired thirteen of them. Success behind the bench didn't mean your job was safe, as my father was the first to find out. Dick Irvin had been a Rosebud, and he became the first captain of the Chicago Blackhawks. In his rookie year as a coach he had taken the team to the 1931 Stanley Cup finals, losing to the Montreal Canadiens in the fifth game of the best-of-five final series. The following October, he was actually packing his bags to leave for training camp when a telegram was delivered to him in Regina. It read, "As the directors desire to make a change, your services as coach will no longer be required." It was no secret McLaughlin made all the decisions, while the directors, mainly a group of his old army cronies, nodded in agreement.

Tommy Gorman coached the Blackhawks to their first Stanley Cup victory in 1934. No matter, he too was fired. Three years later McLaughlin decided he would ice a team made up totally of American-born players. He laid this one on his coach at the time, Clem Loughlin. There were several native-born Americans already on the team, who were then joined by strangers named Ernie Klingbiel, Milt Brink, and Bun Laprairie, who had been recruited from various leagues in Minnesota, Wisconsin, and Michigan. The all-American Blackhawks did manage to win one game, beating the Rangers 4–3 in New York. But the experiment was, in all, a disaster.

The Major, naturally, fired Loughlin and replaced him with an American, Bill Stewart, whose grandson Paul Stewart is now a referee in the NHL. This time McLaughlin was vindicated. Stewart became the first American coach to win the Stanley Cup.

Paul Stewart

My grandfather had been working as a National League referee and also as an umpire in the National Baseball League. He had coached and organized both men's and women's hockey at the college level.

[As coach of the Blackhawks] he won the Stanley Cup in '38, an upset over the Toronto Maple Leafs. That was the time he had a fistfight with Conn Smythe in the corridor at Maple Leaf Gardens before one of the games. He was a fiery, feisty guy.

The next season, around Christmas, Major McLaughlin had one of his brain-waves and suggested to my grandfather that he sit upstairs during the games so he could get a better view of the ice and direct the team from there. My grandfather said to him, "What are you, nuts? What am I supposed to do, pull strings and tell them where to go?" Everybody thought McLaughlin *was* nuts and at that time maybe more than usual because he was going through a bitter divorce with his wife, the famous dancer Irene Castle.

During the first intermission that night, the Major walked into the dressing room and started to tell the players what they should do. My grandfather said, "Who the hell do you think you're talking to? They're playing for me." They had a real row, and after the game my grandfather was fired.

He had two years left on a contract that called for $5,000 a year, so it wasn't a bad payday for him. But there was a stipulation that he couldn't coach any hockey team within five hundred miles of Chicago. That somewhat limited his chances to coach. So he went back to baseball umpiring and the NHL hired him back and he worked as a referee until they brought in the red line a few years later. Somebody decided he was too slow a skater to keep up at that time, so they let him go. Overall, he worked twenty-four years as a

Major League baseball umpire and fourteen years as a referee in the NHL. He coached hockey again in 1957, the U.S. National team, and they had a record of 53–4. The nucleus of that team won the gold medal at the Olympics in 1960.

In the fifty years between the Blackhawks' Stanley Cup victory in 1938 and the hiring of Mike Keenan in 1988, the team changed coaches twenty times. That's one of the reasons the Hawks won the Stanley Cup just once during those fifty years. One of the coaches was Billy Reay, who has the record for the most wins as a coach in Chicago. But you won't hear from him in this book because I don't speak to him. Why? My mother told me not to, that's why. More on that later.

On November 6, 1992, the owner of the Blackhawks, Bill Wirtz, held a news conference to announce that Mike Keenan was no longer with his hockey club. After four seasons as both coach and general manager in Chicago, Keenan had relinquished the coaching duties to Darryl Sutter, who had been his assistant coach for two years. There were reports that Sutter was being offered head-coaching jobs elsewhere. Wirtz didn't want to lose him and the only way Sutter would stay was as head coach, so Keenan moved upstairs.

Wirtz and Keenan had been at odds over a contract since the previous June, shortly after Keenan had coached the Hawks into the Stanley Cup finals where they were beaten by the Pittsburgh Penguins. It had been the Hawks' first appearance in the finals since 1973. In his statement Wirtz said, "Mike wanted more authority than the Blackhawks have traditionally given anyone that has held the position of general manager. Mike continued to express second thoughts about giving up coaching, which is a very difficult thing. To give up coaching and become a general manager, after coaching for many years, is a terrible transition."

Wirtz was right. Mike Keenan wasn't going to be happy working for a hockey team but not coaching it. He had been a high-profile coach for twelve years, the last eight of them in the NHL, first with Philadelphia and then with Chicago. Before that he had coached college hockey at the University of Toronto, junior hockey in Peterborough, and had spent three years as the coach of the Buffalo Sabres' farm team, the Rochester Americans, in the AHL, when Scotty Bowman was running the Buffalo hockey operation.

Mike Keenan has been a very successful coach, and a very controversial one. He won the Canadian college championship at U. of T., reached the Memorial Cup finals with Peterborough, and won an American League championship in Rochester. In his eight years in the NHL his teams finished in first place five times and reached the Stanley Cup finals three times. In 1987 and 1991 he had the pressure-filled job as head coach of Team Canada in the Canada Cup, and was a winner both times.

Mike is a favourite camera subject for those of us in the television business. Behind the bench, he is, as Frank Boucher described Lester Patrick, dramatic, emotional, sometimes arrogant – in some ways much like Scotty Bowman, who, Keenan freely admits, had a big influence on his coaching style. Scotty always chews ice cubes during games. Keenan chews ice cubes too. Like Bowman, he isn't universally loved by the men who play for him, nor by the media who cover his teams. The cameras often catch Keenan openly and animatedly criticizing players during games. In his years in Chicago he became famous for a lack of patience with his goaltenders, pulling his starter and then pulling the back-up and putting the starter back in, leaving them little room for error or comfort.

I interviewed Mike for this book a couple of weeks after he had left the Blackhawks. Understandably he was still upset over what had happened, and how it had happened.

MIKE KEENAN

I was asked six days after the Stanley Cup finals, "Do you want to coach? And if you do you have to sign a three-year contract." I said, "I'm too tired. I can't make that decision right now. I think it's unfair that you're asking me right now. But if you're worried about Darryl Sutter not getting a chance to coach, and if that's what you want, a commitment for three years right now, I can't give it to you. So we'd better hire Darryl. I don't know if I can give our team, our organization, my best abilities, if I'm asked to make a commitment right now, after six days, to coach for three more years."

The change was made. Sutter became the Blackhawks' head coach with Keenan as general manager, and the new season began. But the problem of a long-term commitment was still there.

MIKE KEENAN

I kept saying, "I want time. I don't want to sign a contract now. I'd like you to give me till the end of March because of the way I'm feeling right now. I expected it to be extremely difficult to be able to walk away. I can't answer the question now, I can't tell you if I am prepared to walk away. I don't think you should ask me after fifteen games. Ask me after sixty and I can give you a better answer." I didn't want to sign the contract until March because, as I'm sitting here, I can tell you right now I want to coach again.

When he left the Blackhawks, Keenan had a supporter, of sorts, in the team's vice-president Bob Pulford, whom Keenan had succeeded as general manager and who now was taking over as GM again. Pulford coached in Los Angeles and Chicago and he obviously sympathized with Keenan by saying, "I went through the same thing. Certainly, if you have coached as long as Mike has, you have withdrawal pains and they are very difficult. You are still watching a game as a coach and you are still thinking as a coach."

That's exactly what Mike was doing when we got together at the Montreal Forum. He was thinking as a coach as he answered my questions and talked to me about what he likes to do best of all.

MIKE KEENAN

The thing you have to be for sure is a student for life so you continue to learn about the coaching profession on an ongoing basis. If you can't accept new ideas, if you can't accept change, then you're not going to be a very effective coach, particularly now in the '90s. You have to be flexible in your thinking.

I've coached in the league for eight years. That's not a very long period of time, yet the tactics have changed. The skill level has changed. You need the ability to adapt to the changes that you see in the people you're handling and in the business aspect of the game. You walk into a locker room now and for sure there are four or five millionaires looking at you. If I had the opportunity to write a book about coaching, that's the number-one thing I would stress to young men and women who want to coach, adapting to the way the game changes. It's not whether you've won or lost in the past.

It's whether you're winning or losing now, whether you're getting better or worse.

The single most important element of motivation for a professional athlete is pride in himself. I've learned this from having the opportunity to coach some of the best people in the game and the best example I can give is Wayne Gretzky. The motivating factor for Wayne Gretzky is his pride in his performance, pride in his ability to be the best player in the game on a daily basis. I don't know if he even knows it but he has a tremendous sense about positive rivalries. I'll give you an example.

In 1987 I had both Wayne and Mario Lemieux on the Canada Cup team. Mario was an excellent hockey player then but hadn't won on a consistent basis. So there they both were and Wayne said to himself, consciously or subconsciously, I don't know, "I need to get better as a player because I see this rising star and I'm going to tell him and show him everything I know about the game for two reasons. One, our team will be better. Two, he's going to force me to be better because I want to be the best." And I saw that happen right before my eyes.

You could see that Mario was coming, getting better, and Wayne just kept getting better. Wayne was by far the best player on the Canada Cup team in '87. Mario was very important, the second-best player and the top goal-scorer. But the best player for us, in terms of the leadership that was responsible for us winning the Canada Cup, was Wayne and his contribution to the team overall. Mario helped him raise his play to a level that was absolutely necessary for us in order to win.

I'll tell you a little story about Wayne that year. It was here, in the Montreal Forum, our first practice. I had called it for 10:30, and you know the stories about how Keenan is known for discipline so you had better be on time, and so on.

It's 10:29 and I'm standing at centre-ice watching the clock. Wayne isn't on the ice yet but he's coming from the locker room to the ice and he's surrounded by what looked like about fifty media people. He's being accommodating, as he always is, but he was watching the clock too. He stepped on the ice just before 10:30. I was looking right into his eyes, and his eyes, they just went like saucers. They were wide and glowing and I said, this is it. This is his place of solace. This is where he loves to be, what he wants to do with his life right now. As soon as his left foot, his left skate, touched the ice at the Montreal Forum for the first practice for Canada Cup '87 his eyes went just like that and he saw everything in that building. It hit me instantly. I said to myself, "I'm in for a treat." And I was.

Those of us in the broadcast booth often use the word "emotional" to describe a game, or the performance of a team or a player. Mike Keenan spoke about the role of emotion in an athlete's game.

MIKE KEENAN

You have to have an emotional state of readiness to be a high-performance athlete. That comes with preparation. You have to be prepared to take your play beyond what you expect at normal times and beyond the expectations you have for yourself as an athlete. You have to be at that state of readiness where you can perform at your best possible level.

There have been many times when I have walked into the locker room before a game and realized that the players weren't ready, that they were not emotionally up for the game. You can sense it, no question about it, and you know there's going to be trouble. It's a scary feeling when you're going out for competition and you know they're not prepared. You sense they didn't have the mental discipline to prepare themselves for that particular evening, whatever the reason. It might be fatigue because of travel, or they're over-confident or they're not confident, or they're fearful of the situation.

The good coaches have an intuitive feel for the game, have a reading of their team at all times and know what state they are in as a group. To a certain extent it's a gift, like a player with hockey sense. You have to work at it, you have to stay in tune with the group you are working with. But you can defi-nitely sense where your team is at.

Tom Landry, long-time head coach of the Dallas Cowboys, says coaches get too much blame when their team loses and too much credit when they win. He says you can't win with-out talented players, that coaching "genius" is overrated. Mike Keenan agrees.

MIKE KEENAN

You can never win anything at the professional level unless you have players with the ability to win. In the end you can be effective in terms of the management of your club and pre-pare them as well as you possibly can. If you work from the premise that no one knows what the human potential level is, you probably will do as well as you can with the people you have to work with. But you ultimately can't win it all without the talent base. If a player doesn't have that intrinsic pride in his own performance, as we talked about earlier, then you can do anything you like as a coach and you and he won't sustain or maintain his skill on a long-term basis.

The players are ultimately responsible for success or lack of success. Somehow the media structures or slots a coach and says, well, the coach did this to be successful, or he didn't do this and that's why they're not successful. The coach has some influence but it's the performers on the field, in Landry's case, or on the ice, in a hockey coach's case, that have to execute to get the job done.

It's during a game that I enjoy coaching most. It's more important at the professional level because you expect more from your athletes at that time. Scotty Bowman, my mentor to a certain extent, is the master at it. You have to have the ability to read the game while you're standing there, know the personnel you have and the personnel you're working against. You have to be able to know which performer on a given day is at his best because they're not all at their best all the time. You have to be able to decipher that quickly, spontaneously.

It has a lot to do with sequencing. Scotty can sequence in his mind the rotation of the players in a game whether it's changing on the fly, or who should be up and on the ice next, and how all that plays out in terms of the score of the game at the time.

The first time I explained this to a team was the Canada Cup team in '91. I started off a meeting by asking them, "How many minutes are there in a hockey game?" They all give me that "What are you talking about?" look because they've been playing the game all their lives. Right away: "Sixty minutes." I said, "No, that's incorrect." And they're all still sitting there with that "What does he mean?" look in their eyes.

I said, "There are 360 minutes in a hockey game, unless you play overtime. That's because there are six of you on the ice at once. Now we're gonna start and we're gonna give our goalie, Bill Ranford, 60 minutes. There's 300 minutes left. Wayne will get at least 27 minutes, maybe 30, so now there's 270 left." I said, "Mark [Messier] will get 25 minutes," and so on. Now I start going through every member of the club and the guys I haven't named yet are wondering how much time they're going to get. Three minutes? Four minutes?

I said that if we get 10 minutes in penalties that leaves 350 minutes, so any undisciplined play takes time away and detracts from our ability to perform as a group. I went through the whole process to make them understand the sequencing or judgment a coach has to deal with standing behind the bench, and how it's all predicated on the amount of ice time you have to work with.

I put it all up on the blackboard. When I put 60 minutes beside Ranford's name they started to laugh and said that I pull goalies more than anybody else. [Laughs] I went down the whole line-up. I explained that, because he will be on the power play, Paul Coffey will get more time than, say, Eric Desjardins, and so on. I said, "What we're getting at here, fellows, is that you are all stars on your own teams. When you go back to Boston, or Chicago, or Philly, wherever it is, you're going to get Wayne's ice time. But here some of you will have to learn to accept 6 minutes, or 8 minutes. You're now a role player and that's the ice time a role player gets. You'll have a better appreciation for the role players on your team."

That was the first team I had ever done it with. I don't know how it occurred to me, but I had to figure a way of explaining to these stars why some of them were going to be role players. Dale Hawerchuk, for example, was a role player on that Canada Cup team. When I'm coaching I can tell you, probably within fifteen to thirty seconds, how much ice time everyone received. When I check on the ice times after the game my guess would almost be right on. I'm sure Scotty can do it too.

When Mike Keenan was coaching the Philadelphia Flyers, his number-one goaltender, Pelle Lindbergh, was killed in a car crash early in the 1985–86 season.

MIKE KEENAN

It was a devastating blow for our club, and that means no disrespect for the other goaltenders I had. I can still remember walking into the arena the next day and being totally devastated. I was leaning up against the wall in my office and Bobby Clarke was there with his wife, Sandy. I turned to Sandy and said, "I don't know how we're going to keep this team together because he meant so much to all of us."

That was in November and we were on a tremendous winning streak. Our team ended up in first place with 110 points that year but we got beaten in the first round by New York, by a hot goaltender. In terms of the heartache, the hardship, the stress, there is no real way of describing the effect that tragedy had on all of us. It was really difficult. It was ever-present.

Mike agreed with the thought, expressed by several coaches I talked to, that there is a big difference between coaching in the playoffs and in the regular season.

MIKE KEENAN

I think there is because the athletes are better prepared, emotionally [in the playoffs]. They know it's crunch time for them and they're very proud. Some of them have a fear of doing well and they don't understand it. Once you explain it to them they can handle it a lot more readily. Once they have had some winning experiences they can handle it.

And they can also handle it once they have had some losing experiences. They almost need both to develop a depth of confidence.

The regular season is like a marathon. It's a question of, can we get through it and perform well? But the playoffs are special, and always will be special. I liken playoff games to a package, two games in one. All the emotion and all the work you do for two games in the regular season is packed into one game in the playoffs.

Unlike all the other men I interviewed, Mike Keenan didn't mention hockey when I asked him about the start of his coaching career.

MIKE KEENAN

My first coaching job was with a high-school lacrosse team at Don Mills Collegiate, in Toronto. We went to the city finals and that's really where I found out I love to coach. I had been teaching at hockey schools all through university and at one time I owned my own hockey school. My first hockey coaching job was with a senior-A team in Whitby. In fact I was a part-owner of the team. I had won a championship as a player at the University of Toronto. I was drafted by Vancouver of the WHA and played a year for them in Roanoke. I was qualified to teach school and so was my wife. I went back to Toronto and started teaching and was making $6,000, which was about twice what I was making in hockey. A few guys from my old U. of T. team were still around and we entered the Whitby team in the Senior League. We all became shareholders.

I started out as a player, then became player-coach. That's probably where I had the most gut-wrenching of all my experiences. I'm a very mediocre player and I'm trying to coach the other players. I felt I owed it to my teammates to be able to play well and coach well. I found that very difficult. A broken shoulder ended my playing in the first year. I tried to play again the next year but I couldn't get over the bad shoulder. After that season I went into coaching in junior hockey and that's where it all started.

The image of "Iron Mike," the tough-guy disciplinarian, has always been associated with Keenan's coaching career. But Mike says he really isn't quite what the image has made him out to be.

MIKE KEENAN

I think it's just a misunderstanding and it's partly my fault. I have matured as a coach and an individual, but coming into the league I had certain fears. The fears weren't about my ability but about the process of the NHL where so many coaches were being dismissed. I wasn't a former player so I thought if I didn't maintain a hard, stern structure in the early part of my career I was going to be out like everybody else.

In my early years I found it very difficult to make the transition in the ten-minute time period you're given after a game to open the door to the media. After sustaining a tremendous level of concentration during a game I found it extremely difficult to flip out of that and become congenial and approachable so soon after the game ended.

I still remember Red Fisher being upset with me because I wasn't talking much and he said something about Keenan being aloof and arrogant. I told him it had nothing to do with that. I was thinking, what does Mike Keenan have to say in his first year? He's thirty-five years old, never played in the league, and now he's coaching at the Montreal Forum where they've had so many great teams and great players. I thought about the coaches that had been there, Scotty, Dick Irvin, Toe Blake, and I felt humbled by it all. I felt I had nothing to say, and people thought I was being arrogant. That's part of the reason. I brought a lot of it on myself, but I was just a new kid on the block.

I've matured since then, I've been able to make that transition. I understand it more, and certainly with my players I've been able to understand it better. My approach is still firm, discipline-oriented, demanding. Yet I've shown them the other side, that I care for them as people. I had more fun coaching that last year in Chicago than I had in my whole career. When I left the team so many of them called me. Chris Chelios said he'd take me out to dinner. I enjoyed the group I had and I was the most relaxed I'd ever been in the NHL.

When I coach again I think I'm going to have a different perspective. I consider this to be a sabbatical. I'm reading a lot, trying to educate myself about hockey, the changes that have taken place, the influx of the Europeans and Russians, the new rules and how they are going to impact on the game. There's a tremendous amount of money involved and there is such an emphasis by the people paying that money to win, win now. If one guy signs a huge contract he throws the whole salary scale of the team out of whack. A coach has to deal with that sort of thing. These days a tremendous amount is expected from the coach.

I'm being a student right now so when I come back to coach I'll be a much better one. There's no question about it. I'm going to coach again.

*Coaches, including Mike Keenan, have had their problems
with the media. Chicago's Charlie Conacher laid hands on a
reporter in the 1940s as did Hartford's Jack Evans and
Toronto's Mike Nykoluk in the '80s. In the distant background their confreres were no doubt secretly applauding.
Which leads me to a brief story about me and Billy Reay, as
promised earlier.*

*Billy Reay played several seasons in Montreal while my
father was coaching the Canadiens. He was a journeyman
but an effective centreman who was on Stanley Cup-
winning teams in 1946 and 1953. Our families were friendly
and, when Reay became a coach in the NHL, he and I got
together often whenever our paths crossed. He coached
briefly in Toronto, then in 1963 settled in for a long run with
the Chicago Blackhawks, coaching them in a team-record
1,012 games. In 1973 the Blackhawks played the Canadiens
in the Stanley Cup finals. Danny Gallivan and I were the
boys in the booth for* Hockey Night in Canada.

*The series opened in Montreal. During the second period
of the first game the Canadiens' Jacques Lemaire scored a
goal on a play that the Hawks loudly claimed should have
been ruled offside. Early in the third period our producer,
Ralph Mellanby, told me on the intercom from the TV
mobile that they had heard that during the second intermission Reay had gone to the door of the officials' room to complain to referee Bruce Hood about the Lemaire goal. I
relayed that item to our viewers as follows: "We have had a
report that during the intermission Billy Reay was seen
headed in the direction of the officials' room to perhaps further comment on the play leading to the goal scored by
Lemaire. I guess at playoff time the magic word in a final
round is 'tension.'" There was no further comment on the
incident during the rest of that show or at any other time in*

the series. (In light of what transpired later I reviewed the tape of the game to confirm what I had said.)

The next day a newspaper, Le Journal de Montreal, *carried a picture showing Reay, closely followed by a Forum security man, confronting Hood as the referee walked down the corridor leading to the officials' room. The caption under the picture, translated, read: "Between the second and third periods Billy Reay did not hesitate to speak his mind to referee Bruce Hood. 'Didn't you see that Lemaire was offside when he scored the fourth goal?' yelled Billy. The referee did not reply. . . ."*

Normally during a playoff series the Hockey Night in Canada *announcers are in fairly close touch with the coaches. During the '73 finals I was bodychecked by a flu bug that laid me pretty low. So, with the permission of my bosses, I had to skip most of the scene except for the games. I wasn't around for the between-game bull sessions with Reay and the Canadiens' coach, Scotty Bowman.*

Montreal had a 3–1 series lead when the teams played what most of us thought would be the final game of the series in Montreal on May 8. The Canadiens' management was so confident they booked a hotel and ordered the champagne for the post-game victory party. But, in what turned out to be the best-remembered game of that series, the Blackhawks stayed alive. Ken Dryden and Tony Esposito, the two goaltenders on the legendary team that had defeated the Soviets in the historic '72 series the previous September, took turns outfumbling one another all night. The Hawks finally prevailed 8–7.

After the game I spied Reay holding court with a dozen or so reporters. I joined the group. The minute Reay spotted me he forgot all about everybody else and with fire in his eyes said to me, "I want to talk to you!" My friend Billy didn't mean at some later time, man to man, friend to friend. He meant right then and there, complete with a live audience. In the next few minutes I became the centre of everyone's attention as the suddenly furious Chicago coach lit into me with a tirade the likes of which I had never experienced. It was all because of what I had said about his trip down the hallway to meet Bruce Hood in game one.

"Who do you think you are, saying something like that? Who told you that story? How can you talk about something you don't know anything about? I've got family out there watching. How do you think they felt when they heard somebody like you talk like that about me?" Along the way he used an expression I had never heard before, and have never heard since. He said: "You're a cheap cheat. You're nothing but a cheap cheat." He called me that four or five times before he was through. The only thing I remember saying was, "It happened, Billy. What did I say that was wrong?" But he kept hammering away at me, implying the incident I had mentioned on TV had never taken place.

At one point Jacques Berube, a CBC producer who was standing beside me, said to Reay, "There was a picture in the paper." Billy didn't let that stop him, and I was a "cheap cheat," plus other things, for a few more minutes. Berube muttered to me, "This is unbelievable."

I guess I stood there and took it. I can't remember how it finally ended. I probably left after he levelled the lowest blow of all by saying, "Your father would be ashamed of you if he knew how you talk about people on TV."

My mother was at the game and I gave her a ride home. Her normally talkative son was unusually quiet and it wasn't long before she asked me, "What's wrong with you?" I told her what had happened. Her only comment was a terse, "If I were you I'd never speak to him again." For once her son did exactly as he was told.

In 1976 the ghost of Major Frederic McLaughlin paid a visit to the Reay household, which was in an apartment building owned by the Wirtz family, the same Wirtz family that owned the Blackhawks. A day or two before Christmas, Billy awoke to find that some time during the night a note had been slipped under his door. It was from the Wirtzes. The gist of their holiday-season message was, "You're fired."

I was doing the sports news that night on CFCF-TV in Montreal. I read the story and finished with a brief editorial comment: "Merry Christmas, Billy."

7

Some Surprise Winners

AL MacNEIL JEAN PERRON

JOHN MUCKLER

When the Stanley Cup is finally won, the climax of the ever-lengthening NHL season, the outcome is rarely much of a surprise. Favourites, or near-favourites, almost always emerge victorious. However, once in a while a "Cinderella team" comes from far back in the pack to surprise almost everyone, even themselves.

Since the expansion of 1967, there have been three teams in particular that have slipped their feet into the glass skate-boots: the 1971 Montreal Canadiens coached by Al MacNeil; the Canadiens again, in 1986, coached by Jean Perron; and the 1990 Edmonton Oilers coached by John Muckler. MacNeil and Perron were rookie head coaches and to a large degree so was Muckler, who had coached Minnesota for only a few games in 1968–69. Interestingly, each coach had also elected to use a goaltender who was a virtual stranger to Stanley Cup competition. All three goaltenders ended up winning the playoff MVP award.

In 1971 the Boston Bruins were favoured to repeat their easy Stanley Cup win of a year earlier. The Bruins, led by Bobby Orr, who was at the peak of his greatness, had finished the season with all kinds of records, including 121 points in the standings and 399 pucks behind their opponents' goaltenders. Phil Esposito had scored the previously unbelievable total of 76, a record we were certain nobody would ever match. In the first round, the Bruins played the third-place Montreal Canadiens, a team that had finished the season twenty-four points behind Boston. To make the Bruins' task seem even easier, Montreal coach Al MacNeil said he would start the series with a goaltender, a law student at McGill University, who had a grand total of six games' experience in the NHL. Kid by the name of Ken Dryden.

In 1985–86, under first-year coach Jean Perron, the Canadiens had won forty of their eighty games, but so had the Hartford Whalers. This edition of the Habs had Larry Robinson and Bob Gainey from the glory days of the late 1970s, but overall, the team gave little indication it would go very far in the playoffs, especially when Perron named a twenty-one-year-old rookie to start the first series against Boston. Kid named Patrick Roy.

If the 1986 Canadiens seemed a far cry from the glory teams of that franchise, the 1990 Edmonton Oilers appeared to be an even farther cry from the team that had won the Stanley Cup four times in five years in the 1980s. Grant Fuhr had been called the world's greatest goalie throughout that era. But in 1990 Fuhr was injured and unavailable for the playoffs. Bill Ranford, with four games of playoff experience, would have to carry the load. The Oilers had finished nine points behind the defending champion Calgary Flames. There really seemed no way the Oilers could come close to the Stanley Cup in 1990, what with Grant Fuhr injured,

Paul Coffey playing for the Pittsburgh Penguins, and Number 99 spending his winters in Los Angeles.

Now let's hear from the three chaps who coached three teams named Cinderella.

Al MacNeil is a Maritimer who had a lengthy playing career as a defenceman. He played junior for the Toronto Marlies and began his professional career in the Toronto Maple Leafs organization. He was traded to Montreal, went from there to Chicago, then to the New York Rangers, and was the second pick of the Pittsburgh Penguins in the 1967 expansion draft.

AL MACNEIL

When I was playing in Rochester the team was co-sponsored by Toronto and Montreal. They were the first teams to get together in running a farm club. I had known Sam Pollock from junior hockey and we hit it off pretty good. I always felt that I was going to eventually end up back with Sam. He traded for me from Pittsburgh and asked me if I wanted to coach. I told him I thought I was ready and he offered me a choice, Cleveland or Houston. I had been in the American League before. I thought I would try something new so I said I would go to Houston. I was always interested in the dressing room and I felt I had a pretty good idea of what was needed to win.

I had a mix there of kids and veterans. Tony Esposito and Phil Myre were the goalies. I ended up as the playing-coach. You talk about work – being a playing-coach is the hardest thing you can ever do. You have to play, and at the same time you have to tell your players what to do. Then you have to go out and do it yourself. You put yourself right on the line, and that's the hardest part. But I had a pretty good rapport with the guys. We got in the playoffs and then got knocked off by Dallas. It was a good learning year for me.

The next year they moved the team to Montreal, in the American League, and called it the Voyageurs. I was still the playing-coach and they brought in Ronnie Caron to help me. He went behind the bench. The season after that [1970–71] I joined the big team and started the year as the assistant to Claude Ruel. Then in December he relinquished his job and I took over.

I was surprised when it happened. I guess I was naive, but I thought Claude had a good support system with Sam and Ronnie. I didn't think there were any problems that we weren't going to be able to get through. I couldn't see any big difficulty in the coaching area but I guess Claude found the pressure was getting to him. So I moved in and I was glad for the chance. I was happy to do it. I felt up to the challenge because I had two good years of coaching behind me, and through Ronnic and Sam I had a pretty good idea of what the organization wanted from a coach.

When I took over there were several young guys who had played for me at some time during the previous two years, guys like Reggie Houle, Marc Tardif, Pete Mahovlich, Pierre Bouchard. All the young guys were my guys, plus I had only been away from playing in the NHL a couple of years so I had played against a lot of the older guys in the room. I was familiar with them and they were familiar with me. They didn't give me an assistant. I was all alone from then on.

I really didn't think we were going to win the Stanley Cup. We were really struggling and for everyone it was a hard time. The goaltending at that time was sporadic. We had Rogie Vachon and Phil Myre. They were good, but it never got going. It was almost out of desperation that Ken Dryden was called up from the Voyageurs. I didn't know Dryden. But

I was in on the decision with Sam and Ronnie. They were saying, hey, there's got to be someone else that we can at least look at. So we brought him up and he played a half-dozen games in the final few weeks of the season.

I found it humorous that everybody thought it was such a great decision on my part to start Dryden in the playoffs when we played Boston in the first round. Anybody who had watched him closely in the games he played for us shouldn't have been surprised. I remember distinctly the one game that made up my mind. I started him in Chicago, which is an intimidating place to play, especially for a rookie goaltender. We hardly got out of our own end all night yet we won the game 2–1. I mean, this guy just stood on his head to stop the shots. So for me there was no real big decision as to who was going to start the first couple of games in the playoffs. As it worked out he ended up playing every game.

People often ask me about the best game I ever broadcast. I don't have one particular "best game" but even now, over twenty years later, I still say that 1971 was the best playoff year. The Canadiens upset the favoured Bruins in seven games, then eliminated the Minnesota North Stars in six. They played Chicago in the finals and won the Stanley Cup with a 3–2 victory in the Chicago Stadium in the seventh game.

The scenario was the stuff movies are made of. Start with an underdog team, add an unknown, untried, rookie goalie who ends up being chosen the MVP of the playoffs, throw in victories over teams with stars such as Bobby Orr, Phil Esposito, Stan Mikita, and Bobby Hull, and top it off with one of the greatest players in history, Jean Béliveau, retiring after carrying the Cup off the ice in his final game.

Looking back on it now it seems surprising the Canadiens were considered long-shots. There were seven players in their line-up who would be elected to the Hockey Hall of Fame, including Béliveau, Frank Mahovlich, Yvan Cournoyer, and Jacques Laperriere. Perhaps the presence of so many greats was what made it tough for the rookie coach. The fiercely competitive John Ferguson gave MacNeil problems. Fergie put on a stick-breaking tirade directed at his coach in full view of the crowd at the Forum after the Canadiens lost a home game in the Minnesota series. That drew attention but, for Al MacNeil, the worst was yet to come.

During the fifth game of the final series Henri Richard had very little ice time. The Pocket Rocket, his pride cut to the quick, fumed as he sat on the end of the bench watching the Canadiens lose the game and fall behind 3–2 in the series. Afterwards, in reply to the first media type who asked, "How come you didn't play?", Richard exploded. In a quote heard round the hockey world, especially in the Province of Quebec, Richard called MacNeil "the worst coach I've ever played for." Today Henri Richard will tell you that he said it because he was "so goddamn mad." He has no quarrel with Al MacNeil, who he says is a good guy. But the damage had been done.

The crisis-loving Quebec press and fans had a natural on their hands as their beloved team appeared ready to lose the Cup to the Blackhawks. It was guaranteed to sell newspapers and raise radio stations' ratings with a French-Canadian hockey hero pitted against his unilingual English-speaking coach. The headlines screamed, and the phone lines were blazing on the hotline shows.

People called the Forum threatening to kill MacNeil. Bodyguards were hired and they were at his side when the Canadiens won the sixth game on an emotion-filled Sunday afternoon in Montreal. The drama continued in Chicago two nights later when the Canadiens came from behind 2–0 to win the game, and the Stanley Cup, 3–2. To complete the seemingly impossible scenario, Henri Richard scored the game-tying goal in the second period. Then Henri Richard scored the Stanley Cup-winning goal in the third period. That's right, the stuff movies are made of. Through it all the beleaguered rookie coach of the Montreal Canadiens, amazingly, stayed cool.

AL MacNEIL

I handled it by putting myself on another plain. I just ignored it. I said to myself, hey, something has happened. I can't worry about that. I can't concern myself about the repercussions of something that I did, that I thought was the right move. But I didn't anticipate the reaction.

When I played, and even when I coached, I was never aware of the crowd. I tried to block them out. I appreciated them but I never let them influence my thinking. When I was behind the bench I tried to wrap myself in whatever I was doing just to get through it. It wasn't that I had disdain for them or anything like that. It was just the only way I could deal with it.

The thing that bothered me was that it bothered my wife. That was the ugly part of it. You know, the death threats. We had bodyguards sitting in the living room of our house twenty-four hours a day for about ten days. When the calls and threats came in I laughed it off at first. But the reaction from my wife, I didn't want that.

I had no problem with Henri Richard. I had no problem playing him again in the last two games. That's the hard part of coaching. I knew Houle and Tardif, all the young guys. I knew what they could do. It's like everything else, the changing of the guard, anywhere, is tough to do. Old ways die hard.

We had a kid on our team named Bobby Sheehan, a real

character who came from Boston. In the first or second game of the Bruins series I took Jean Béliveau off the power play and put Sheehan on. Boston had the juggernaut and we weren't exactly overwhelming. Sheehan had unbelievable speed and he was in his home town. I always put a lot of stock in a situation where a player is back home because he's going to maximize his efforts. So when I made the change Jean came to the bench and looked at me like maybe I had just gone to Mars or something. Of course the power play didn't work. We hardly got over centre-ice for the whole two minutes. The next day I grabbed Sheehan and said, "What did you do to me last night?" He said, in that Boston accent of his, "Sorry, coach. I just couldn't get it together." [Laughs] With Sheehan, I died a thousand deaths. He was a funny guy.

When the Stanley Cup champion Montreal Canadiens reported for training camp the following September Al MacNeil wasn't the coach. Scotty Bowman was. MacNeil was still coaching, but he was with the Voyageurs, the Canadiens' farm team in the American Hockey League, now based in Halifax. Al MacNeil is the only man who, after coaching a Stanley Cup winner, began the next season back in the minor leagues.

AL MACNEIL

I was the one who brought that subject up with Sam. It was a combination of a lot of things. At the time there was a lot of baloney: the FLQ stuff was heavy, and there was a little bit of the language crap and everything else, although the language wasn't going to be a problem. I was going to enrol in a French-immersion course that summer. If I had stayed with the club I would have been bilingual within the next six months. But looking at it realistically, it just wasn't the place for me to be at the time. I went to Florida for ten days after the playoffs to kick it around in my mind. Looking at all the things, at the ugliness that came out of it, I didn't think I was going to be able to bury it all. So I thought I would move on.

It was tough. It was a kick in the pants. There was great magic about the Canadiens coaching job. It was the best club in hockey to coach, the most prestigious. But I grew up in the game. I had been away from home since I was fifteen years old and I had fought for anything that I had. I won some and I lost some. I just rolled with it.

MacNeil spent the next eight seasons in Halifax, then returned to the NHL as the coach of the Atlanta Flames. The Flames are now in Calgary and Al is still with the team, in the front office.

AL MACNEIL

I love hockey and the game has been good to me. One of the great joys of being in the business is that you get up in the morning and you know you'll like what you'll be doing the rest of the day. You're a lucky guy if you're able to say that.

Jean Perron first earned recognition in Canadian hockey as a successful college coach at the University of Moncton. He left Moncton to become an assistant to Dave King with the Canadian national team at the 1984 Winter Olympics. The following year Perron moved into the NHL as a seldom-seen-or-heard-from assistant to Jacques Lemaire with the Montreal Canadiens. When Lemaire quit in the summer of 1985 Perron was named to replace him. He coached in Montreal for three years before being released. After a short stint with the Quebec Nordiques late in the 1988–89 season, Perron became a sportscaster in Quebec City. In a bit of an ironic twist, he is now the colour commentator on radio broadcasts of the Nordiques games, because Jacques Demers happily gave up that job to return to the NHL as coach of the Montreal Canadiens.

JEAN PERRON

I got my Master's degree in Phys. Ed. at the University of Sherbrooke and then a Ph.D. at Michigan State. My goal was to coach university hockey, which I did, at the University of Moncton, for ten years. We won two national championships. We would have won a third but, during the finals, the National Film Board was shooting some kind of a weird movie about college hockey, and they used my players as actors. It was very distracting to everybody.

One of my big dreams was to coach in the Olympic games, to march with the athletes in the opening ceremonies. I got a call from Sam Pollock, who was with Hockey Canada, and he asked me if I would like to be an assistant coach for the Olympic team in '84. I said, "When's the next plane?" So I went to work with Dave King. We had some good players on that team: Patrick Flatley, Kevin Dineen, James Patrick, Kirk Muller, Russ Courtnall, and J.J. Daignault.

Just before the Olympics the Nordiques had offered me a three-year deal to coach their farm team in Fredericton. But that wasn't in my plans. After the Games they were still after me and so were the Canadiens. Jacques Demers called me and asked me to join him in St. Louis. I had supper one night with Marcel Aubut in Quebec and then the next night with Ronald Corey and Serge Savard in Montreal. I chose the Canadiens and would have gone to a minor-league team for them. Jacques Lemaire told me I would learn three times as fast if I stayed in Montreal with him, so I became an assistant coach with the Canadiens.

I spent that first season in the press box relaying information to the other assistant, Jacques Laperriere. The season ended with a loss to the Nordiques in the playoffs. Jacques Lemaire didn't like the part of being a head coach that meant he had to deal a lot with the press, so he quit. It was announced that same June day that I was going to be the head coach. They called me to a meeting in Serge Savard's office. He asked me if I was ready for the job. I said I wasn't, that I wanted a year as an assistant behind the bench so I would get to know the players better. He said, "Ah, come on, Jean, you're ready. If you want the job you've got it right now. Let's get on with it." So I took the job.

I wasn't nervous when I first took the job. Then I went on a holiday, a fishing trip, and I can remember sitting there fishing and I started to shake. My fishing line was in the water and it was shaking and I was saying to myself, "Christ, what did you do? What kind of a decision was that?"

When I started I had a pretty good feeling. There were a lot of good veterans on that team, Bob Gainey, Larry Robinson, Mats Naslund, Mario Tremblay, Chris Nilan. We didn't start out too good, but about Christmas we had a big meeting and Gainey assured me the team was behind me and we got rolling. But you know what it's like in Montreal. One time we lost three-straight games and a reporter asked me if I had heard the rumour that if we lost four straight I would be fired. There were a lot of things like that but I never shook in my boots.

First of all, in the first year you don't pay attention to the open-line shows. You don't read the papers very much. You concentrate on the games. You want to analyze everything. You study all the videos, and that was something I did too much of, now that I think of it. But in that first year I really paid a lot of attention to all the details.

I feel the season turned around in March, in Winnipeg. We had lost three straight and I was pissed off. So I told the players they weren't in shape. I told them a few things were gonna happen. I was going to practise them twice a day and I told them the bars on Crescent Street in Montreal were out of bounds for the rest of the season. After I said that Larry Robinson said I was acting like a junior coach, that I treated the players like juniors. I feel that was the best move I ever made because I had so many rookies. And basically the team leaders were all behind my decisions. The two-a-days went very well. We worked on our systems, power plays, penalty-killing. They were long sessions but with high intensity, and that's how we went into the playoffs.

We had three goalies that year, Steve Penney, Doug Soetaert, and Patrick Roy. After the training camp Serge Savard told me I had to send Patrick Roy to the minors. I said, "No way. I can live with three goaltenders." But you can't do that in the NHL. There was a lot of turmoil.

Penney had been good in the playoffs before and he was supposed to be the starter. We played our first regular-season game in Pittsburgh. Penney was injured so I started the rookie, Patrick Roy, and we won. Then Penney came back. I didn't like Penney's style, didn't like his trapper. He couldn't grab the puck. Every time I started him I didn't have confidence. Soetaert was hot and cold.

I started putting Patrick into tough situations, especially on the road. We played one game in Long Island and, let me tell you, he won the game for us. So when we approached the playoffs I said, "This is the kid I've got to have in the net." Even in practice I could see he was so much better than the other two guys. The year before, they had brought him up from junior to play for Sherbrooke in the American League playoffs and he was outstanding. I saw those games and he was something else. I proceeded to convince Serge Savard he was the man of the future. When the playoffs started there was no doubt in my mind he was gonna be my goalie.

In the first period of the first playoff game, against Boston, we were outplayed and outshot. I think the shots were something like 15–3, but we came into the dressing room tied 1–1. Patrick was stopping everything. He was really on top of his game. But the rest of the team had played poorly. Instead of going into the back corridor to let the boys cool off like I usually did I decided to go right into the dressing room. Bob Gainey was our captain and he's the best leader I've ever seen in my life. Let me tell you, I had a chance to work with Mark Messier and Wayne Gretzky at the Canada Cup and I'll still take Bob Gainey. He was always thinking about the club. So in the room Gainey stands up and says, "For chrissake, coach, what are we gonna do?"

Right away I said, "You know what we're gonna do? First of all, we're gonna play disciplined hockey. We have to stay away from stupid penalties, and that means you, Chris Nilan. Do you understand? And second, you're gonna shorten your shifts. They're too long. A minute and twenty-five seconds is too long in the playoffs. That's it." And I left the dressing room. After the game the guys told me Nilan was so upset he threw his stick against the wall and took off to have a smoke in the bathroom. Anyway, that seemed to settle everybody down. That was the start of our trip to the Stanley Cup, the turning point for us. No question about it. And there's also no question that in that Boston series Patrick Roy became Patrick Roy.

The Canadiens eliminated the Bruins with three straight wins in the best-of-five series. Roy allowed only six goals in the series. They then played the Hartford Whalers and won when another rookie, Claude Lemieux, scored the series-winning goal in overtime in the seventh game. In the Wales Conference final series they eliminated the New York Rangers in five games. The best-remembered game from that series was played in New York when Roy made thirteen saves in the first nine minutes of overtime before Lemieux won the game with another overtime goal. Meanwhile, in Alberta, the Calgary Flames upset the best team in hockey, the Edmonton Oilers, which meant everyone left had a chance. It got down to the Canadiens against the Flames in the finals. Montreal won in five.

JEAN PERRON

During the playoffs we made the players stay in a hotel outside Montreal. They called it Alcatraz. When we came back from New York leading the series 3–1, instead of letting them go home as usual we took them to Alcatraz. They guys started looking at me like, "Is this guy out of his mind, or what?"

Bob Gainey kept telling me that the playoffs are long, very long, and rest was important. Anyway, we won the next game and that series was over and we let them go home for the next four or five days. Then we brought them back to Alcatraz.

When we were getting ready for the finals we had a meeting out there and Bobby Smith made a heck of a good comment. I let all the players talk if they felt they had something to say. Bob Gainey and Larry Robinson talked about what it was like to win the Stanley Cup. When it came to Smith's turn he said, "Fellows, I was in the finals once in Minnesota and I missed the chance of a lifetime. I missed a chance to carry the Stanley Cup. Right now I feel we can do it, we can touch that big trophy. Let's not miss our chance because, if we do, it's something we'll regret for the rest of our lives." That's something that struck me and I guess it struck the players too because everybody pulled together from then on.

I've got a small souvenir Stanley Cup at my house with all the names on it from that team. I can count thirteen first-year players who played on that club at one time or another. I think that's a record. In the finals, Stephane Richer didn't play because he broke a curfew. Petr Svoboda didn't play much because he was still adjusting to NHL life. Dave Maley came in, so did Serge Boisvert and Steve Rooney. Gaston Gingras became a big part of our power play and scored some important goals.

I had a good mix of young guys and veterans. Ryan Walter was a good leader for that club. Some people thought I had trouble with Larry Robinson because of what he said about me treating the players like juniors, but that wasn't the case. He knew I was being paid to make decisions. After we beat Hartford he was the first player to come to the bench and congratulate me. When the playoffs were over he told me I had made a helluva move with what I did and that he wanted me to be just as tough the next year because he wanted another Stanley Cup. You know, even though those two-a-days were tough, Larry was always the first one on the ice. He was great around the guys, always making jokes and relaxing everybody. We called him "Big Bird" and I used to think he was the oldest teenager on the team. When he said what he did I know he was just upset. I'm sure that deep down he didn't mean it.

The other day I watched a tape of all the playoff games in '86. Ronald Corey sent it to me. When I was watching the final game in Calgary, when we won the Stanley Cup, I said, "Is this what happened?" My only real memory was the plane ride home, everyone in the big plane having fun.

Twelve-year-old future hockey broadcaster spiffied up and posing with his all-time favourite coach. The Irvins, Dick Sr. and Jr., 1945. *(Hockey Hall of Fame)*

Dick Irvin in a typical mood during a game, circa 1948. Notice the hat, winter coat, scarf, and gloves. The arenas were colder in those days. *(Mac McDiarmid Collection)*

Two members of hockey's "royal family."
Lester Patrick and his son Lynn, when Lester was the coach and Lynn
the star left-winger with the New York Rangers in the late 1930s.
(Mac McDiarmid Collection)

Lester Patrick with his two brother acts on the 1940 New York
Rangers Stanley Cup-winning team. Neil and Mac Colville are on the
left, Lester's sons Lynn and Muzz on the right.
(Mac McDiarmid Collection)

Art Ross, with his ever-present cigarette, in the Bruins dressing room
in 1941, with Milt Schmidt, on the left, and Frank Mario.
(Mac McDiarmid Collection)

Art Ross and four Bruins in the early 1930s. On Ross's right is the
team's first superstar, Eddie Shore.
(Mac McDiarmid Collection)

Jack Adams, who ran the Detroit Red Wings for 35 years. He was "Jolly Jawn" as long as things were done his way. *(Mac McDiarmid Collection)*

The man who built Maple Leaf Gardens, Conn Smythe, front and centre as always, flanked by two of his Stanley Cup-winning coaches, Hap Day on the left, and Joe Primeau. In the back row, Reg Hamilton, King Clancy, and Bob Davidson, Maple Leafs stars in the '30s and '40s. In the photographs behind them, Syl Apps and Ted Kennedy. *(Mac McDiarmid Collection)*

Bill Stewart, the baseball umpire and hockey referee, with some of his Chicago Black Hawks during the 1938 playoffs when they upset Toronto in the finals. Stewart was the first American to coach a Stanley Cup-winning team. *(Mac McDiarmid Collection)*

Hector "Toe" Blake, hockey's all-time Stanley Cup-winning coach. Blake won eight Cups in his thirteen years as coach of the Montreal Canadiens. *(Mac McDiarmid Collection)*

George "Punch" Imlach, with his familiar fancy hat and in his familiar jaunty pose during the early 1960s when his Toronto Maple Leafs were winning three-straight Stanley Cups. *(Mac McDiarmid Collection)*

Emile "The Cat" Francis during the longest of his many hockey lives, coaching the New York Rangers. *(Courtesy E. Francis)*

Milt Schmidt struck this pose for a publicity shot after he ended a great playing career in Boston to become coach of the Bruins in 1954. *(Mac McDiarmid Collection)*

Harry Neale coaching the Vancouver Canucks. Looks like Harry is checking the clock, hoping a long night is coming to an end.

Tom McVie, the much-travelled professional rink rat, during his days as coach of the Washington Capitals.

Don Cherry behind the bench of his beloved Bruins in the late 1970s. His shirt collar wasn't as tight in those days but the sports jacket was vintage Grapes.

My best memory is the parade they gave us in Montreal. You know, before that fifth game in Calgary, I called my wife and told her I thought if it went on one more game I wasn't going to be able to make it. I was pooped, exhausted. A season in the NHL is so different from college hockey. It lasts so long. So when that one was over and we had won, imagine how I felt when we got home and there were twenty thousand people at the airport. Then they had the parade and they said there were close to a million people on the streets of Montreal. That's when it hit me just how big hockey is in Montreal. It's out of this world. The day of the parade, that was the nicest day of my life.

John Muckler's coaching CV reads like a road map. He started in the Eastern League in Philadelphia and remained in that area with teams called the New York Rovers and the Long Island Ducks. Then Muckler hit the road for real, with stops in Memphis, Minnesota, Cleveland, Jacksonville, Providence, Dallas, and Wichita, before becoming an assistant to Glen Sather in Edmonton. Two years after the Oilers traded Wayne Gretzky Muckler head-coached them to a surprise Stanley Cup win. A year after that he was on the road again, shuffling off to Buffalo.

JOHN MUCKLER

I was a playing-coach with the Long Island Ducks in the Eastern League and broke my foot. Ronnie Howell, Harry's brother, came in to take my place and I hobbled around behind the bench with a cast on. We went twenty-eight games without a loss. I wasn't sure if that happened because I was such a lousy player or such a good coach. [Laughs] That ended my playing career and I started to coach full-time.

You mentioned to me that Al MacNeil had bodyguards when he was coaching in Montreal. That happened to me too. I was coaching in Providence and we were playing at home against Rochester. Don Cherry was coaching them. A big fight broke out and Don sent John Wensink out on the ice. One of our guys in the fight was Bert Wilson and Wensink came up behind him and gouged his eyes. Bert was disabled for about a month. After the game I called for Cherry's hide, and Wensink's too, and it was all over the papers. I received three letters from Rochester and they all said I would be killed the next time we played there. So I turned the letters over to the FBI.

We played three more times that year in Rochester and FBI guys would pick me up at the airport, come with me to the hotel, and then to the game. We had two of them dressed in Providence Reds colours standing beside our bench pretending to be stick boys. There were two more behind our bench, and another two sitting directly across the rink from our bench. They were there for all three games.

The first time we played there I started Wilson and Cherry started Wensink. Right off the bat they went into the boards and Wensink hit Bert from behind. Bert came off the boards, hit Wensink with a short left, and knocked him out. Don never put him on the ice for the rest of the night. We won that game. They had about eight thousand there, as many as the building would hold, and they sold it out the rest of that year every time we played there.

My first head-coaching job in the NHL was in Minnesota in '68–69, the second year of expansion. I wasn't ready, no question about that. Wren Blair was the coach and general manager at the time. He became ill and asked me to come up from Memphis and take over. I think we played every one of the old six teams at least once. One time we played them six games in a row. The first game I coached we lost 1–0 to Toronto. Paul Henderson scored the goal.

There are a lot of ways you find out how you've been fired in this business. That time I was at a party some time around the All-Star break. It was about 2:00 in the morning and somebody turned on the TV set. The news was on and that's where I learned that I was gone as coach, although I did stay with the North Stars in another capacity for about a year.

Then I went back to coaching in the minors for several years before I got another opportunity to coach in the NHL. I had a certain amount of success, won a couple of championships, and was named Minor League Coach of the Year in Dallas. But after a while, even though you are successful, they put a tag on you. They think of you as a good minor-league coach but not able to coach in the National League. You get stereotyped.

There are benefits that go with coaching in the minors. One of the kicks you get is developing players for the NHL, seeing them get the opportunity to play there and then being able to stay and become a regular. Charlie Huddy was one I had who was in that category.

Fortunately for me Glen Sather gave me the opportunity to go to Edmonton as his assistant. I had been coaching their minor-league farm team in Wichita. One summer I was interviewed for the Edmonton job three times. They didn't tell me I had it until late in August when Glen called and told me. I hung up the telephone and then said to myself, "Hey, what's the salary?" [Laughs] So I had to phone him back and ask him how much am I going to make, and what's the length of the contract? We came to terms and I ended up going to Edmonton.

During my time there as an assistant Glen and I had different roles. Glen was the motivator, the bench coach. He didn't want any part of the practices at all, and rightfully so, for the simple reason that he was the GM and president of the hockey club. His duties never really gave him any spare time to run the practices. So I ran them and the longer I stayed there the more authority I had at practice and it worked out very well.

Ted Green was the other assistant. He represented great success as a player, ran some of the practices along with me, and developed into a head coach, which he is now and doing a good job. We had different personalities, different reasons for being there. I don't think you can design something like that. We were all in the right place at the right time, with our own reasons why we were there. I never did get a job description. I don't think Teddy ever had one either. We just fitted in very well and did things on our own, or Glen would give us the opportunity to do the things we did well. You have to give him credit for being a good administrator.

I really wanted to become the head coach. The reason I stayed was that I enjoyed myself so much being around the players there. I enjoyed the organization, and the bottom line was that they paid me very well. They paid me like a head coach. I went there with the promise that I would become the head coach. When that wasn't provided to me, then I became the associate-coach, or the co-coach, whatever you want to call it. I had the authority, other than on game nights, that a head coach has. That pacified me then. They were a great bunch of hockey players and a great bunch to be around. Knowing that I was part of their success satisfied whatever ego I had at the time.

After Gretzky was traded I think Glen stayed as head coach one more year for the simple reason he knew it was going to be a difficult time for everybody involved. He knew the effect the trade would have on the team. Some people were very bitter that Gretz left and I guess understandably so when you see a great person and a great player leave your hockey club. I don't know anybody who could keep something like the life of Wayne Gretzky in perspective the way Wayne has been able to do, considering who he has become and what he has gone through over the years.

As it turned out we played Los Angeles in the first round that year. We had won the Stanley Cup four of the past five years and we were leading the series 3–1. But they came back and beat us four games to three. The enjoyment that Gretz got out of winning that series, not just beating the Edmonton Oilers but just winning the series, and the emotion he showed on the ice after they had their victory, I think that taught everybody on our team a lesson. He was going to go about his business and he wanted to win very badly and we saw that we should treat him and all our opponents the same way.

The year after that was when I became the head coach, the year we won the Stanley Cup nobody thought we would win, even ourselves, I guess. We went to training camp and we didn't look at ourselves as a contender. I think a lot of the players were still getting over the loss of Wayne. Some of them had a tough time playing against him even then. It took some convincing that it's fine to be friendly, it's fine to appreciate what Wayne did for the organization, but at the same time he was on another team trying to beat us.

I think it turned around late in February when we played a game in L.A. I started Messier, and Marty McSorley was on the ice for them. We lost the opening face-off. Mess went back into our zone and McSorley ran him right through the end of the rink. Before the game was over there were about four hundred minutes in penalties. The teams fought all night. It was a record for the most penalties called in one game and we set a record for most penalties by one team in one game. Gretz was there, not fighting, but in the middle of it. Our guys realized that they were gonna try to defeat us and we should be doing the same things to try to defeat them. We had to go about our business, had to treat Wayne the same as we would treat everyone else. After that game we seemed to settle down. The players seemed to forget about the past.

We had had our ups and downs all year, and we ended up only eight games above .500, but we were playing awfully well at the end of the season. Grant Fuhr was injured but Billy Ranford was playing well in the nets. Mess had a great year and ended up winning the MVP. Kevin Lowe was strong all year, and Jari Kurri started to play very well at the end. You could feel something was going to happen.

We had made a deal with Detroit which brought us Petr Klima, Joe Murphy, and Adam Graves. Klima was a problem practically all year long. His work ethic wasn't up to our standards. But the two kids, Murphy and Graves, gave us more speed and toughness. We had another young player, Martin Gelinas. The three kids were playing on separate lines and at times not playing very well. We thought that if we put them on the same line it would get rid of some peer pressure. There wouldn't be that pressure to move the puck to a veteran player and they'd feel more comfortable playing with each other. That's what we did. We wouldn't have won the Stanley Cup without that line. In the second series we beat L.A. four straight. In the final game Murphy scored the winning goal in overtime. The kids dominated that series.

The big series that year was the first one, against Winnipeg. They beat us pretty good in the first game. Bill Ranford was just horrible. Our back-up goalie was Pokey Reddick and I remember Peter Pocklington coming in after the game and asking me why I didn't pull Ranford at the end of the second period. I told him I didn't think we could win the Stanley Cup with Pokey, and I was going to stick with Billy and go all the way with him. The next game Billy was shaky for maybe half the game. Mark Lamb scored the winning goal in over-time. We went to Winnipeg and lost two, then won the next three and Ranford was terrific. In the fifth game, in Edmonton, we were ahead by one goal. Dale Hawerchuk had a breakaway in the last minute and Ranford stopped him.

I remember in the sixth game in that series, we were leading 3–0 and they came back to tie us in the third period. If they win that game it's all over. I called a time-out and Jari was standing right in front of me. I said, "Jari, this is it. We've got to show what we've got now." The next shift Jari is on the ice and he comes down the right side and beats Essensa with a shot over the right shoulder. I don't care what goalie was in the net – Terry Sawchuk, Turk Broda, Jacques Plante – they weren't going to stop that shot. School was out after that. I knew it was all over.

We played Chicago in the next series and split the first two in Edmonton. We lost the next game in Chicago and now it's the fourth game there and that's probably the best game I've ever seen Mark Messier play. He took two penalties on his first two shifts as if to let everybody know that this was going to be Mark Messier's night, so everybody had better get out of his way. After that he was the most feared player on the ice and he had all kinds of space. He scored three goals and did everything a player could do. He scored, he backchecked, he was physical, he just dominated the game. It was the best game he'd ever played and I don't think he's played one like that since. That turned the series around for us.

We went into Boston to open the finals, and everybody had picked them to beat us. Anybody in an Oilers uniform, or associated with the Oilers, couldn't understand that. I don't know if you'd call that being cocky but we were sure we could beat anybody at that particular time.

The game most people remember from that series was the first one. It went into the third overtime period and Billy

Ranford put on a show that night that was unbelievable. The only other performance I can compare it with was when Grant Fuhr shut out the Islanders 1–0 when we won our first Stanley Cup.

Petr Klima scored the winning goal and everybody said I was a genius because I had hardly played him and that I had put him out because he had fresh legs. I hadn't been playing him because he wouldn't backcheck, and it's true he was the only fresh guy on our bench. I knew he had great offensive ability and at that point in the game it didn't matter if he wouldn't backcheck because everyone out there was so tired. He had a couple of shifts in the overtime and afterwards everyone claimed they were his only two shifts or maybe his only one all night. That's not true. He'd had eight or nine during the regular three periods. On the winning goal Kurri set him up nicely on a criss-cross. Petr came in from behind, Jari went from his left to right, and that took Andy Moog with him, and Petr shot it through Moog's legs.

When that series was over and we had won, it was my biggest thrill. I keep remembering that nobody picked us to win. That was a team that grew and got better as the year went along. We got better in the playoffs, kept getting more confidence in ourselves, and I don't care who we were playing. It was a real team effort, and it showed me that coaching in the playoffs is the best time. That's when you can tell your players anything and they'll believe you. It got to a point where if I said black was white, they'd say, sure, black is white. When you tell a player, or your whole team, the way you think they should approach the game they're going to play, and watch it work in the game, it's a great thrill.

I coached one more year in Edmonton but I never had a bad ending. It wasn't a great ending there for me, but it wasn't bad. We finished at .500, then came on awfully strong in the playoffs. We had our first series against Calgary and it was probably one of the best ever played in the history of the NHL. We won in overtime in the seventh game. Then we played Los Angeles and in the sixth game we scored a goal in overtime and we thought the series was over. But the referee disallowed it. The face-off was just outside their blue line. We left the same players on the ice, won the draw, threw the puck back to the front of their net, scored again, and eliminated them.

Now we're in the Conference final against Minnesota and our hockey club was beat up pretty good. Messier had a bad knee and a bad thumb. We just didn't have anything left. By the time it was all over I had gotten the feeling that I had maybe gone as far as I was going to go in the organization. With a lot of players leaving there was a big changeover. It seemed like a new era was about to begin and I wasn't supposed to be part of it.

I still had another year to go on my contract. I met with Glen and said I would like the opportunity to negotiate with other teams to see if I could become a general manager in the NHL. That's one of the reasons I went to Buffalo. I wasn't brought in there as a coach. I was promised I would eventually become general manager.

After a couple of months in Buffalo I became a coach again but not because I wanted to. I became a coach in Buffalo for the simple reason of necessity. I walked into the Buffalo organization because they wanted to change the personality and outlook of their hockey club. They wanted a fast-skating, offensive, good puck-handling team.

Rick Dudley was coaching when I got there. We sat down five or six times and talked about what type of team we wanted. I think we put him in an unfair situation. We were asking him to become something that maybe he didn't understand at that particular time, or maybe he just didn't want to do it. I don't know which it was. He tried to change the team concept but fell back into the pattern in which he had a great deal of faith and you can't blame a person for that. But that wasn't the direction they wanted to go in, so they asked me to coach for the remainder of '91–92. Then they came to me before the next season and asked me to coach for one more year. I thought that somewhere down the line it would make any future job I had in a different capacity much easier if I went back and coached another year.

I think eventually I will be comfortable not coaching. At the start in Buffalo I kind of enjoyed it. I enjoyed having dinner at 6:00 the night of a game and not having that feeling in the pit of your stomach you get when you're a coach. But now that I'm back coaching I enjoy those feelings all over again. I enjoy coaching, no doubt about that. I believe coaching is like playing. You can only coach for so long and then your time is up. But I still get a big kick out of it. I like being around young people. It keeps you young yourself.

8

The Youngest and the Oldest

GARY GREEN BILL DINEEN

Those of us in the television business tend to forget that new, young fans are tuning in, we hope, from season to season. We take too much for granted, including a proper identification every once in a while of the men who work as colour commentators and analysts. We don't remind the viewers often enough that Harry Neale coached in over four hundred games in the National Hockey League. Today's new viewers might not realize that John Garrett tended goal in pro hockey for ten years, or that Steve Shutt scored over four hundred goals for the Montreal Canadiens. Another well-respected hockey broadcaster in recent years is Gary Green, who has the distinction of being the youngest head coach in the history of the NHL.

Green's credentials as the "youngest" go even further than that. Lou Boudreau was twenty-five years old when he became the playing-manager of baseball's Cleveland Indians in 1942. When it comes to non-playing coaches or

*managers, Gary Green is the youngest man ever to have
held that position in the history of professional sport. When
"Greener" became head coach of the Washington Capitals,
November 14, 1979, he was twenty-six years old.*

GARY GREEN

A lot of credit for that goes to Roger Neilson. I was twenty
years old and went to Roger in Peterborough and begged him
to let me be his assistant coach with his junior team [the
Petes]. I had had a tryout with the Vancouver Blazers in the
WHA and they sent me to the Charlotte Checkers. When
you get sent there, and then get traded to the Roanoke
Rebels, and you're the seventeenth player on a fifteen-man
roster, that kind of tells you where you stand as a player. I had
a university degree in my back pocket, a degree in psychology, but I really wanted to be part of hockey. So I went to
Roger and came in at the right price. I told him I would do it
for free for the whole year so I could learn from him. So I was
able to talk Roger into letting me be his assistant coach.

During that time I was learning from another great coach,
Fred Shero. I was running back and forth to Philadelphia in
my car, or, I should say, my wife's car. I'd take a box full of
flyers for the hockey school I was running and leave them
at rinks along the way. Then I'd get to Philly, and if Fred
Shero was alive he'd tell you that I would stand outside his
dressing-room door or outside the rink after his practices.
Never could get into the games but I was able to get into
some of the practices. Then I would walk him to his car and
I'd have four or five questions that I would ask him. First of
all, he must have thought I was totally nuts, but then he
started giving me a few more minutes, then a few more, and
I ended up learning an awful lot from Fred Shero and then
from Roger Neilson.

I really wanted to learn a lot about coaching, but I also thought there was a void in there where coaches didn't have a chance to get together and express opinions. So I put together an international coaching symposium in Belleville, Ontario. I got Roger and Fred to go, and Bob Pulford. I had a sports psychologist there, and Tommy Woodcock, a veteran trainer, because I wanted somebody from every department in the hockey world. It lasted five days and it ended up with 150 coaches from all over North America.

The biggest surprise was when I got a special-delivery letter from Boris Kulagin, the Russian national coach, asking if he could come. So he did and he stayed with me and my wife. I was a young kid then and had no idea, really, of how it all worked, but that's how I really got into coaching, by being around all those people, listening and learning from Kulagin, Shero, Neilson, Bob Pulford, all those types.

At the end of the year that I worked with Roger I got a $1,000 honorarium for having done a pretty decent job, I guess. Then Roger moved on to coach in Dallas and Gary Young got the head-coaching job with the Petes and they promoted me to paid assistant coach and assistant general manager. Around that time I had gotten to know Max McNab and Tommy McVie of the Washington Capitals. I was twenty-two at the time and went to Washington to see about an assistant-coaching job with the Caps. It was my pushing for it more than their wanting me, but they were curious and interested enough to bring me down there to talk. But then Gary Young got released and the Petes ended up making me the head coach and general manager, so I went back to Peterborough.

That was when I lied about my age. I wasn't proud of that because my father would have killed me. I didn't outwardly lie. It was at my press conference and I worded it very well at the time. The Petes' executives were all there and they had never really asked me how old I was. They thought I had to be twenty-five or twenty-six because I had a university degree. They didn't know that I did my degree in two years. They signed me shortly before my twenty-third birthday. At the conference a writer asked about my age and I got around it by saying that I was nearing the quarter-century mark. So they wrote that I would be turning twenty-five shortly, which meant that shortly was a few years down the road.

When that year ended we had reached the Memorial Cup finals and lost the final game. After the game Bud Robertson, the team's president, asked me why I lied about my age. I said I really didn't lie, I just insinuated I was a little older. He told me it wouldn't have made any difference, but try and tell a kid just about to turn twenty-three that twenty-five doesn't sound a helluva lot older. I really had thought it would lose me the job.

I stayed two years in Peterborough and was fortunate to have very good teams. Keith Acton played for me, and so did Larry Murphy. In all, eleven or twelve players I coached there ended up in the NHL. After my first year John Bassett arranged for me to meet Bill Dewitt, who owned the Cincinnati team in the WHA. He offered me $25,000, but I was making that much in Peterborough. I didn't think I wanted to go to the WHA, but more important than that, what was gnawing away at me was that I hadn't won the Memorial Cup. The Petes had always come close. Under Scotty Bowman and Roger Neilson they had come close, and I had been one win away in my first year.

So I stayed in Peterborough and all that summer I kept sending the players postcards. Every single Thursday I'd send them a card knowing they'd have it in the mail Monday morning. I kept writing to them, "We have to be one game better next year. Have a good summer. Greener." I'm sure it used to drive them crazy getting a card in the mail every

Monday. But the next year we were fortunate and won the Memorial Cup, beating Brandon.

After that year I had a lot of inquiries from pro teams. The previous season Gary Darling, who was with the Bruins, had asked if I wanted to leave the Petes right away and coach the Rochester team in the AHL. I didn't have any interest in doing that, but that summer, at the draft in Montreal, I did sit down with Harry Sinden, and he asked me if I wanted to coach the Boston Bruins. Don Cherry had just been fired and Harry was surprisingly interested in this young coach.

Norm Kaplan and Art Kaminsky were my agents and they had already made a deal with Washington for me to coach their farm team in Hershey. The contract hadn't been drawn up yet and when they told Harry how much I was going to get from Hershey, which was $55,000, he called them liars, saying that was too much money. The last thing I wanted to do was upset Harry Sinden. I looked at the Bruins roster and realized it would be a case of a young, rookie coach coming in to take over a veteran team. I figured the up-chance there was pretty slim. So I went to Hershey.

When the season started in Hershey it was still like a dream come true for a guy just turned twenty-six. I kind of looked at that job as a two-year stint. My wife was pregnant and in November we had just moved into a house I rented from Ron Schock. I had just got back from a road trip and we were unpacking the boxes when I got a call that evening from Roger Crozier, who was working in the Caps' front office. We had the radio on and were listening to a Caps game and Roger asks, "Greener, are you ready to coach in the NHL?" I said, "When?", and he said, "Right now. They're going to fire Danny Belisle tonight." The game was on the radio, the Caps were playing at that moment, and they knew what they were going to do. I said, "Of course I'm ready. I can coach in the NHL. I feel sorry for Danny, but I'm ready."

I got off the phone and I can remember my wife was sitting on the couch and I said, "Sharon, I think I'm going to be asked to coach the Washington Capitals tomorrow." She was sitting there, belly out to here, the boxes half unpacked, and she just looked at me.

The next morning at practice the Hershey general manager, Frank Mathers, called me off the ice and asked me the same question Roger had asked the night before. I just looked at him and he said, "I know it's the big league and I know you're young. But there is no question in my mind that you can do the job. You've shown me in a couple of months you know what you're talking about."

So I left for Washington. I remember flying from Harrisburg to Washington that night and I guess I really realized this was the big league because there were a lot of cameras and reporters at the Washington National Airport. All I had been thinking about was coaching and had never even thought of the media attention. In Hershey there was only one media guy around, Steve Summers. But all the lights and cameras and everything didn't bother me the least bit because I understood the magnitude of it right away. What didn't help was the fact that the airline lost my bags and I didn't get them for four days.

I had asked that the players meet me that evening at the Sheraton Hotel. They had had a terrible start with only four wins in their first sixteen games and we were going off on a road trip the next day. All I had been thinking about was what I was going to say to these guys. I was twenty-six and I had guys who were thirty and thirty-five years old and I wasn't quite sure how to approach them. I had to keep focusing on the fact that they were hockey players, the ice surface was the same size, you used the same number of players, and regardless of how much they were being paid they still really wanted to perform well.

So when we were all there at the meeting I simply said to them, "Fellows, I'm not an Al Arbour and I'm obviously not a Scotty Bowman and I didn't play in the NHL. I know you know all that. There's just one thing I'm going to ask you for and that is your respect. I'm asking for the opportunity to try and gain your respect. If I don't have it after the first month or two, if I haven't proved to you by then that I can coach at this level, then you'll chase me out of here anyway. So just live with me. I can't change my age for the same reason that I can't change your ages. So please give me that. That's all I ask for."

Did I get their respect? I don't know. You'd almost have to ask them. But I think I read and heard about it enough times to know that they did respond well. I mean, as a teacher I could tell at my hockey schools which kids were responding and which weren't. And I liked it because I saw the guys on the Capitals really wanted to learn. They wanted to play better, they wanted to win. They liked to be organized and they liked, at times, to be yelled at when the team wasn't playing well. I was full of emotion because that was my style, whether I kicked over garbage cans or patted them on the back.

Most of my philosophy revolved around teaching. It was execution, getting from point A to point B and believing the other guy is going to do it too. Most of the players reacted positively. I can remember Jean Pronovost saying that through all his years he never really had it explained to him as accurately and simply as I was able to do. That's not patting myself on the back. It was just my style, what I wanted them to do.

When it came to coaching so soon in the NHL I wish I could go back and say to you that I was in awe, but I was mainly focused on my own team and my own players. Later on I understood just how good coaches like Scotty Bowman

and Al Arbour were. Like Scotty. He used to amaze me and
just drive me nuts because all of a sudden I would get my
fourth line on the ice and it was just like he read my mind
and he'd have his best players come flying out. He'd have
his first line against my fourth and I would wonder how
could he possibly have been able to react that quickly. It
was almost like he knew beforehand. But at the time I
didn't have a chance to dissect the other coaches. I had too
many struggles of my own.

*Unfortunately Gary Green wasn't a complete "wunder-
kind" in his tenure as hockey's youngest coach. The team
did improve after he arrived and was over .500 in the sixty-
four games he coached with a record of 23–20–11. But they
missed the playoffs by two points. In 1980–81, with Gary
coaching the entire season, the Capitals finished with
seventy points in eighty games, missing the playoffs by just
one point. The following season began badly for the team
and, after thirteen games, with the Caps having won just
once, Gary Green was fired.*

GARY GREEN

There was a lot of turmoil within the organization. We had a
lot of veteran players, we were giving up a lot of draft choices,
and there were battles between Roger Crozier, Max McNab,
and Jack Button, the people in the front office. I saw this
whole political warfare going on at the top. All I wanted to do
was coach. In Peterborough I controlled my own destiny. In
Washington, after a pretty good first year, there was a lot of
tampering going on.

In my second year we had a tremendous amount of injuries. We had over 450 man-games missed that year and it was
a struggle. I used five different goalies. We picked up guys

like Rick Smith from Boston at thirty-seven years of age. There were players like Jean Pronovost, Denis Maruk, and Bob Kelly I had to use a lot. I think we were in the top ten by Christmas, but I had used these guys too much and then lost them in the latter part of the season. That was my inexperience, not understanding the rigours of the schedule.

We missed the playoffs by one point and it all came down to the eightieth game, on the final Sunday. Saturday night we had played against the Islanders and lost 2–1, and that was just a kicker. But we still had a chance on the final night. If we beat Detroit, and Quebec beat Toronto, we would be in. We won our game big, 7–1 or 7–2, and then on the telescreen they piped in the game from Quebec.

I remember walking across the ice after our game hoping like hell we'd be okay. At that time Toronto was winning. We all went back into the dressing room and watched the game, and the Leafs won and we missed the playoffs. The old cliché rang home with me loud and clear that you've got to take care of yourself. You can't keep hoping the other guy is going to win games for you in professional sports. So that was a very depressing time because we came so close again.

The most difficult thing I ever experienced was in my last year and that was what I felt was a confrontation between religion and sport. It was really difficult because we had players like Jean Pronovost, Ryan Walter, Mike Gartner, and a number of others who had become born-again Christians. I had absolutely no difficulty with that whatsoever. But as far as the team was concerned, and I might be wrong about this, I felt there was a real split going on.

There were players like Bob Kelly, Dennis Ververgaert, Mike Palmateer, and others who weren't particularly religious. They felt the other guys were Bible-thumpers and, even though they wouldn't say it to their faces, they were saying it behind their backs. It was all new to everybody. The guys were carrying their Bibles with them into the dressing room and there was absolutely nothing wrong with that. But we had new players coming in, like, for example, Bobby Carpenter and Gaetan Duchesne, and one night they would be going to the coffee shop for discussions with one part of the team, and the next night going to a bar with the other part of the team. I was looking for common ground there.

I decided to hold a meeting, and that was the toughest for me ever in my life because it was a meeting where I discussed religion in the dressing room. I called the meeting "the Christians versus the Lions" and that made the lions just roar in the background. There was a lot of resentment over what I did. I know Jean Pronovost was very upset. So was Ryan and so was Mike, I think, because it seemed I was insinuating it was their fault. I wasn't trying to do that at all but I had a very rough time.

My comment at the time was that I didn't feel there was room for religion between the hours of 9:00 and 5:00, that when it was a working day religion should never be talked about. I have never talked to the guys to this day about how they felt about what I did but I felt that I caused a real problem as a coach just by bringing it up. Yet I didn't know what to do. I still don't have the answer to this day. But it was the toughest thing for me as a coach.

The next season we went to Europe to train for the second year in a row. The players didn't want to do that. I remember Denis Maruk yelling in the back of the plane on the way over, "Guess we're not going to play any road games this year, eh, coach? Are we gonna stay home and play?"

It wasn't so bad being in Sweden, but we went to Oolu, which is one hundred miles south of the Arctic Circle in Finland, to play one exhibition game and that pretty well did it for the players. We flew back to JFK, got on a bus, because they didn't even have a charter for us, and went to

Hershey, and then went on the road for more exhibition games. Then it was right into the season and we started losing right off the bat.

I had a bad problem then with our goalie, Mike Palmateer. I used to pull Mike two or three minutes into a game. He wasn't happy in Washington, even though he was making a lot of money, because he didn't feel he was recognized. It wasn't like Toronto for him. Mike needed the fans to motivate him.

This is an example of a real frustration for a coach. We played a home game on a Friday night and I pulled him about three minutes into the game. We were down 2–0 and again he had let one shot in from the red line and one from the blue line. We lost that game, travelled to play the Islanders the next night, and lost again. I didn't play him in that one. Our next game was in Vancouver on Wednesday but I had decided that we weren't going to take the team back to Washington. We went straight to Vancouver on the Sunday and we were going to take the time to regroup.

On Monday morning we were on the ice at 9:30. Nobody was there from the media. I had sent my assistant, Bill Mahoney, to Winnipeg to scout a game, so I was the only coach on the ice. Our general manager, Max McNab, was the only one in the stands. Just before the practice Mike Palmateer came to me and said "Coach, you know that 1:00 meeting we've got this afternoon? I'd like to get out of that meeting if I could. I know you're just gonna have us ride the bikes and have a meeting. I'll do that some other time."

I can remember being absolutely livid in the dressing room. But I wanted to start everything fresh so my comment to Mike was, "Tell you what, Mike. I'm having a helluva morning. It's a great morning here in Vancouver, and I'm going to pretend you never asked that question. So you just get ready for practice."

I went on the ice and guys like Ryan Walter and Bob Kelly were really bearing down, trying to get their scoring touch back. And Palmateer refused to stop any pucks. He lifted his arms, his legs, he wouldn't stop any. I was at centre-ice so I blew the whistle and yelled down, "Mr. Palmateer, are you going to stop any pucks for us this morning?" And he screamed back, "Fuck off!" So I went racing down and I grabbed him. I wanted to choke him, I wanted to strangle him, and then the rest of the guys ploughed in.

I threw Palmateer off the ice and I met with the team. Some of them wanted to kill him too. Bob Kelly wanted me to let him finish him off. I asked the players to run the practice while I went to the dressing room to deal with Mr. Palmateer.

I had it out with Mike, and Max McNab had two cigarettes going at the same time, he was so upset. Mike walked back out and our trainer said to me, "I never say anything on the players, but this is killing us all. Last night when we were helping the Pittsburgh trainers flip over" – the Penguins had played there the night before, using the same dressing room – "one of their trainers asked me why Palmateer had two bags. I said he's only got one, and he said, no, he's got two. So we opened it up and the bag was full of scuba diving equipment. We asked Mike how come, and he said he had rented a boat for 1:00 that afternoon and was going scuba diving."

So I said to Max, "I want no part of this guy on my team. Send him home now. Just get rid of him." Max said he would. I'm not much for walking but I remember taking a long, long walk back to the Bayshore from the rink, I was so furious.

When I got back to the hotel Max called me and said he had just talked with our owner, Abe Pollin, and he had said he didn't think we could trade Mike Palmateer, and that he would talk it over with me when we got back. I thought, "Screw you. Who do you think is running this hockey team?" So we played in Vancouver and then in Los Angeles, and I didn't play him.

We lost both on the coast, by one goal in L.A., and then went to Colorado and tied Grapes's team. The day after we got home we were playing Minnesota and I got called off the ice when we were practising and told to go to a meeting with all the head honchos, including Mr. Pollin. I can remember Jack Button pointing a finger at me and telling me it was all my fault because the players had lost respect for me. They went after my assistant coach too.

I remember being told at the meeting that Mr. Palmateer is like a piece of real estate and that I would have to play him until his value rises so they could recoup some of their losses on this piece of real estate. They told me it was my job to get him going. That's when I told them that, seeing as we had a game that night, instead of sitting in a meeting for a couple of hours, my place was with my team. So I got up and went back to the practice.

I was forced to play Palmateer that night against Minnesota. They hammered us, one goal, two goals, three goals, four goals. I had always yanked him [before] and the players on the bench were yelling at me to hook him, pull him out of there. I just stood behind the bench and kept looking at him thinking, "You go ahead. You show Mr. Pollin and everyone else exactly what I've been telling them." I left him in, but I knew it was all over for me.

I got a phone call the next morning about 8:00 from Jerry Sacks, who was Abe Pollin's president of the Cap Center. Jerry told me Mr. Pollin wanted to meet with me at 9:00. I got off the phone and said to my in-laws, who had been visiting us and were just getting ready to go back to Ontario, that I was going to be fired.

I went to the meeting – it was just Mr. Pollin and me – and sure enough he told me he was going to relieve me of my position. That was that. There's one thing I regret, that I didn't fight for my job. I also regret something else. I walked into Max's office and said, "Well, Max, you went through another coach."

Max looked at me and said, "What are you talking about? I was fired an hour ago." That really hurt me. Max and I had a great relationship and he was very good to me.

I told the guys on the team right away. Bobby Carpenter came into my office and cried like a baby. Ron Weber did his final interview with me and he was in tears all the way through. [Ron Weber is the Capitals' play-by-play radio announcer. He has never missed a game in the team's history.]

When I went out of the office there were all kinds of media people there, cameras, lights, just like the night I arrived to become coach of the team. Glenn Brenner was the big sportscaster in Washington but he didn't care about hockey and never gave us any coverage. Even he was there, so I turned to him and said, "Hey, Glenn, what's going on around here? Is there a basketball game or something?" That broke everyone up.

I had been the youngest coach ever hired in the NHL and now I was the youngest ever fired. I walked out the front door, the way I always did.

Hockey may be a young man's game but some older chaps have done all right in the coaching department. Two of them, my father and Bob Johnson, coached Stanley Cup winners when they were in their sixties. During the 1991 playoffs I mentioned to Bob that he would be the second man to coach a Cup winner after turning sixty, if his Pittsburgh Penguins did it. A few days later the Penguins won the Stanley Cup. In the hubbub following the championship game in Minnesota Bob spotted me in a corridor, gave me a big hug, and said, "Now there's two of us." I knew what he meant but didn't say much in return because I was a bit choked up, what with the moment of triumph for Bob and the memory it evoked of my father. A few months later the memory of that meeting became bittersweet following Bob's untimely death.

Scotty Bowman coached the Penguins to a second-straight Cup in 1992, when he was fifty-eight. Toe Blake was fifty-five when he won the last of his eight Stanley Cups in Montreal.

Early in the 1991–92 season I ran into Bill Dineen before a game at the Montreal Forum. He was working as an advance scout for the Philadelphia Flyers. Bill looked great, and I kidded him about his new, relaxed life away from the rigours of the coaching profession. He had spent the previous sixteen seasons as a coach or manager in professional hockey. He began in the Western Hockey League, then coached in the WHA with Houston and New England. For the seven years before he joined the Flyers, Bill had coached or managed the Adirondack team in the American Hockey League.

A couple of weeks later the Flyers fired their coach, Paul Holmgren, and replaced him with Bill Dineen. The day that happened Bill was fifty-nine years, two months, and six days old, the oldest man ever to make a head-coaching debut in the National Hockey League.

BILL DINEEN

I guess they felt like they were going to make a change and they asked me to do it. I had to think a bit, ask myself if I really wanted to get back into that kind of a life. I was fifty-nine and had to take a couple of days to think it over. It was discussed a bit at home, but I usually end up making those decisions anyway.

Why would I want to do it? It wasn't like I had to do it, but they asked me, and I guess you do anything to help out the organization. It was nice to know they thought enough of me to give me the opportunity. And I guess one of the big reasons I took the job was that it was my first chance to coach in the National Hockey League. After all those years in the Western League, the WHA, and the American League, I certainly thought my coaching days were over. So I thought I would give it a try.

The first couple of weeks after I came in I wasn't too sure of myself. But I gained a little momentum, and I think the team did at the same time. My theory was that some of the guys were a little uptight. I told them to just go and play hard, enjoy yourself, and let's have some fun. We didn't make the playoffs but from the All-Star game on we had the third-best record in the league.

As I look back certainly one of the highlights was coaching in Houston when Gordie Howe played with his two boys. That's when he came out of retirement. Mark and Marty were under-age when we drafted them and we had phoned Gordie ahead of time so it wouldn't be a surprise. I knew him pretty well because we had played together in Detroit. So when I called the last thing he said was, "What do you think about a third Howe?"

The way he tells the story is that he heard the sound of the phone hitting the floor first, then the sound of me hitting the floor. But the truth of the matter is, when we drafted the boys, I sort of felt he wanted to come back and play, even though he had been two years into retirement.

It was a pretty good situation, Gordie being as easygoing as he is. Gordie wasn't too interested in the new style and the new systems in hockey, all he wanted was the puck. So in practice Gordie'd be shooting pucks up against the glass and just having a good time enjoying himself. He really mixed in well with the young guys on the club. We had some good ones, like John Tonelli, Rich Preston, and Terry Ruskowski.

Things are a lot different now than when Gordie and I were playing on those Detroit teams in the '50s. Now you've got three or four coaches, a special-teams coach, a goalie coach. You've got to delegate responsibility and make your assistants feel part of it. There's a lot more changing of lines now and you've got to get involved with the systems or else I think you will lose ground.

You used to see a lot more of the other teams. When I played, teams played each other fourteen times in the regular season. You got to know what they were going to do. Now you have to make adjustments almost every night. Teams that aren't in your division, usually you haven't seen them for a couple of months or more. We tape their previous two games and watch those tapes, plus the one of the last game we played against that particular team. There's a lot to prepare for: how they change lines, how they come out of their own zone, how they play in the neutral zone, how they forecheck. You've got to change with the times.

I think teams worked harder in the old days due to the fact that they were on trains together. There was a lot of card-playing, a lot of joking that went on. I think it really comes down to the same thing today, that the good teams are the tight teams.

For me, the most important thing for a hockey player is to do the best he can at all times. I think that is somewhat of a coach's responsibility. You have to make sure you detect a trouble spot and you've got to step in and look after it right away.

I coached a father playing with his sons in Houston, and now I'm coaching my own son, Kevin, in Philadelphia. You

know, we hardly ever talk. When my wife comes down from
Lake George we might go over to his house. That happened
about a month ago. We pretty well keep our distance during
the season. I don't really communicate with him a whole lot
unless he needs to be told something.

I probably get mad at him more than anybody else, but
that's not right either. I've got to guard against that. He's like
anybody else. He makes his share of mistakes but I'm pretty
easygoing. I don't believe in yelling at a guy at the moment. If
a player makes a mistake he knows it himself ninety per cent
of the time.

I think the players watched out for the father-and-son
thing when I first got here. But then everybody accepted the
fact that it wasn't happening. I like to think it's not happening and I don't think it is. But I'm very much aware of it. I certainly protect myself, and him too.

All my boys played hockey. Shawn is the oldest. He played
in the American League and the Central League for seven or
eight years. Peter was the next guy. He was drafted by the
Flyers and played in the American League for ten years. He
had short stays with L.A. and Detroit. Gordie played for the
Islanders for six years. This is Kevin's eighth year in the
league. Our youngest, Jerry, played in the Eastern League the
last two years. So they've all played pro.

I didn't force it on any of them. Actually, their mother is
more responsible for them being hockey players than I am.

KEVIN DINEEN

I was traded to the Flyers from Hartford, so I beat my dad
here by about two weeks. Typical of him – I went to the
rink that day and found out that Homer was fired and they
said they were going to have a meeting with the players.
Kjell Samuelsson told me that Bill was going to hold the

meeting. I said, "Bill who?" and he says to me, "Bill, your dad." Then he says, in that big Swedish accent of his, "C'mon. You know. You must know." But I didn't have a clue. I knew Homer's job was in jeopardy but I certainly had no idea my father was being considered for the job. And I don't think he did either. Just like everybody else, I didn't see him until he walked into the room.

It was a bit uncomfortable at the beginning but after a couple of weeks it was pretty easy for me. I wouldn't even call him a player's coach. He's just an outgoing guy, talks to everybody whether he's happy with their play or not. He's very approachable so there is no sniping or talking behind his back. I can honestly say that even if I wasn't here there wouldn't be any of that and that's made it a lot easier for me.

For the most part the players have accepted it. There's a lot of kidding that goes on about the coach being my dad, but I get more of that from the other teams than I do from our own guys. A couple of weeks ago he sat with me and Rod Brind'Amour because we were struggling and he spent about twenty or thirty minutes with us and he was tough on both of us. He talked about our game, gave us advice, and I think it helped a lot. He can play the heavy, but for the most part he's a pretty positive and upbeat guy.

I talked with the Dineen boys before the Flyers played the Canadiens on a Saturday night, at the Montreal Forum. The coach told me he wasn't too pleased with the way his son had played the past game or two. That night the Flyers defeated the Canadiens 4–3, in overtime. Kevin scored the winning goal.

9

Scotty

SCOTTY BOWMAN

I was part of the Hockey Night in Canada *broadcast team for the 1992 Wales Conference final series between the Pittsburgh Penguins and the Boston Bruins. Prior to one of the games in Boston I was in the hallway outside the Pittsburgh dressing room when an underwear-clad Penguin sidled up to me and whispered, "What was Scotty Bowman like in Montreal?" I smiled and thought, "Scotty hasn't changed. He had us baffled in Montreal when he coached the Canadiens, and he's got them baffled now, in Pittsburgh."*

William Scott Bowman has won more hockey games than any coach in hockey history. He started coaching in the NHL with the St. Louis Blues November 22, 1967, at the age of thirty-three. He spent four years in St. Louis, then coached the Canadiens for eight years, winning the Stanley Cup five times. The Bowman-coached Canadiens of the late 1970s that won four straight Cups are considered by some, this writer included, the greatest team of all time.

Scotty worked as both coach and general manager for almost seven years with the Buffalo Sabres. When he was fired by the Sabres he became a commentator for Hockey Night in Canada, *returning to the NHL in an executive capacity with the Penguins in 1990. After the Penguins' Stanley Cup win in 1991, their coach, Bob Johnson, was stricken by a brain tumour, which took his life a few months later. Bowman took over as interim coach, and after a so-so season, while Mario Lemieux and friends were trying to figure out their new coach, and vice versa, the Penguins got their act together and won the Cup again. The following year, after waiting until after training camp to make up his mind, Bowman was back coaching in Pittsburgh.*

The Penguin who sidled up to me that night in Boston has plenty of company. Ask five of Scotty's former players about him and you'll get five different answers. Steve Shutt, the Canadiens' top left-winger during Bowman's time in Montreal, says players on that team had one thing in common – they all hated Scotty. In the next breath Shutt will tell you Bowman was the key to their four-straight Stanley Cup victories. The most-often-heard line from ex-players is, "I didn't like him, but I respected him."

In his book, The Game, *Ken Dryden, the perceptive goaltender on Bowman's Stanley Cup teams in Montreal, described his coach: "Abrupt, straightforward, without flair or charm, he seems cold and abrasive, sometimes obnoxious, controversial, but never colourful . . . He is complex, confusing, misunderstood, unclear in every way but one. He is a brilliant coach, the best of his time."*

Bowman is a product of the school of hockey management-training which first Frank Selke and then Sam Pollock ran at the Montreal Forum. They spotted Scotty early as a young man with a good hockey mind. When a head injury ended Bowman's promising playing career in 1951, when he was only seventeen years old, Selke recruited him into the Canadiens' organization as a minor-hockey coach. For the next several years Scotty worked in all areas of the organization, except directly with the NHL team itself. When the NHL expanded in 1967, Lynn Patrick, who had been hired to run the St. Louis Blues hockey operation, hired Bowman as his assistant.

SCOTTY BOWMAN

When I agreed to go to St. Louis, Lynn Patrick said I would be coaching the team. It was a tough decision to leave Montreal. It was my home. I'd coached the juniors and they were a pretty visible team and of course the Canadiens had a good team at the time. Then one day before the first season in St. Louis, Lynn said to me that because of tradition, the Patrick name and all that, he would like to coach the first year and I would be the assistant. Then I would take over in the second year.

By that time I was already up to my neck in work. There was a lot of work involved in setting up a new team, so it sounded okay to me. I was the only assistant at training camp and Lynn was running the team. We had some veteran players like Jerry Melnyk, Bill McCreary, Fred Hucul. I wasn't intimidated by them because I was just the assistant coach. But I really got scared one night, which turned out to be the night Lynn decided to quit as coach.

We were playing the Flyers and they were the top team in our division. I was changing the defence and Lynn was changing the forwards. We were nursing a 2–1 lead and there were a couple of minutes left in the second period. I went down the bench and told Lynn I thought there was a forward we should take out, Norm Beaudin, because he wasn't a strong defensive forward. I should have said I thought we should double-shift Gerry Melnyk, but I didn't. I guess I got flustered, and I wasn't supposed to be coaching the forwards anyway. Lynn put out a rookie named Roger Picard and when he was on the ice the Flyers tied the game and then he was on when they scored the winning goal in the third period.

Lynn knew I was upset when the game was over. He called me at home at 2:00 in the morning and told me, "Scotty, I'm going to relinquish the coaching job. I can't do it any more." I felt very bad about what had happened in the game, but he told me not to worry about that. He said, "You're ready to coach the team."

We had won only four out of our first sixteen games and that's why I got really nervous. The next morning I called Sam Pollock in Montreal. I was sort of looking for some support, that I really didn't have to take the job. Sam was very astute. He said, "Well, you know it's not coming at a good time. It's coming about a half-year earlier than you expected. But if you don't take it now, somebody else will." I was nervous, but I took Sam's advice.

In the first few years of the Blues the team's line-up would include some great names, veteran players who went there for one last hurrah. These included Glenn Hall, Dickie Moore, Al Arbour, and even the legendary Doug Harvey, who joined the team when he was forty-three years old. The colourful and unpredictable goaltending great, Jacques Plante, was talked out of retirement. Plante and Hall combined to give the Blues the best defensive record in the league in 1968–69. They gave up only 157 goals against in 76 games. The New York Rangers were the runner-up, with 196 against. When they were presented with the Vezina Trophy, Hall was thirty-seven years old, Plante was forty.

SCOTTY BOWMAN

Those players were at the end of their careers and had all come from winning teams. I think they just had a lot of fun. I don't think I ever did anything that was foolish with them, but I wasn't intimidated by them either.

The first time I ever coached Jacques Plante was after he retired and came back to play with the Junior Canadiens in an exhibition game at the Forum against the Russians. He really worked to get in shape. He went to the blackboard and told our defence what he wanted them to do. He had probably studied the Russians, he was that kind of a goaltender. He wanted to make sure they knew he was going to play the shooter and leave the other players to the defencemen. He explained it all very well, then went out and played a great game. We won 2–1.

When I had Plante and Hall in St. Louis they had different ideas about how to play. Glenn was the only goalie I can remember who wanted the defence to rush the puck-carrier because he thought that way it diminished his chance to make a perfect play. We got to the point where we knew the day before the game who was going to play, so we would tell our defence to get ready for whatever style each guy wanted in front of him.

They gave us some interesting moments. We always had a third goalie with us, a young player. He dressed as the back-up but Glenn and Jacques were playing all the games. If we played at home one night and then on the road the next, we would send one of the two ahead to get a better sleep and then he would play the next night.

There was one time when we played in St. Louis on Saturday and in New York on Sunday. Hall had gone ahead to New York, and he started the game. We were down 1–0 early and then Vic Hadfield scored a goal from centre-ice that took a real big curve. We had received a penalty just before that, so after the goal went in Hall blew his stack. He went after the referee, Vern Buffey, and Buffey threw him out of the game. We were down 2–0 after only five minutes. The name of the kid we had dressed as the back-up was Robbie Irons.

In those days they let you warm up a new goalie if he came in during the game. We were in the warm-up and Doug Harvey came over to me and said, "Scotty, you know we can't go with this kid. Why don't we get Jacques?" Jacques was watching the game in the press box. Doug says, "You want me to tell him to get hurt?" I said, "Okay, if you can."

So a couple of minutes into the warm-up Robbie Irons goes down, injured, just like Doug told him to do. He's down and he won't get up. The trainer jumps on the ice, and they end up taking Irons off on a stretcher. [Laughs] We had Plante paged on the PA system. He went down to the dressing room to get ready and the whole thing took about twenty-five minutes. The worst part was that Bill Jennings, who was president of the Rangers, kept coming by my bench, and so did Emile Francis. Emile was the manager and I can't remember if he was the coach then too. Anyway, they wanted me barred from the league and everything else. I said, "The guy's hurt. What are we supposed to do?" So Plante makes his grand entrance about twenty-five minutes later and the big story was we won the game 3–2.

Now the other story with Jacques Plante was in the season when he suffered an injury in the All-Star game. He had a terrific All-Star game. He and Bernie Parent played and the shots were something like 50–12 against them. Plante hurt his knee in that game and he made a slow recovery. He came back with about four games left in the season. He was gonna play half the game for the first three that were left and then maybe the full game in the last game of the season. His goals-against average was below two a game.

We went to Oakland and about halfway through the game, just when we were going to put Jacques in, we got a penalty. He yelled at me to leave Glenn in for the power play because he was too cold to go in at a time like that, which was right. They scored on the power play and we were down 3–0. Then Jacques went in and they scored two more and we lost 5–2. But his average was still below two a game.

We went to Los Angeles to play the next night. It was our final game of the season and the deal was that Plante would play the whole game. That morning in the hotel, one of our players, Camille Henry, came to me and told me that Jacques didn't want to play because he said he had a twinge in his knee. I said that he was going to play. We went to the rink and came back to the hotel and Doug Harvey also told me that Jacques really didn't want to play. I was kind of upset and I said, "Well, he's gonna play."

About an hour and a half before the game Doug and Camille came to see me and Jacques was with them. Doug told Jacques to tell me how he felt and Jacques said, "I don't think I can play tonight." We had a third goalie with us, Ted Ouimet, and Glenn wasn't going to dress. The game meant something for Los Angeles in the playoff picture. The president of the league at the time, Clarence Campbell, was a big stickler on dressing your strongest line-up. There was no way you'd rest guys unless they were legitimately hurt. So I was obligated to play Glenn and when I told him he was very upset. He said he had a sore back, sore foot, sore everything else. I said I wanted him to go in and if the game got out of hand Teddy would take over. We won 2–1 and Glenn played a terrific game.

The players were upset with Plante so they put all kinds of white tape around his luggage and painted a big red cross on it. Somebody wrote on the tape, "Win # 76 for Jacques." He came down to the room about two minutes before the game was over and he was upset the players felt that way. [Plante's final goals-against average was 1.96 in 37 games.]

That was on a Saturday. We went home the next day to start the playoffs Wednesday. On Monday Plante came in and told me he wouldn't be able to play. By that time we had all had it with him, I guess, so we went out of town to a hotel and told him to stay in St. Louis. The day of the game we're getting off the bus at the Arena just as Jacques was pulling into the parking lot. Camille Henry, and I give him a lot of credit for this, came to me and said, "I know how you feel. But he's not coming back, Scotty, unless we make a fuss over him, make him feel wanted. I know everybody's cheesed off with him, but I'm telling you I know what he's like. He'll coast right through the playoffs unless we appeal to his pride."

I thought that was a pretty good idea so I talked to Plante and asked him how he felt. He had received a special treatment that day for his knee at the clinic run by the football Cardinals. I tried to sympathize with him and that seemed to pep him up. He told me that he thought he could dress as a back-up that night but he still didn't think he could play.

We were playing Philadelphia in the first round and when the game started Plante didn't want to sit on the bench. He stayed in the dressing room and watched on TV. We were ahead 1–0 in the second period and Gary Peters of Philadelphia broke in on Glenn Hall. Glenn made a great save but he stretched right out, to the limit, and pulled his hamstring. It was terrible, really a tough injury. He came to the bench and said, "Scotty, I don't know about this." He was nauseated. He went back in, played about thirty seconds, came out again, and said, "Sorry, Scotty, but I can't go."

So we had to go to Plante. I didn't know it, but he was in the dressing room with hardly any equipment on. So he had to put his pads and everything on and it took about ten or fifteen minutes. Then he made his big entrance in the St. Louis Arena. He always had the crowd on his side and they went for it as if he was Napoleon coming in. And he played, well, you can check the records, but he played just great. We beat Philadelphia four straight, and then we played Los Angeles and beat them four straight. We won eight straight games and they were eight of the greatest games I've ever seen a goalie play.

(I checked the records. In those eight St. Louis victories Plante allowed only eight goals and had two shutouts. In the finals against Montreal the Blues lost four straight. Plante gave up twelve goals but he didn't get much help. The Blues scored just three on the Canadiens.)

You won't find much mention of a "Bowman system" of playing hockey. But he always has a plan for every game. During his final few years in Montreal I did a radio show with Scotty before every Canadiens game. I usually asked him about his "game plan." Whether his team was playing its toughest opponent, or its weakest, he always had one.

SCOTTY BOWMAN

I have to break coaching down into preparation, practice, and motivation. Practice is a lot different now because you have a lot of help. I think back to the days when one coach was running the show. Now, times have changed. Twenty-five years ago the travel was on trains and I'm sure they missed practice because of that. They didn't skate the morning of a game. I remember when I first started coaching in junior hockey, Bobby Orr was playing for Oshawa and we went to Boston to play them in an exhibition game because the Bruins wanted to showcase Orr down there. When I was there I watched the

Bruins practise and they went at it for two hours. I thought it was a terrific practice, it was like a game.

The thing I fear the most in practice is, when do the players have enough? When have you given them enough to keep their conditioning, their mental sharpness, and to get them ready for the next game? I think it changes from day to day.

Sometimes I think back to teams that maybe I was trying to prepare too much. I don't think it's all X's and O's. Hockey is an impulse game. I remember when Fred Shero took over the Flyers and everyone started to talk about systems. One of the funniest lines I ever heard was, when I was coaching in Montreal, somebody asked Henri Richard about the system we used to get the puck out of our own end. Henri said, "The Canadiens' system hasn't changed much. We try to get it out of our end as fast as we can." And really, that's about what the system should be.

When I was in Montreal we used to like to have a scrimmage. [A practice game. In the old days, Scotty mentions, scrimmaging was almost all that teams did at practice and there were times when the competition became very hot and heavy. In those days teams had fewer travel days and more time between games than today.] I liked to have one good scrimmage a week. It isn't good to have one the day before a game. But if you play on Saturday or Sunday and don't play again until Thursday, then Tuesday is an ideal day for a scrimmage.

When we scrimmaged I liked to have our top offensive line, which was Shutt, Lafleur, and either Pete Mahovlich or Lemaire, play against people like Jarvis, Gainey, and Robinson. It was a good challenge for Gainey to go against Lafleur, who at that time was the best offensive player in the league.

Today teams don't scrimmage very much. I often question that because I like to practise within a game situation, even to the extent of changing players on the fly. When a team is playing well and making good changes, the players aren't staying on the ice when they're tired. These are important factors. It's very important for a coach to have drills that could turn out to be game situations. I've talked to goaltenders about this, about the shooting drills they've gone through. There's no way in a game a player is going to be allowed to do what they do to goaltenders in a practice. When you get into a game it should be an extension of what you've been doing in practice. I always worry. I don't want to leave too much on the practice rink.

Scotty said the magic words, "changing on the fly." Almost every coach I spoke to who had gone head to head with Bowman talked about his skill at manipulating his players during a game. They all admit that, without question, he's the best.

SCOTTY BOWMAN

When I first started coaching in St. Louis I had a veteran team. We were in a division that didn't have a lot of offence to start with. We were blessed with a lot of experience, players who could really shut down the opposition in a defensive way. Plus we had great goaltending. The goaltending was superb. So it gave me a chance, when I first started, to work on matching those veteran players against the best offensive players on the other teams. And Lynn Patrick was there to help, to advise me how to use certain players in certain situations.

When I went to Montreal it was a different game altogether. They had players like Frank Mahovlich, offensive players, and we had a good defence as well. I was able to have enough players, I mean, you can't match up if you don't have enough players, offensively or defensively, to do well.

Then, as time wears on, you get to know the other coaches. There are some coaches who are obsessed with trying to get a certain player into a certain situation. But you have to be ready to try things, to test the other coach. I've always felt that what wins or loses games are the great players on either side. If you can keep the other player off the ice for whatever reason, or if he is on the ice and you can combat him with a certain amount of strategy or with players who are doing what they should do, then it's going to help you win the game.

We always played Gainey against Lanny McDonald when he was in Toronto. They only had Sittler and McDonald for us to worry about. One of the best lines I ever coached against was the one in Philadelphia – Barber, Clarke, and Leach. They went through a season one year, one of the years they won the Cup, and they were on the ice for only twenty-nine goals against when the teams were at even strength. Mind you, if you analyzed it, you might find most teams had players on the ice against them who never could score. One year we tried Mahovlich, Lafleur, and Shutt against them for a while but it didn't work. When we finally defeated them in the playoffs, in that series in '76, we decided it wasn't going to work with just one centreman against them. So we'd give them Lemaire, then Riseborough, then Jarvis, just little bits at a time. Riseborough was a good, feisty centreman, Lemaire had offensive ability, and Jarvis could check. It worked. We seemed to keep them off balance.

I think match-ups are often exaggerated. There are players on every team that obviously have certain jobs to do every night. If they're great scorers they have to score goals. So you don't worry about that player. But there are others who you have to give an assignment to, who you have to get to commit to a certain job if they are going to be effective. The easiest way to coach is just to put the lines on in turn, one after the other. What you have to do is talk to your team. You don't ever want to put the seed in a player's head that he can't play against a certain player on the other team. You could shatter his confidence. I think the majority of players are better if they have a certain assignment. My job is to try to get them to fulfil that assignment by using them the right way during a game.

Other coaches might read that and mutter, "Easy for him to say. Look at all the great players he has coached." True enough. There haven't been many coaches in hockey history who have coached as many superstars as Scotty Bowman. In Montreal he stood behind a bench that had players on it named Lafleur, Robinson, Savard, Lapointe, Shutt, Gainey, and Lemaire. He had Gilbert Perreault in Buffalo. In Pittsburgh the names changed to Stevens, Tocchet, Jagr, and Mario Lemieux. But great players don't necessarily make a coach's job that much easier.

SCOTTY BOWMAN

I think the thing about great players is you've got to realize there's a lot of pressure on them. I mean, every player is different but there's really a lot of pressure on the really great players for them to perform. There's the media, the hype, everything. I think as a coach you can make it easier on yourself, and on them, by getting them into situations that can help them and at the same time help your team. I remember in the early expansion days I was talking to Wren Blair, who was running the team in Minnesota. I was asking him how I could get some of my guys to check, to play better. He said, "Scotty, when you've got a guy that's got forty goals, try to make him better so he can score fifty. Don't try to make him into a checker, because he's not a checker."

I think what you have to do with your top players is you have to make them responsible, make them feel that the team isn't going anywhere unless you guys do it. Sam Pollock used to refer to baseball and say he could take a lot of aggravation from a .300 hitter but none from a .200 hitter. I guess that's the way you have to think, as a coach. I don't think you can let a star player run a team but you can take a little more aggravation from him if he's going to perform to his ability. I think a coach has got to say that if a guy is having a good year, you feel part of it, if he's having a bad year, there's maybe something you should do to help him. It's a two-way street.

The compartment in Scotty Bowman's brain marked "hockey" never stops working. When the 1992–93 NHL season began, the league changed its policy concerning time-outs for TV commercials. Instead of stopping play for thirty seconds seven times in a period, they stopped it for sixty second four times. Bowman immediately figured out how this would help Mario Lemieux get more ice time. Knowing the play would be halted approximately at the four-, eight-, twelve-, and sixteen-minute marks of each period, Bowman knew that if he took Mario off just before the commercial was called, he could put him right back on when play resumed. In effect, Lemieux could get two consecutive shifts. Bowman even calculated how much more ice time this would mean for his superstar over the entire season. In the first few weeks of the season three coaches asked me

how the new rule worked – Are they stopping for sixty sec-
onds now? Scotty had figured it out and had his "plan"
working by the first game of the season.

Yet, with the respect there is for Bowman's ability to
coach a hockey team, before and during games, there is also
the perception of Scotty Bowman as a calculating taskmas-
ter, aloof and distant from his players. As I awkwardly
worked the conversation around to this, Scotty trained his
eyes about six inches above mine. He kept nodding his head,
slightly. He knew what I was getting at – the Ken Dryden
description of him. It's a part of his persona he doesn't enjoy
talking about. But he did, briefly.

SCOTTY BOWMAN

Well, I think it comes from the coaching. I never felt comfortable really trying to – I mean, I could talk to a player one
on one about the game or something else. But I just didn't
feel comfortable being buddy-buddy, if you want to call it
that. Saying things that maybe you didn't mean or couldn't
back up.

I think a coach has a lot of tough decisions to make in a
tough position. The players, maybe it's not easy for them to
play sometimes for some coaches. I just think it worked better for me that they knew I wasn't going to stroke them and I
demanded that they had to play well. Most of the time it
worked. It would be nicer if you could get along and be
friendly with the players, if you could try to do it. But I don't
know. I don't think you can change off. Everybody has their
own personality.

I think there are players and coaches who don't get along.
You can't be a patsy for your players. But if the players are
going to perform to the best of their ability there has to be
some kind of common ground. I mean, you know, you can't

go around with a wounded tiger. You either have to patch it up, or shoot it down. I think that happens with players if the coach is demanding.

Probably the toughest part of coaching is when you have a team and, on a given night, you don't know which players are going to play to their capabilities. Could you say a coach is responsible for that? Maybe he is, maybe he hasn't bridged the gap for those players, hasn't motivated them some nights. Coaches have an affinity for some players over others because the guy brings his stick and skates every night. You know you're gonna treat him a little differently because you appreciate what he does.

Another tough job for a coach is to keep a good team good over a long time. It's even tougher to keep a great team great, as Bowman was able to do with his team in Montreal, which won the Stanley Cup five times in eight years, including four in a row starting in 1976.

SCOTTY BOWMAN

In Montreal the expectations are very high for the team and the players. I think that's an edge for the coach. The Buffalo Bills lost the Super Bowl two years in a row and then when they got there the next year everybody said they'd win because it was their third-straight year in the game. I said to myself that they were the team with all the pressure on them and they got beaten badly. You have to have a winning tradition and with Montreal it helped in certain situations.

You knew when the playoffs came the team was going to give an ultimate performance. You expected it and I think it spurred them on. Everybody demanded it. There was no place to hide. That helps a coach when you have a really strong team. What makes the big teams really good is that they get a group of very talented players to forget about the individual accomplishments a great part of the time and play as a team. It's still a team game. One man's not going to be able to do it all by himself, and I think that's a key part for a championship team. The coach has to make sure he has everyone, whether it's four, six, or seven top players, he's got to make sure that they're all on the same page.

Following his fourth-straight Stanley Cup in Montreal, in 1979, Scotty left the Canadiens, mainly because he didn't get Sam Pollock's job after Sam retired. He got the kind of front-office job that he had wanted with the Buffalo Sabres, but it didn't work out very well in the long run. From there he went to Hockey Night in Canada, *and then to Pittsburgh, where he eventually coached again, winning his sixth Stanley Cup in 1992.*

SCOTTY BOWMAN

I think if I have a regret it's that when I went to Buffalo in 1979, I ended up coaching. I wasn't going to coach. I was going to be the manager but I ended up saying I would be coach for a year. It may have been folly for me to think that I wasn't going to coach again after my eight years in Montreal. I think when a guy has been a coach it's a little more difficult for him to become a manager. And when you try to do both, it's a pretty tough job.

When I went to Pittsburgh, I was really happy the first year working in the personnel and scouting areas. Then Bob Johnson became sick and Craig Patrick called me in and talked about coaching. In my wildest dreams I never thought I was going to coach the team for very long. What I thought would happen was that I would go there and if Bob passed away, which he did in November, they would want to get someone else, probably a younger guy. But that didn't work out. It all happened so fast I didn't have much of a chance to think about it.

The team had won the year before so I didn't feel the usual kind of pressure because I wasn't replacing someone who had been removed from the job. I felt at the time I was more interim than anything.

I don't know if you can coach today for very long in any one city. I left St. Louis after four years. I was in Montreal for eight, Buffalo for five or six. Now I'm in Pittsburgh. I think players get tired of coaches and coaches get tired of players. I think there's a common denominator there.

There are parts of hockey I don't like, the travel and other stuff. I'm a lot older than the guys who are starting out as coaches. I'm not as comfortable as I used to be in the hour leading up to the game. It takes about three hours to play a game and there are nights when you feel things are going well and it's fine. But there are other nights when the game can't end soon enough. Coaching is a lousy job if you can't win maybe one out of every two games. But once the game starts, until it's over, it's a special time. I still like going to games and now I'm coaching again. I mean, you've got to have something to do at the games.

IO

Dominating the '80s: Al and Slats

AL ARBOUR GLEN SATHER

When the Montreal Canadiens won the Stanley Cup in 1979 it was their eighth in the space of twelve years. They have won it just twice since. When the Montreal dynasty ended, the New York Islanders began its own by winning the Cup the next four years. When the Islanders' championship run ended, the Edmonton Oilers took over, with Cup victories in four of the next five years. The mighty Canadiens had faded, but dynasties were alive and well elsewhere in the 1980s.

The Canadiens of the '70s were "Scotty's team." The Oilers of the late '80s had the imprint of their head coach, Glen Sather, front and centre in almost every media report of their success. We didn't talk in quite the same way about Al Arbour of the New York Islanders, but if the NHL soon finds its elusive goal of parity, Arbour may stand as the last coach to win the Stanley Cup four years running.

The Islanders' 1992–93 media guide describes Al Arbour as a "journeyman defenceman" during his twelve seasons *as a player in the NHL. (Media guides are usually kinder to head coaches.) Nevertheless, he played on three Stanley Cup-winning teams, Detroit in 1954, Chicago in 1961, and Toronto in 1964. One of the few players in league history to wear glasses during games, Al preferred to stay in the background while teammates named Howe, Hull, and Mahovlich grabbed the headlines.*

It hasn't been much different during his coaching career. Far from being a "journeyman," Al Arbour has been a very good and very durable coach. When he stood behind the bench during the Islanders' final game of the 1991–92 season, he was coaching in a regular-season game for the 1,438th time and breaking Dick Irvin's "most games coached" record that had stood for thirty-six years. Arbour is second to Scotty Bowman in coaching victories, both in the regular season and in the playoffs. Not bad for a guy who had trouble deciding if he really wanted to be a coach in the NHL.

AL ARBOUR

I never coached in the minors. Amazing, isn't it? I kind of helped Joe Crozier when I was playing in Rochester but I never really coached the team.

Scotty Bowman was the one who got me interested in coaching. I was playing for him in St. Louis at the end of my career, and he wanted to step aside and become the general manager. He wanted me to take over. There was a bit of conflict. Syd Solomon [Syd III, of the family that owned the Blues] wanted his man to coach and Scotty wanted me. Scotty won so I coached that year (1970–71) until about February. Then I went back to playing, of all things, and Scotty coached. After that year they let him go. There was controversy all the time.

I was under contract and stayed as assistant general manager. At Christmas the team was in last place, so they fired the coach, Bill McCreary, and asked me to go back. I really didn't want to but I ended up coaching again. We got in the playoffs and we beat Minnesota in the seventh game, in overtime. Kevin O'Shea scored the winning goal. Then we played Boston. They had their big team then and we didn't stand much of a chance.

Over the next summer I got into a conflict with Syd. I had just signed a three-year contract but, when I went back to St. Louis in August, we got into some heated arguments about players and things like that. I knew I was a marked man because we weren't hitting it off very well. It was just a matter of time. I coached thirteen games and I was gone. [Syd Solomon III deserves some kind of place in hockey history for firing coaches named Scotty Bowman and Al Arbour.]

After I settled my contract I scouted for Atlanta for a few months. I had a couple of offers to coach in the NHL. One was to be the coach and general manager in Vancouver. I had to deal with two guys, Coley Hall and Tom Scanlon. We had a meeting. I'd go into one room with one guy and he'd tell me I could do this and I could do that. Then I'd go into another room with the other faction and they would tell me things completely different. I said to myself, "What am I getting into here? This thing isn't going to work out too well." So I passed on that one.

Later on, either at the Memorial Cup or at the draft, Bill Torrey asked me if I would be interested in coaching the Islanders. I told him no. I said I had four kids and I wouldn't want to move them to New York. I had never been to Long Island but I thought it was just like Manhattan. There was no way I was going to move my family to a place like that.

Shortly afterwards we went to Florida and I bumped into people from Long Island. We started to talk and they were telling me how nice it was to live there. I thought, maybe I should give Bill a call. I did and I asked him if he had found anybody yet to coach and he said he hadn't. He told me the job was mine if I wanted it. So we went to Long Island and saw that it was a very nice area. I took the job and the rest is history.

That started my association with Bill Torrey and I guess you could say it was a unique one. No doubt about that. We were on the same wavelength, but we still had our fights, our arguments. But it was all for the good of the team. We were heading in the right direction and we were very patient. We drafted Bryan Trottier and then sent him back to junior. We were the only team to do that at the time and it certainly paid off. We built the team from the defence out, one here, one there, through the draft. We took a lot of flak, especially Bill. I didn't get there until the team's second year. They had won only twelve games in the first year and Bill was under a lot of pressure. But his patience paid off. We were together a long period of time and we worked well together. We had some great years.

You could see a good team in the making. We got Denis Potvin for the defence, Trots at centre, other young bucks like Clark Gillies, Bob Bourne, John Tonelli. Then came the arrival of Mike Bossy. You could see we were putting together the core of our hockey club and that we were going to have something special. We kept getting better, finished first overall in '78–79, but we still couldn't get very far in the playoffs. We got knocked on our can by Toronto one year and by the Rangers another. The club really hadn't found an identity yet. At the trading deadline the year we won our first Cup we got Butch Goring from L.A. He was the final piece in the puzzle. We had a very young team and he was the guy we needed with just the right kind of experience. That year we played Boston in the playoffs. Before then we might have been pushed around, been nervous and uptight. It was a tough, physical series and we won it. The club settled in after that. We were on our way.

During the four years we were winning the Stanley Cup I tried a lot of things to keep the team at that level. That year we finished in first place [1978–79] we had really tried hard to do it. We did, then got knocked off in the playoffs. I said I would never do that again. I said I was gonna start in the second half, around the end of January, and build the club to a real crescendo. We wanted to play well but if we didn't finish first it was no big deal. We always felt the first playoff series was our toughest. After we got by the first series we got the machine rolling and we were in good shape.

The thing is, you had to be tough on the players and you also had to ease off. You had to find the right time to do it. Timing is everything to a hockey team. I mean, I had some lively guys, guys that enjoyed life and had good times, things like that. You give them a little leeway, then you pull them back. They knew once we got to the end of January we meant business. We started preparing ourselves at that time and we ground them down pretty good for the timing to hit perfectly. We won four-straight Stanley Cups and got to the finals in the fifth year.

When people ask me about what made that team so great for so long I keep going back to what terrific competitors we had. They just wouldn't lose the big games. Bobby Nystrom would do anything. Mike Bossy, great scorer that he was, was a great competitor too. Same thing for Trottier, Potvin, Tonelli. It extended to guys like Ken Morrow, the silent one, on defence. The chemistry was great. If things weren't going well for certain players on a certain night the other guys would make up for it. We had enough character on the team to do that. We won nineteen-straight playoff series. I want to see that duplicated. Edmonton didn't win four Stanley Cups in a row. They won two straight, then lost.

At the conclusion of the 1985–86 season Al Arbour retired as coach of the New York Islanders and moved into what looked to be a lifetime job in the team's front office. They held "Al Arbour Night" at the Nassau Coliseum. They unfurled a big banner which read, "Thanks Al for 13 great years." Then, two and a half seasons later, fifty-six-year-old Al Arbour was coaching the New York Islanders again, a team whose skill level was a far cry from what it had been in the glory days of the early 1980s. It's another case when you have to ask, "Why?"

AL ARBOUR

I wasn't thinking of coming back. The team was struggling. Terry Simpson was the coach and he was doing a good job but the owner wanted to make a change. I was away in Florida at the time. Bill called me and asked if I wanted to take over. I said, "Just a minute here." I had never given any thought to coaching again. I told him I would finish the year to give him a chance to look around. We didn't want to tell the players I was an interim coach. The thing was, they were going to get another coach. So I finished the year and then Bill said he hadn't looked for anyone else and the job was mine if I wanted it.

I thought about it and said, well, why not. The big thing I had to consider was how I was going to be able to handle losing a lot of games. I knew the type of club we had. We had to rebuild, and it wasn't going to happen overnight. That was a big question for me. I was never a very good loser and I knew it was going to be tough sledding. So I gave it a shot but, you know, it's been very hard, very tough. When you're not accustomed to losing it certainly does a job on you. It eats you up. You've got to be very careful you don't get caught in a trap. You have to adjust and it's very difficult. When I came back I said I was going to handle it better than before. I used to take the game home with me and it used to stay with me. I'd always be thinking ahead. I had to make peace with myself and I've worked quite hard at controlling myself much better.

There's so much more to coaching these days. It's all changed dramatically with the videos and all. In the old days you coached a lot by using fear. It doesn't work now with the modern player. Society has changed and players have changed. Now they talk so much about money, comparing themselves with others, what they can and can't make. At times it grates on you a little bit. But I find that the kids today are pretty good kids overall. They work hard and take good care of themselves. It's like a business, a big business. I've got nothing against them. I think they're great. The thing I like best about coaching is the association with the players.

I enjoyed playing the game too. I enjoyed the fun of it, the highs, the lows, the feeling that you had after you won a hockey game. You get it as a coach but there's no greater feeling than the one you get when you're a player and you go out there and win a real tough game. I mean, you have this feeling inside and it's just fantastic. I've had great feelings coaching and winning the Stanley Cup but it never seemed to be the same feeling I got when I was a player. That's what I enjoy, the competitive thing. When you're winning, how great it is, and when you're losing, how bad it is.

In coaching there are things I could do without. There's a lot of aggravation, but that's part of the game. I'm not a PR man. I'm a loner type of person. I possibly haven't been that good with the press either. I kind of like to be left alone, so dealing with the press and all that is not one of my favourite things. But it's part of the job, and you do it. Everybody's been very good to me all through the years but that's not my strength at all.

I don't know about a second retirement. I haven't set any target. But it's getting close.

If Al Arbour was a "journeyman" player in the NHL, the same can be said about Glen Sather. "Slats," as he is called, toiled for six teams in ten seasons. One of his stops was in Pittsburgh. In later years one of his teammates there, Les Binkley, recalled Sather as "a tough, arrogant kid who worked really hard in practice and never gave an inch against anyone. He was clever as hell. He knew the game inside-out." Slats is no longer a kid but those words can now be used to describe his work as president, general manager, and coach of the Edmonton Oilers.

Sather's career in Edmonton began as a player when the Oilers were in the WHA. On March 3, 1977, he became coach of the team. Except for eighteen games at the start of the 1980–81 season when Bryan Watson coached the team, Slats stayed behind the Oilers' bench until he gave up the coaching part of his duties following the 1989 playoffs. While his team was winning the Stanley Cup four times, Glen Sather had the unique opportunity of coaching Wayne Gretzky at the peak of The Great One's greatness. It doesn't get any better than that for a coach.

GLEN SATHER

I suppose there really isn't any great series of adjectives left to describe Wayne, particularly when he was at the peak of his game. What it was like was watching something unfold, like watching your children grow up. You see what they can do every day, you see them change. With Wayne, I saw him evolve into what he has become, a legend.

Yeah, I used to watch him in practice do things that you couldn't imagine anybody could do and do them at full speed, move so well from side to side, which nobody has been able to do like him. He overcame guys with size even though when he came in he was around 160 pounds.

His biggest advantage was his intelligence. He was so much more intelligent than anyone else, could see the ice and know what was going on and remember things better than anyone I've ever seen. He was really a pleasure to be around.

When he was young he was very impressionable and the things we wanted him to do were designed to take advantage of what he could do the best. When he first started setting up behind the net, I mean, that was purely his instinct. We made it easier so he didn't have to go back into his own end all the time. We'd have him wait at the point so he would always have a jump on guys. It was intimidating to the opposing players.

Wayne never missed any practice time. He always watched the films with the guys, he was always there at all the meetings. He was treated like everyone else on the team. He wasn't given a lot of special attention away from the building. We watched what he did, but as far as coaching him was concerned, we treated him much like the other guys, except that we adapted our style around him. We had the other players change while we left him pretty much alone.

When we were winning the Stanley Cup my assistants were John Muckler and Ted Green. But in the beginning they weren't there when Wayne was. The first five years, I pretty much did things myself. Then I hired John Muckler and as the process evolved we gave him more and more responsibility because there were a lot of things going on. But the whole situation of how we developed our style of play, a free flow, switching sides, and the defencemen being involved, that was pretty much a concept I thought of when those two assistants weren't even there. We developed this because we had Wayne, and we had Paul Coffey and Messier and Anderson, guys that could do things that a lot of other people couldn't do.

I remember the first day we were in the NHL we had a meeting with the team and I told them our goal wasn't to make the playoffs, it was to win the Stanley Cup. I told them that, for me, that attitude came from the Montreal Canadiens. The year I played in Montreal Sam Pollock came into the room when the season started and told us, "We don't expect just to make the playoffs. We expect to win the Stanley Cup." Of course when I told that to the reporters in Edmonton they all thought I was nuts. But we did it after five years and I think it was a great tribute to the attitude those players had. Right from the beginning they developed the attitude that they wanted to be winners, they wanted to be great players. They weren't interested in just being so-so.

When I was coaching I liked the competitive part of the game. I particularly enjoyed coaching against Scotty Bowman and Bob Johnson. I knew that when you got into a game against them they could change things, they could compromise. They would come back at you with something new. Because we played against Bob Johnson so much when he was in Calgary I always knew he was the kind of guy who, if we had won, would try and change his style to make it more difficult for you the next game. I had a lot of admiration for him because he was a guy that could change right in midstream. Not a lot of coaches do that. I found over the years that a lot of guys were very predictable about what they were going to do, whether you aggravated them or you just didn't do anything. You pretty well knew what was going to happen. But with Bob Johnson and Scotty, they were always changing and I liked that about them.

The best time for me as a coach was in training camp, because even then we were getting ready for the playoffs. I don't think you can get your team into the right frame of mind in the last month and a half. You've got to do it right from training camp on. It's almost a slow process of manipulation. You have to play a role, so the players get impregnated with the thoughts you want so it becomes second nature to them. If you think that in the last month you're gonna change your team into being a great competitor, you're wrong. You've got to start that right at the beginning of the season.

A lot of things changed in recent years. We really couldn't afford the kind of great players we developed. We were trapped in a no-win situation. We couldn't afford them so we had to move them. That's the unfortunate part of it. But I really enjoyed coaching them. I enjoyed the games and the bus rides and the kibbitzing around in the airports. It was all a lot of fun. But as we got into our tenth and eleventh years Wayne was traded and things started to change. Attitudes changed and the million-dollar contracts came into place. You could see what was going on as far as Canadian teams were concerned and a lot of changes had to be made. That's not to say it couldn't be done again. It just has to be done in a different way.

When you're a coach you have to analyze each player as an individual and treat him as an individual inside a team concept. Each guy has different situations away from the rink. We've had a lot of guys that have had enormous, I don't know if you want to call them problems, but enormous aggravations. Some of those situations could really destroy a player. But if the coach handles them properly, you know the player appreciates what you do for him, and he performs for you on the ice. On the other hand, if you don't handle it right, you create a lot of problems.

An awful lot of talking goes on between coaches and players, one on one. Today they have a lot more needs and you really have to cater to them. When I was a player the coach might say two words to you in a month. There's a certain amount of tension when personality conflicts develop between a player and a coach. I've seen it with teams I've managed but not coached. You've got to try to get them to mend those things. Today, there's not the same attitude towards the team concept. The one thing I enjoyed about the Super Bowl this year [1993] was that after the game you heard guys talk about the team concept, how they did things together. I think in the NHL we're getting away from that a little bit. That's what really makes winners.

Every year we won the Stanley Cup we had a good team. One year we beat Philly in the seventh game of the finals. It was satisfying but I expected to beat Philly. That year it was fun coaching against Mike Keenan. He's a good coach, a good tactician, and he pushes the guys hard. He coaches an awful lot like Scotty Bowman, even chews ice like Scotty.

I suppose winning it the first time is the toughest because you have to develop the attitude that you can win it. Players have a lot of doubts and you've got to get them over that. You've got to trick them, con them, push and prod to get them to go the way you want them to go. I guess when you get there that's probably the most satisfying point.

I particularly enjoyed one year when we didn't win the Stanley Cup – 1981, the year we beat the Montreal Canadiens when we were a very young team. It was a best-of-five and we won the first two games at the Forum, then went

home and won the next game in Edmonton. That was the
year we brought in Andy Moog to play goal. Nobody knew
anything about him and we fooled them. I think that was
probably the most memorable time I had as a coach, beating
the Montreal Canadiens when they were in their heyday.

Luck of the Irish –
Thirty-five Games, No Losses

PAT QUINN

Pat Quinn has two offices in the Pacific Coliseum, home of the Vancouver Canucks. The one upstairs is somewhat presidential, befitting his role as the president of the Canucks. He also occupies the coach's office. It's located at ice level and is, well, like most coaches' offices. None of them will ever rate a spread in **Architectural Digest.** *Hanging on the wall above Quinn's desk in his coaching quarters is a sign reading: "A total commitment is paramount to reaching the ultimate in performance." Credit for that saying is given to a football coach, Tom Flores.*

Pat Quinn is an imposing figure who dwarfed me, and my tape-recorder, as we sat at his desk in the ice-level office. Quinn played over six hundred NHL games as a defence-man. While with Toronto he levelled Bobby Orr with an elbow that earned him a major penalty and knocked Orr out of that game and the next one too. It's one of Don Cherry's favourite video replays.

Vancouver is Quinn's third stop as a coach. He first went behind the bench with the Philadelphia Flyers late in the 1978–79 season. The following year he coached the Flyers to a record that will likely never be equalled: thirty-five consecutive games without a defeat. It began October 14, 1979, and ended January 6, 1980. Thirty-five games, twenty-five wins, ten ties. Shortly after it was over Quinn put a sign up on the Flyers' dressing-room wall that read: "It's impossible. But it's not impossible because they've done it." Credit for that quote went to Scotty Bowman.

PAT QUINN

What I remember vividly is the first game in the streak. The season started against the Islanders, at home, and we won in a very tight game. Then we went to Atlanta and we got beat 9–2 and, boy oh boy, was I devastated. We had just spent a month at training camp and then to get beat 9–2. I thought, holy smokes.

We came back home, we've got Toronto, and Toronto was a pretty good club with Sittler and that crew. We get into a hockey game that's going our way pretty much. We've got a 4–2 lead when all of a sudden the parade to the penalty box starts and we're down two men with two minutes to go. Bob Kelly took things into his own hands and jumped over the boards to mix it up with someone. He figured they couldn't penalize us any more and we'd still be down by two men. He went on his own. I didn't even see him go. Well, the rules call for a penalty shot if that happens. None of us knew that. So Lanny McDonald takes it and scores and it's 4–3 and now we're tight. Fortunately we squeaked through it and won. That was the first game, the starting game, but of course at that time nobody was thinking about a streak.

Montreal had the record with twenty-eight straight. I

don't think it became a factor with us until we got into the twenties and then, boy, it's just strange how it goes. You don't do anything different as it goes along but certain individuals would come along in games that maybe we shouldn't have won, they would come through and win it for us. Rick MacLeish was one. I can recall him not having very good nights and then all of a sudden snapping one in to win us a game. I can remember after we had gone twenty-seven games and it was Behn Wilson. Pittsburgh had never won in our building and they had a 2–1 lead with maybe thirty, thirty-five seconds left in the third period. They'd cleared the puck successfully down into our end. Behn got it and he skates from one end to the other and puts the darn thing in to tie it up. That allowed us to go into the game in Boston where we broke the record.

I didn't have to mention it as a coach because the media certainly picked it up as it went along. It became quite a topic of conversation in our city. If you remember that was the time of the situation of the hostages in Iran. A writer compared the length of what was happening to the hostages to the length of our streak, so it picked up a kind of identity of its own.

As it got going along our guys really surprised me. We had a mixed bag of players on that team. We had a defence that had some unknowns on it. They used to call them the "3 B's": Bathe, Busniuk, and Barnes. They didn't play too long in our game but they were regular players then and we had a good team. I think it really had a lot to do with us pulling together as a team.

We had two goaltenders, Pete Peeters, who was a rookie, and an old vet in Phil Myre, and they basically flip-flopped. They both played their share. Phil played the game in Boston. We could never win in Boston but that night he played a real strong game for us and we won 6–2. That was a special night for Phil Myre, especially in light of the fact that young Peeters was a rookie. Obviously we had the great Bob Clarke and Bill Barber and they were great leaders through that whole stretch. That game in Boston, when it was over, it meant something to those guys, it really did.

When it ended, well, we had played in Buffalo in the thirty-fifth game and won it. A real good hockey game. We went to Minneapolis two nights later and they beat us soundly, 7–1. It almost seemed like we were ripe for it then, you know, in spite of all the valiant cries on the bench: "Yeah, we can do it. We've done it before." We just couldn't do it. Interestingly, Lou Nanne, who was running the Minnesota team, gave his players a trophy for breaking the streak. And that's how it ended.

After that there was a letdown. The streak had a life of its own and it sustained our players. In fact, as a young coach, some days I was getting frustrated. I still believe that you win your games through your practices. We'd come on the ice for practice and they needed me less and less because they were on such a roll. I guess as a coach your ego gets in there and you think, "Maybe we should get rid of this thing, lose, so I can have some value." For a good three weeks after the streak ended we lost our edge. The same hockey team couldn't win the kind of games they had been winning easily before. But we rebounded and it turned out to be a great year for us because we got to the Stanley Cup finals. Unfortunately we lost to the Islanders.

The '80 final was quite a series. The games were close, well-played. The first game was in our building and we played well. We went into overtime and we had a penalty called against us. I had never experienced a penalty in overtime before. I still think it was a rather chintzy one, and they scored on the power play to win the first game. We came back to beat them 8–3 in the next game, and it went like that from then on.

They could win it in the sixth game on their home ice and it was a real good hockey game. We felt Potvin hit the puck into the net from above his shoulders on the first goal of the game. Later on there was the goal they scored on the infamous offside. It wasn't a foot offside, it was ten feet. I have the film. The overtime winner by Nystrom was offside as well, so it was just one of those things. You can't do anything about it. Maybe that's why I dislike referees and linesmen to this day.

Quinn was voted 1980's coach of the year because of all of that. Two years later he was fired by the Flyers. They replaced him with Bob McCammon with eight games remaining in the 1981–82 season when the team had a record of 34–29–9.

PAT QUINN

I wondered about that. Obviously you wonder. Our team was in first place in January and then we ran into a lot of injuries. We lost Clarke, Bob Dailey, Paul Holmgren, key people in our line-up, and we weren't winning. I guess they felt they had to make a change to salvage their season. It was a pretty drastic move because the year before they had given me a five-year contract. You know, like that old Sinatra song, "Riding High in April, Shot Down in May."

It seems too easy to blame coaches in our business but unfortunately it happens. I think our game is a little more sensible towards coaches now. You and I can both remember the days when you'd have someone like Punch Imlach coach the same team for ten years. Look at your father, fifteen years in Montreal. Sure there are some bad coaches, guys that maybe get in over their heads. But for the most part the quality of men who are coaching in our game today is tremendous.

After parting company with the Flyers, Pat completed studies at the University of Delaware and obtained a law degree. He was then hired to coach the Los Angeles Kings, and he held that job from the start of the 1984–85 season until halfway through 1986–87. That's when he became the central figure in a bizarre off-ice situation that was called "Quinngate."

On January 8, 1987, the owner of the Kings, Jerry Buss, advised NHL president John Zeigler that Quinn had signed a contract to become president and general manager of the Vancouver Canucks the following season and had accepted $100,000 from the Vancouver team. Quinn confirmed this to Zeigler. After much legal wrangling and assessing of fines Zeigler's decision was that Quinn was suspended for the balance of that season and would not be allowed to coach in the NHL until the start of the 1990–91 season. When it was all over, Quinn, who felt he had acted within his rights, said, "I was looking for some justice to a ruling I thought was incorrect. A man works his whole life to establish a reputation for honesty. This has been tough on me."

Quinn didn't become coach in Vancouver at the beginning of the '90–91 season, but he did take over for the final twenty-six games. The coach he fired was Bob McCammon, the man who had replaced him when he was fired in Philadelphia nine years earlier. The following season, after the Canucks finished in first place with a franchise-record ninety-six points, Pat Quinn won his second Coach of the Year award.

Pat Quinn

When I first started coaching the coaches weren't paid all that well. Fred Shero had a reasonably good salary, but for the most part coaches were making in the $30,000 to $40,000 range when players were making up to $200,000 in some cases. There have been so many changes the last little while that you ask, where does a coach fit into the organization? What's his value? Certainly your best players should be compensated. They're the ones the fans pay to see. They don't pay to see the coach, although they pay to see the product the coach can bring together. Is he your fifth most valuable person? Is he your tenth? I'm not sure. Last year our average [player's] salary was around $375,000. Most coaches don't make that so I would say, yes, the coaching profession is probably lagging behind.

I've had some great players to coach. When I started in Philly I had Bobby Clarke. In Los Angeles I had Marcel Dionne. Marcel had a reputation as a guy who thought about himself ahead of the team. I found out that was a bad rumour because this guy was as good a team player as I have ever been around. He wanted to do anything that would help our hockey club.

You don't coach the great players too much. You allow them to use their skills to the best of their ability and you hope you have the players who can play with them. Right now I have Pavel Bure and there are a couple of problems. One is that he is a creature of habit. He was trained in the Soviet Union and they are taught differently there. We have worked on his play without the puck, tried to get him to adapt to our system. Here I think I'm lucky again because I've got an individual who really wants to be a team player. The good players want to be team players. But at the same time you have to give them the freedom to use their superior individual skills. With Pavel there is obviously a little bit of a communication problem. But for the most part he really wants to be part of the group and you can't have a better joy, coaching a talented guy who wants to be a team man.

I think I could have stayed away from coaching once I got here. I looked at coming here as another step I wanted to accomplish in this game. Being president was a bonus because that's basically the business side. The general manager's job is where you can actually build a team. I was lucky here. For three and a half years the owners were patient and allowed us to ride through some tough times. That's what I wanted to do. I didn't want to coach. I wanted to have a coach who could handle the players.

When I was just a coach I didn't want to make trades. I wanted to discuss everything with the general manager, but in the dressing room I wanted to have the authority. I wanted to be able to deal with the players as if I was their leader. As a general manager I wanted to do the same thing, take a hands-off approach, get the players and let the coach coach them. I think of good two-man combinations that worked well together, like Bill Torrey and Al Arbour with the Islanders. You can look at some organizations, not to be named, and see where some GMs have a bigger presence than they should when it comes to the actual handling of the club. It's a fine line.

I think you learn from just about all the people you're involved with. I played for Punch Imlach. He wasn't the greatest communicator on a day-to-day basis, but in those days you had the six teams and you could readily be moved out. There was no real waiver protection and a guy like Punch always had that hammer, play our way or you get the highway. Today, players have a lot of movement available to them. So you appeal to them. You try to teach and hope the players will give their best. Now, saying that, two of the best coaches in the last decade and a half have been Scotty Bowman, who was an iron fist, and Mike Keenan, who was also an iron fist. So I don't know that there is a right way to coach. You have to use your own personality, your own beliefs. The fear element is gone. Some of the guys still use it to some degree, but now, for the most part, it wears out fast. Fear and intimidation are not long-term tools any more.

Today's players are coachable. I don't think the boys of today are a lot different from the boys of my time or even prior to that. They all want to win, that's the bottom line. Some of them are brought in too young, they don't have a good base of team play and sometimes you stub your toe getting those guys to play that way. Unfortunately, managers sometimes bring in eighteen- and nineteen-year-olds and tell the coach he has to play them. Then when they don't play to a good level it's the coach's fault. In our day we played in the minors and learned our craft down there until we were twenty-four or twenty-five, unless you were a star. That's one of the big differences today.

I think the thing I like best about coaching is the contact with the kids. I've really enjoyed that. I've been lucky with veteran players like Marcel and Bobby Clarke. I can name a whole bunch. Right now, here in Vancouver, Ryan Walter is a treat to work with, to have around the team. And we also have a bunch of young guys who are meeting some challenges. If you can help them do it, that's the greatest satisfaction.

12

Professional Rink Rat

TOM McVIE

One of hockey's true characters is Tom McVie, who has been coaching professionally for twenty years. Before that he had a fourteen-year playing career, all of it spent as a rough, tough right-winger in the rough, tough Western Hockey League. There are many stories that make the rounds in hockey about Tom McVie, most of them starting with Tom himself. Like when his wife says to him, "I think you love hockey better than you love me." And Tom replies, "But I love you better than I love baseball."

McVie's first coaching job was with the Dayton Gems in the International Hockey League. Halfway through his third season there he moved up to the NHL to take over the Washington Capitals. When he arrived the Capitals had won just three of thirty-six games in the 1975–76 season. It wouldn't be his only NHL experience with a team of that calibre.

Tom McVie

A lot of people asked me why I would take a job with a team like that. My answer was that the Montreal Canadiens had Scotty Bowman coaching them and they hadn't asked me to replace him. Nobody else asked me to take any other job in the NHL. I'm the one guy walking around who has coached three expansion teams and can actually carry on a half-decent conversation. Anyone who's coached as many as two is usually with Jack Nicholson in the cuckoo's nest.

Max McNab came in with me as the GM and we won some games from then on. [Eight out of forty-four.] The next year, with the same players, we won twenty-four games and finished with sixty-two points, and some of the guys thought I could actually walk on water. I came second to Scotty that year in the Coach of the Year voting. Then the next season wasn't so hot and we only won seventeen.

The following year I took the team all the way through training camp, which lasted three weeks. You've got to remember that in those days there weren't any assistant coaches, just me and the trainer. We had a lot of guys in camp, sixty or seventy, and I was on the ice all the time, four shifts a day, two hours each. Eight hours a day on the ice – but that's what I like to do anyway.

The day before the season started I was called into Abe Pollin's office. He's the owner. So I go in and he looks at me for a minute, then says, "We're making a change in the coaching department." So I said, "I guess this wouldn't be a great time to ask for a raise, but I am the coaching department." He said, "That's what I mean," and just sort of pointed to the door.

I was dumbfounded. Then I asked, "Well, am I going to be scouting?" and he kept pointing to the door. Then I asked, "Am I gonna be helping Max McNab?" And he was still pointing to the door. So I said, "When I walk out of the Cap Center, you mean, that's it?" And it was. I was out of there. Gone. Fired. A change in the coaching department.

I went five months without a job after that. That's the longest I have ever been out of hockey and I can see why. The season was starting the next day so it was pretty tough to get a job. Then John Ferguson hired me. Thank God for Fergie. He had been fired by the Rangers, then went out to Winnipeg to take over the Jets in the WHA. I had always been an NHL man and was never very big on the WHA. It was around the end of February and it didn't look like they were going to make the playoffs.

We got going pretty good and made the playoffs right at the end of the season. We played Quebec in the first round. Jacques Demers was their coach, and we beat them four straight. Then we played Edmonton in the finals. Sather was there with Gretzky, who was just a kid, eighteen or nineteen. We beat them in six games for the last WHA Championship.

Winnipeg got in the NHL the next year but had lost a lot of players to teams that owned their NHL rights. So it was expansion for me all over again and I knew what was gonna happen. They said they had a five-year plan, then they offered me a two-year contract. I'm not a mathematician but it didn't quite add up.

There was a big fan-club rally after we had won the WHA and everyone knew we were going into the NHL the next season. It was almost like a Jimmy Hoffa union meeting with people yelling all the time. I told them they'd take a lot of our players and they said, "We don't care. We don't care." I told them the ticket prices were going to double and it would take a long time to make the playoffs in the NHL. They just kept saying, "We don't care." But after a few games the next season, they cared all right. We only won twenty games out of eighty.

That was the year they had "Tuxedo Night" at the Arena the first time the Montreal Canadiens played in Winnipeg. They were the Stanley Cup champions with Lafleur, Shutt, Robinson, Gainey, and that gang. It was on a Saturday and *Hockey Night in Canada* was going to show it coast to coast, so that on Tuxedo Night Winnipeg could show the whole country that they weren't just a bunch of farmers. They sold sixteen thousand tickets and they could have sold another sixteen thousand.

That same night Bobby Hull, who had said he was going to retire, was supposed to make his comeback with the Jets. He'd been practising with us and that night was going to be his first game and it was a big story. We had a rule that the players had to be in the dressing room one hour before they went on the ice for the warm-up. We were strict on this rule and it's less than an hour before warm-up and Hull hasn't shown up. I asked my assistant coach, Billy Sutherland, what we should do and he said there was only one thing we could do and that was not play him. I told him that was easy for him to say because he was going to sit out of sight in the press box. I was the guy who would be standing behind the bench.

So the team goes out to warm up and Hull isn't there. Even in my office I could hear the people buzzing in the Arena. Then Hull comes running in, taking his tie off. I said, Bobby, c'mon in. He charges into my office and says, "Geez, I forgot that the game was at 7:00 because it's on TV and they moved it up an hour." I said I figured that was it, then told him he wouldn't be playing that night. He's got his tie off and now he's taking his shirt off and he's got that big chest and he keeps undressing. And I said, "Look, you can't play."

He was hot, really steaming, but he handled it like a pro. He put his clothes back on and out the door he goes, right out of the building. I figured that the rest of the guys on the team were waiting to see what kind of balls I had. You know, rules are rules, for everybody.

So now, here comes my boss, Fergie, smoking a big cigar, and he says casually, "Where's Hull?" I told him that Bobby had come in late and he can't play. Fergie tells me to quit screwing around and I said, "I'm telling you, he's not playing. He's gone home." Fergie says, "Are you crazy?", walks out, and kicks the door as he goes. It was one of those doors with a hollow panel and he put his foot right through it.

A couple of minutes later he's back and says, "I'm gonna ask you one thing. Do you know this game is on *Hockey Night in Canada,* coast to coast?" I said I did, but the guy came in late and he can't play.

Fergie leaves again, then comes back about a minute later. "I'm gonna ask you once more," he says. "Do you know that *Sports Illustrated* is here to cover the Bobby Hull story? Do you know this is Tuxedo Night? Do you know they have a ceremony planned at centre ice for the Manitoba Sports Hall of Fame?" I said I did, but that I didn't care because the guy had come in late.

So he leaves again. I knew he'd be back and he was, quickly. He says, "I'm gonna ask you one more thing. Just one more. Do you know he's one of the owners of this team?" I said that I had heard that but I didn't care if he owned the whole team. Rules are rules and that's that. He goes to the door, turns around, and says, "I knew you had big balls but I didn't know they were this big. And by the way, where do you think you and me will be working tomorrow?"

When I look back at that game I guess I could say somebody up there likes me. I remember watching the tape afterwards and you were commentating and saying, "The Winnipeg Jets are completely outskating and outworking the Montreal Canadiens." We outshot them 48–18 and won the game 6–2. The people went nuts.

After the game Fergie was all happy and, I couldn't believe it, the media guys hardly asked me anything about Bobby Hull. We were going to Edmonton to play the next day and later on Fergie asked me if Hull would be playing. I told him he would if he was on time for the plane. But he wasn't on the plane. He did play a bit for us after that, then we traded him to Hartford and that's where he finished his career. But I knew then that when I would be talking to a player telling him he wasn't going to play he'd be thinking that I was the guy who benched the greatest left-winger who ever played.

There's a strange follow-up to that story. Ten years later I'm coaching in New Jersey and we've got a kid from Winnipeg on the team, Kevin Todd. When he was growing up he was a big Bobby Hull fan and his father had saved up some money and bought tickets for Tuxedo Night so Kevin could see Bobby play. He was about ten years old then and when he found out Hull wasn't playing he cried. Now I'm coaching him and he hears this story and he says to me, "So you're the guy who wouldn't let Bobby Hull play that night." Small world.

The next season we won our first game, then didn't win in the next thirty. That set a record and that got me fired. I guess everyone's misery is humour later on in life but at the time you just cannot believe the misery when you're involved in something like that. I know there are people starving and people who are sick but at that particular time you just don't care about people. You care, but – you know what I mean. It's just hell. It's tough on your family, the kids going to school. You don't know unless you've been through it. I could sit here and talk to you for two days and never be able to explain the anxiety and misery you go through. It's just unbelievable.

The next season McVie was back coaching, this time with Oklahoma City in the Central League. Then it was on to

*Maine in the American League, the farm team of the New
Jersey Devils. In 1983–84 the Devils brought him back to
the NHL. That stint lasted sixty games. The Devils won fifteen of them. The following year, he was back in Maine.*

TOM MCVIE

The team had come to New Jersey from Colorado and it was
another mess. John McMullen, the owner, told me after that
year that I was going to be his coach again the next season but
I'd get just a one-year contract. I thought, man, the players
are going to smell this and I'm going to be history. So I told
him, absolutely not. I said I'd go back to the minor leagues
and he said, "Okay." Then I said I thought I had done a pretty
good job and I was thinking he'd offer me at least a two-year
deal. But what he meant when he said "Okay" was that it
was fine with him if I went back to the minors. I didn't know
what to say but I figured I had better stick to my guns. He
said, "Before you leave, let me ask you something. You mean
you'd go back to Maine and work for half the money and ride
the buses for twenty-five thousand miles? You'd do that
instead of flying and staying in the best hotels, like we do?"
Now I was stuck, but I said, "That's right." Then he said, "I'll
tell you one thing. You're a damn good hockey man, but
you're really a poor businessman."

So I went back to Maine and it was almost eight years
before I got back into the NHL when I got another chance
with New Jersey. But, come to think of it, I likely would have
been history pretty soon there too because they weren't winning anything.

*After part of one season and another full one with the
Devils, Tom McVie was history again. In 1992–93 he
became an assistant coach with the Boston Bruins. But no*

matter how he gets bounced around Tom McVie keeps bouncing back. The reason is simple. At heart, he's really a rink rat.

TOM McVIE

When I went back to New Jersey and coached the full season, they had a lot of foreign players, especially Russians. The press picked up a quote from me one day when I was pretty frustrated and it went all across the country. That's when I said that I have four guys who don't understand a word I'm saying, ten guys who do understand but don't do a thing I tell them to do, and another four who aren't good enough to do what I tell them to do. Anyway, we had a pretty good season. Finished with eighty-seven points, a record for the franchise. But at the end of the year, I was out the door, again.

I'm fifty-seven now and people ask me when I'm going to retire. I tell them, never. For starters it wouldn't be good for my wife to have me around the house all the time. I'm sort of a fired-up guy. I get up early and usually go right to the rink. Even on the road. I'm at the rink a lot of times around 7:30 having a coffee with the trainers, the Zamboni driver, whoever is there. When they open the doors, I'm waiting to get in. I'm there for our practice, I watch the other team practise, hang around some more, then go for a walk in the afternoon. I'm back around 4:30 waiting for the game to start. I really believe that if I wasn't doing this, and getting paid for it, I'd be hanging around some rink in my home town, or wherever, coaching kids to play hockey.

I guess I'm just a rink rat, always have been. When I was growing up in British Columbia, when I was in school, I was always thinking about hockey. When school was out I was over at the rink. I've been hanging around rinks now for fifty years and I guess for the last thirty-five or so I've never had a real job. I don't know what else I would do. I'm too lazy to work and too nervous to steal.

I went through a lot of misery with those poor teams. I look back and think, sure, I would have liked to have coached the Montreal Canadiens when they had Lafleur, or the Philadelphia Flyers when they were winning with guys like Bobby Clarke, or Edmonton with Gretzky and Messier. But you've got to play the cards you are dealt. I did my very best. We didn't win much but I must have done something right and I must have worked hard because no matter who fired me, I had a job the next year. I know I'll never stop coming to the rink.

13

Captain Video

ROGER NEILSON

While researching and interviewing for this book I was side-swiped by a familiar happening in hockey. One of my coaches was fired.

In mid-December 1992, I was in New York on a broad-casting assignment and asked Roger Neilson, the Rangers' head coach, if I could chat with him for my book. Roger readily agreed and we arranged to get together in Montreal when the Rangers played there a month later. The Rangers played there a month later, all right, but Roger wasn't there to keep our appointment. He'd been fired two weeks earlier. Because of this hazard of the coaching trade our conversation was on the telephone rather than in person. A month before he was fired, Neilson had signed a new contract with the Rangers for a reported $375,000 a year. That made him the highest paid among those who were only coaching and not holding down the general manager's job as well.

*Roger's stint with the Rangers was his fifth head-coaching
job in the NHL. He was also with Toronto, Buffalo, Vancouver, and Los Angeles. He was a co-coach in Chicago with
Bob Pulford for three years.*

*After having become a high-profile junior coach with the
Peterborough Petes, Roger began his professional coaching
career in Dallas in 1976–77. He moved up to the NHL and
coached the Toronto Maple Leafs for the next two seasons.
Late in his last year in Toronto he came close to going into
show business, after a fashion. With the Maple Leafs' eccen-
tric owner Harold Ballard doing the orchestrating, Roger
Neilson almost became the "Unknown Coach," the one
with the paper bag over his head.*

ROGER NEILSON

We lost in Montreal on a Thursday night. After the game
Harold Ballard told the TV announcers that he was going to
fire me. I asked our GM Jim Gregory and he said, "Yeah.
You're done."

The next morning in Toronto I went down to the Gardens
to clear out my stuff and all the players were there plus about
a million reporters. But not one person from the Leafs' management was there. Not one. I told the reporters we'd have a
press conference at noon. I assumed somebody would be
there by that time. Some of the players went out for a skate
and the ones who were interviewed said the usual things
they say when a coach is fired. By noon there still wasn't anybody from the front office. So I had to announce my own
firing. It was a bizarre situation.

The reporters asked me what I was going to do and I told
them I just wanted to coach. They said there was a report
they were going to bring Eddie Johnston up from the farm
team in Moncton to take over and would I be interested in

going down there. I said I could be. The Leafs' radio station, CKFH, wanted me to be part of their crew for the two games that weekend, do the colour, and I said I could do that.

What was happening was that [management] couldn't get anybody to take the job. They tried to get Gerry McNamara and John McLellan and they didn't want it. Nobody wanted it. I found out later that some players like Darryl Sittler, Lanny McDonald, and Tiger Williams had gone to see Harold. He wasn't that bad, you know. They'd told him, hey, it's one thing to fire the coach but now you can't get anybody to take his place. They talked Harold into giving me my job back. In the afternoon Jim Gregory had told me not to go anywhere because they didn't have anybody to coach the team. I wasn't going anywhere anyway.

That night I was still hanging around the dressing room and Harold Ballard came in. He always went there Friday evenings to have his toenails cut by the trainer. He said to me, in his usual gruff way, "What are you doing this weekend?" I told him I didn't have any plans and he said, "Don't go away. We may need you here." That was his way of saying I was back in.

Now it's Saturday and Harold is loving it, loving all the publicity. Nobody knew who was going to coach the team that night. The Leafs still hadn't announced anything and the speculation was starting that I might be back. I kept ducking the reporters. There's a million places you can hide in the Gardens. If you knew all the back ways you could walk around there all day and not bump into anybody. I just stayed out of sight.

In the afternoon Jim called me and said that Harold really wanted to make the most out of the publicity about this thing. By now Harold was telling people he did it just to get the team going. I didn't care. All I wanted was to get back with the team.

Now Jim calls me again and says, "What Harold wants to do is have you go out behind the bench during the national anthem and have a paper bag over your head." I told him I didn't want to do that and he said, "Well, he is giving you your job back. Why don't you do it just for the reporters and then when you get to the bench, take it off." And I said that I would.

In those days you didn't have any assistant coaches. I had hired a kid I knew from Peterborough, Al Dunford. He helped me out with the travel, stats, and the videos, that kind of work. I told him about all this. He was about twenty-one or twenty-two, and he said, "You're coming out of this looking pretty good. You can't join his circus." Al never liked Harold. Harold had fired him three times, mainly because he wouldn't wear a tie. Anyway, I realized he was right, and now it's getting on past 7:00 and the game starts at 8:00.

I went back to Jim Gregory's office and told him I couldn't wear the bag, even for the reporters. He said I would have to tell Harold, and just then Harold came in. So I told Harold and he didn't seem to mind too much. He was just happy there had been all the speculation and all the publicity.

So what happened was I went down toward the bench the back way with Gerry McNamara. When the national anthem was over there still wasn't anybody behind the bench. I walked along the corridor behind McNamara and at the last minute he turned off and I walked out behind the bench. And then there was a huge ovation. All the people who had wanted me fired two days before were now all solidly in my corner.

We were playing Philadelphia and I remember Bobby Clarke was facing off and he backed off until the cheering was over. It lasted a long time. About two years ago a friend of mine in Peterborough who runs the TV station asked me if I had ever seen the TV clip of me coming back. I hadn't so he gave me a copy of the *Hockey Night in Canada* show and I watched it for the first time. It was kind of neat.

Not everyone who was in Roger's corner was still solidly there when the season ended, primarily Harold Ballard. He fired Roger, and Jim Gregory too.

After two years in Buffalo working for Scotty Bowman, Roger headed west to Vancouver for the 1981–82 season as Harry Neale's assistant coach. That was the year, as described earlier by Harry, when Roger took over as head coach late in the season and the Canucks reached their highest height, the Stanley Cup finals, with Roger behind the bench.

In the 1982 playoffs Vancouver fans became a big part of the show by waving white towels inside the rink, outside the rink, indeed all over town. Roger started all that one night during the semi-finals, in Chicago.

ROGER NEILSON

That year in the playoffs was one of those situations where all of a sudden a team with not a great amount of skill goes on a roll. Our goalkeeper, Richard Brodeur, was unbelievable, and it seemed everyone on the team played the best hockey of their career for a period of about twenty-five games. That carried us right from the end of the season to the Stanley Cup finals. In one stretch we lost only two out of twenty-two, and this was an under-.500 team. It was a great roller-coaster ride.

Another incredible thing was that, until we played the Islanders in the finals, we didn't play anybody in the playoffs that had a better record than we did during the season. Los Angeles beat Edmonton that year and Chicago beat

Minnesota, and they were supposed to have the best team in that division.

We played Chicago in the semis. We won the first game in Chicago. In the second game we had quite a few penalties and we weren't very happy with that. The referee was Bob Myers. He gave us a penalty near the end of the game and they scored on the power play to give them a 4–1 lead. So, in effect, the game was over. I wanted to have some kind of a protest, so after that goal I wouldn't put the team out for the face-off. Tiger Williams, who knew me pretty well from a couple of teams, turned around and asked me what I was going to do. I told him I'd think of something. He said we should throw all the sticks out on the ice. But I told him we'd tried that before.

In Chicago they hang the towels on a clothesline in the bench area. It's the only rink where I've ever seen that done. Anyway, I just saw one so I grabbed it and held it up, a white towel, as if to say to the referee, "Okay, we surrender."

He was a veteran so he didn't turn around. Tiger yelled at me that the referee wasn't looking and I told him there wasn't anything I could do about that. So Tiger jumps onto the ice and skates up to Myers and starts yelling, "Look! Look what they're doing!" By this time there were three or four players doing the same thing, and he did look, and then he threw us all out of the game.

Afterwards we didn't think much about it. The next day we were on the only United Airlines plane out of Chicago going to Vancouver. We land and we're pulling up to the gate and a big Air Canada 747 goes by and the pilot is waving a white towel out his window at us. He knew we were on the United plane. We thought that was kind of funny and a couple of players mentioned it. Then we get into the airport and every airport employee has a towel, and there were hundreds of fans there and they all had towels. Everybody, and they kept it up until the finals were over. I just wish I'd had the concession.

The Islanders had a very good team, it's true, but that year in the finals we might have pulled it off. We lost four straight, but the first game went into overtime. They beat us 6–4 in the second but we were winning in the third period. That was on a Saturday night and we had to go back to Vancouver to play on Monday. When we got home I don't know how many thousand people were at the airport. But we had nothing left. We just didn't have any offence at all. The legs were gone. They beat us 3–0 and 3–1. But it was a great ride.

Roger Neilson went from Vancouver, to Los Angeles, to Chicago, and then to New York. This was during the time coaches began using videos to study the play of their teams and their opponents. Roger was the first to delve into this coaching aid in a big way. He dissected and trissected the tapes highlighting offence, defence, power plays, goaltending. A lifelong bachelor with nothing but hockey on his mind, Roger would spend hours poring over the various tapes of various teams and games. It wasn't long before they were calling him "Captain Video."

When he became head coach of the New York Rangers for the 1989–90 season it was the fiftieth anniversary of the last time the Rangers had won the Stanley Cup. When the Rangers played their rivals from Long Island that year, Islanders fans would chant, "Fifty years! Fifty years!" Roger couldn't reverse the trend. In his three full seasons in New York his team didn't make it out of the Patrick Division in the playoffs. They looked to have a good chance at the Cup in 1992 after finishing first overall with 105 points. But in the division final Roger and the Rangers ran into Scotty

Bowman and the Pittsburgh Penguins and were eliminated in six games.

Mark Messier had joined the Rangers from the Edmonton Oilers, was promptly named captain, and produced a Hart Trophy-winning season. When he accepted his award Messier thanked virtually everybody in the Rangers organization, except Roger Neilson. That omission fuelled a fire that had been kindled late in the season by reports that the coach and his captain were not getting along because they couldn't agree on what style of hockey the team should be playing. Sparks were still flying at the opening of the '92–93 season, accompanied by garish headlines in the New York press, which was obviously enjoying what had become a very public spat.

There is a saying within the coaching fraternity, "Never go to war with your star player. You can't win." Roger became living proof of its wisdom when he was let go halfway through the season. It wasn't the first time he had been fired, but it was the one that hurt the most.

ROGER NEILSON

A guy like Messier is brought in to win a Stanley Cup. He's paid a very large salary and there is a lot of pressure on him. He plays a year and they don't quite do it. Now he's looking for reasons and he decides that we're not going to win with this coach. So he goes to management and tells them they're just not going to win with this guy. He says because he is the leader of the team it's his job to make that known.

Some media people said that was right. Well, I think it's entirely wrong. A player is brought in to play and show leadership on the ice. If you have a player stepping into management I think you've got a chaotic situation. I think the player will lose his relationship with the players on the team because all of a sudden he's making decisions on who is going to be the coach and who is going to be on the team. However, with the huge salaries being paid out, I think you're going to see more and more of that happening. All of a sudden these days young guys in their mid-twenties read that they're making three times as much as the President of the United States and I think it affects some of them.

Ten years ago, if a player had ever walked up to Jim Gregory or Scotty Bowman, or whoever was my general manager, and said, "Listen, this coach has got to go," any one of those guys would have told him so fast to get lost and then would have told him to get back on the ice and start playing. But today, it's a different story.

I've been with a lot of teams but nothing like this has ever come close to happening before. It's too bad because the experience in New York was the best of my career. I loved it there. I really loved the team. It has some great character guys. Our practice rink was out in Rye and everybody lives about five minutes from the rink. Sunday was always kind of an optional-skate deal and the guys would bring their kids. We had a big basket of candies in the office and the kids would all come in. It's the only team where I got to know a lot of the wives and kids, and it was a great feeling. There was a real family atmosphere and a good hardworking team. I never had that feeling with any other team. To leave there was really tough.

Right at the same time my dog, Mike, was fighting cancer and he couldn't quite hold on. He died two days after I was released. I waited there until he died and then brought him back home to Peterborough and buried him here, by a lake. He was fourteen years old, a husky-lab. He went everywhere with me. He was never tied up, just wandered freely around

Buffalo and Chicago, everywhere I went. I don't know how he survived all those places. He was an unbelievable dog. I could tell you a million stories about him. I had people phoning me from all over Canada and the United States, more about Mike dying, really, than about my dismissal. He made quite a name for himself.

14

"I Refuse to Accept the Award"

BOB MURDOCH BRIAN SUTTER

In 1981 Red Berenson was voted winner of the Jack Adams Trophy as coach of the year in the NHL. Berenson was listed as the first choice on every ballot filled in by league broadcasters, making him the only unanimous winner in the twenty-year history of the award. In 1980–81 Berenson had coached the St. Louis Blues to a 107-point season, still a franchise record. The Blues finished just three points behind the overall regular-season champions and eventual Stanley Cup winners, the New York Islanders. St. Louis won forty-five games that season. A year later, with twelve games left in the season, the Blues had only twenty-eight victories and Berenson was fired.

The Adams Trophy has not always put a jinx on the winner. After capturing the honour Al Arbour won four-straight Stanley Cups, Scotty Bowman three, and Glen Sather two. But facts like that are usually forgotten by the press, who, almost annually, make the lone award voted on by broadcasters the most controversial of the many post-season NHL trophies.

Having said that, this voting member of the Broadcasters Association has to admit things often haven't gone too well for our coach of the year, especially in recent years. Detroit's Jacques Demers won in 1988, Winnipeg's Bob Murdoch in 1990, and the Blues' Brian Sutter in 1991. All three men were fired after one more season with their respective teams. When Pat Burns won in 1989 after his first season in Montreal he said, "I never wanted to be coach of the year. I just wanted to be coach for a year." In his business, it's not easy. The winner is usually a coach whose team has made a big jump in the standings from the previous season. The jump often translates into "overachieving." When the team slips back into its old ways a year or two later the coach pays the price.

Bob Murdoch paid the price in Winnipeg. The Jets jumped from sixty-four points to eighty-five the first year Murdoch was there. The next season they fell back to sixty-three, missed the playoffs, and Murdoch lost his job. Murdoch was a defenceman in the NHL for twelve seasons, ending his career in 1982 with the Calgary Flames. He was an assistant coach in Calgary and head coach for one year in Chicago before joining the Jets. He credits the late Bob Johnson's positive approach to hockey, and to life, for getting him started.

BOB MURDOCH

When I finished my playing career I was going through a bit of a troubled time. I was a little discouraged. Al MacNeil was the last coach I played for and he got replaced partly because of the response of the players. We had a lot of players who I felt were very selfish. It wasn't a game to them any more, it was more of a financial thing. There was no challenge. They weren't trying to do their best. They hired Bob Johnson and he approached me to become his assistant. The first two times I refused because I had had enough of the game. I wanted to get out. The third time he finally convinced me. It was his enthusiasm, energy, love of hockey. It was the greatest move I ever made because, working with him for five years, I really and truly got to appreciate the game as it should be.

I got the chance to become head coach in Chicago and I made that move the same time Bob left Calgary. They say players get tired of somebody like Bob who is so enthusiastic all the time. There were rumours at the end that the players had turned on Bob, that they were getting tired of him. I don't think that was the case at all. I think what was happening was that some players were growing a bit older, their roles on the team were diminishing, and they didn't handle that as well as they possibly could have. I don't think there are many players in the NHL who do handle that very well. In Calgary we had some players that had been with Bob for five years who were approaching the end of their careers, looking for milestones, and starting to question if they were going to be able to get them because younger players were stepping in. I don't think it was Bob Johnson. I think it was the circumstances.

At the end of my year in Chicago we sat down and reviewed where the Blackhawks were at. We were disappointed with the way the season had ended because we had lost in the first round. But overall we thought we had made progress and were working in the right areas. Supposedly my job wasn't in jeopardy. Then Mike Keenan left Philadelphia and suddenly it was in jeopardy. [Laughs]

Actually, they had hired Mike without firing me. I didn't know if we were going to be co-coaches, or what. It didn't work out that way of course and it wasn't so much a case of me being fired as it was of Mike being hired. In those days co-coaches weren't all that popular or that common. You know Mike is a great coach and a quality person. His record speaks for itself.

They fired me in Chicago and I was pretty bitter. I didn't like the way the situation had been handled. I decided maybe now was the time I should step away and see what normal life was like. So I went back home to Kirkland Lake, stayed out of hockey for a year, and had one of the best years of my life. I got to know my family again and worked in the family business, which involves renting, leasing, and selling cars. I went to work at 7:00 in the morning and usually didn't get home until 7:00 at night. It was the first time in twenty-two years I spent Christmas with my family.

I think every person that's involved in professional sports as a career has a fear that when they step away from the game they might not be able to fit into normal society. It was always a fear in my mind, even though I have a couple of college degrees [physical education and mathematics from the University of Waterloo]. Working like I did that year was a great experience. It really gave me confidence that I could handle myself outside the game. So when the opportunity came up to coach in Winnipeg I felt absolutely no hesitation. I realized there wasn't anything mystical or magical about getting out of the game. I could handle that. So when I went back I had even more confidence in myself and my ability. I knew where I wanted to be and what I wanted to do. I wanted to coach.

In Winnipeg I inherited a team that had underachieved. They had a tradition of a good year followed by a bad year. The first thing I did was meet with the players and I found out they had no identity. They didn't enjoy where they were or what they were doing. I mean, they complained about the weather, they complained about the taxes, they complained about the city. None of them was really looking at the game of hockey. What I tried to do was bring some enthusiasm back into the game for these players. I tried to give them some pride and bring an identity to the team. I had two great assistants working with me, Alpo Suhonen and Clare Drake. They were very capable coaches, great to work with, and the players really responded.

We started off the year with a good, enthusiastic training camp. We didn't have any real star players except for Dale Hawerchuk. We had a lot of journeyman types who were just thankful for the opportunity to try and make the team. We tried to reduce the individual element and make everyone feel he was contributing. It turned out that we had a lot of players who had career years. There was a good feeling.

We seemed to win almost all of our one-goal games. We beat Calgary four times and in all of them we were outshot badly. I remember one game they outshot us something like 53–17 and we beat them 2–1. We won those games because of our goaltending and maybe luck or what have you. But everything seemed to go well. We played Edmonton in the first round and almost beat them. We took them to seven games and they went on to win the Stanley Cup. [And Murdoch won Coach of the Year.]

I know you're going to ask me about the difference between the first year and the second year. We wanted to change the chemistry of the team. Dale Hawerchuk didn't want to be there. Our GM, Mike Smith, wanted to move him, so we made the big trade with Buffalo, Hawerchuk for Housley. That meant we had a lot of offensive defencemen and a lot of defensive centres. So we traded Dave Ellett to Toronto for Ed Olczyk. We got rid of some of the foot-soldiers, Paul Fenton, Doug Smail, Laurie Boschman. These were guys that came to play every night. Suddenly the mix wasn't very good.

We got off to a bad start. Mike [Smith] went public in
November not supporting the coaching staff and it was really
a struggle after that. The focus was back on that good
year/bad year thing. Rather than look at the positives everybody started to look at what was going wrong. We had a lot of
players in and out of the line-up. It sounds like an excuse but
I'm not making excuses. Instead of rotating two or three guys
on merit we were rotating seven or eight just to keep everybody happy. So we made some mistakes that year, went
through some growing pains. Unfortunately, the coach was
a casualty.

One of the things I've never really understood was that
when the Winnipeg Jets fired me after I had spent two years
with the team I was a much better coach than I was when
they hired me. It's frustrating as a coach to get to know your
players, learn from your mistakes, learn from your strengths,
feel you're developing both as a coach and as a person, then
get the rug pulled out from under you. The insecurity and, at
times, the lack of respect for coaches are discouraging. I
guess the best way to sum it up is that we are in the entertainment business and you're competing for a lot of dollars.
You've got to give the perception that there's improvement
every year. You've got to keep the people coming back. The
sports business is a great business but the entertainment
business is tough. That's the bottom line and that's the part
that really kills you.

One of the reasons I took this job as the assistant coach
with San Jose is that I wanted to run the gamut. I played on a
Stanley Cup winner in Montreal but I had never been with an
expansion team. I wanted to work with someone like George
Kingston who is an experienced teacher and an experienced
coach. You have to redefine success with a team like the
Sharks. It's tough because you're taking a bunch of kids and
throwing them into a situation where they don't have much

chance. We take a lot of different stats and try to focus on the process rather than on the outcome of the game. We keep saying to our guys, "Never mind the standings, you're showing improvement." But no matter what anyone says, when you go home and you've lost, whether you're expected to win or not, it's still a loss. It's a helluva lot harder to coach the San Jose Sharks than the Pittsburgh Penguins. I'm not saying that to put down Scotty Bowman, but it's a lot tougher because the greatest motivator is reward.

I compare this situation to the old days when it was the Christians against the lions. The people would yell and scream and if the Christians put up a good fight they'd send in more lions. The lions would go home well fed, the people would be satisfied, but the Christians were dead. Every night when we go into the room and we've lost another game, our guys are like the Christians. They've been fed on and they're dead.

When I went to college I had no intention of playing professional hockey. I was going to teach high school and become a hockey coach. Basically that's what I am, a teacher and a coach. I'm doing what I love and that's why I enjoy it so much.

In 1991 Brian Sutter succeeded Bob Murdoch as coach of the year after his St. Louis Blues finished the season with 105 points, a twenty-two-point improvement. A year later, the Blues slipped to 83 points and were eliminated in the first round of the playoffs, and Sutter was gone. A couple of weeks later he became the head coach of the Boston Bruins.

Brian Sutter had been a St. Louis Blue for sixteen years. In a twelve-year playing career he scored 303 goals. He went straight from being a player to being the head coach. The Blues retired his sweater number 11. But the good times were forgotten in an acrimonious end to his days with the Blues.

After Sutter was fired, Ron Caron, the Blues' general manager, said in an interview with **The Hockey News:** *"Brian Sutter meant a lot to this organization. But this goes back to the issue of success and failure. We did not advance in the playoffs and that is how we have come to be measured by the fans. Brian is a self-made man and I think he had some trouble conceding work to other members of the staff. Also, and I'm being very frank here, we knew we were going to acquire some Europeans and we didn't know how Brian would relate to them. We had some questions about adding this dimension to our team with Brian."*

BRIAN SUTTER

I was fired for a very simple reason. We were expected to win the Stanley Cup. When I took over in St. Louis we had the oldest team in the league. Within two years we went from the bottom third of the league to the top half-dozen and it was anticipated we were going to win the Cup immediately. They can say that's not true, or whatever, but they sold that to the people in St. Louis. We knew as coaches we were just one contender for the Stanley Cup. That's what people forget. One team wins it and everybody else is a contender.

I helped players overachieve. I think if there's a compliment you can give a coach it's that his players overachieve. Not for just a few games but for two or three years in a row. They have so-called career years and then it becomes habit-forming, natural for them to do it all the time. That's what we did in St. Louis. Three quarters of our players in St. Louis were players other teams had no desire to have around.

What they told me in St. Louis was that I lost my job because we didn't win the Stanley Cup. Then all the other

Gerry Cheevers, who coached the Bruins in 204 games, often in a sports shirt or a sweater. The first time he coached he was wearing his goal pads.

Gary Green, on the left, was only twenty-six when he became coach of the Washington Capitals in 1980. Caps GM Max McNab is in the middle, assistant coach Bill Mahoney on the right.

Mike Milbury making a point in practice to his Boston Bruins in 1989. Coaches spend hours on the ice as well as behind the bench.

Roger Neilson during his tour of duty with the Buffalo Sabres. Captain Video has been the head coach of six NHL teams, a record.

John Muckler standing on the Buffalo Sabres bench, not behind it. There isn't a coach in hockey that hasn't protested a referee's call in this fashion.

Mike Keenan, all smiles when he became coach of the Chicago Blackhawks. His smile was even bigger when he signed a bigger contract to coach the New York Rangers five years later.

Brian Sutter deep in thought at the Boston Garden. Sutter took over in Boston after being fired by the St. Louis Blues less than a year after he was named 1991's coach of the year.

Vancouver's Pat Quinn with the Jack Adams Trophy as the NHL's coach of the year in 1992. Quinn also won it in 1980 after coaching the Philadelphia Flyers through a record thirty-five-straight games without a defeat.

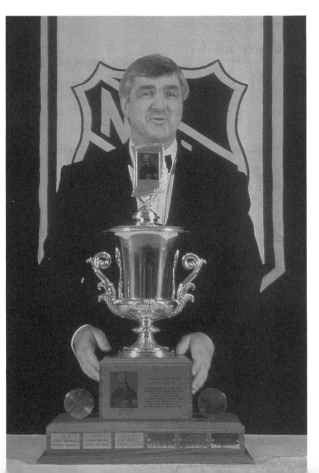

Al Arbour doing something he has done more than anyone else, coaching his team in a National Hockey League game. Arbour is the last man to coach four-straight Stanley Cup winners, with the New York Islanders, 1980-83.

Scotty Bowman, likely on his way to another coaching victory. He has more of them than anyone else.

Scotty Bowman, being congratulated by two superstars, Wayne
Gretzky and Gilbert Perrault, during ceremonies in 1985 honouring
Bowman for becoming the NHL's all-time winning coach.

Dave King was sought
after by several NHL
teams when he was with
Canada's National Team.
After coaching Canada to
a silver medal in the 1992
Winter Olympics, King
became coach of the
Calgary Flames.

In his first season in Toronto, 1992-93, Pat Burns coached the Maple Leafs to within one win of making the Stanley Cup final for the first time since 1967 and won his second coach of the year award.
(Robert Laberge)

Barry Melrose, smiling in the press conference after his Los Angeles Kings defeated the Canadiens in the first game of the 1993 Stanley Cup final. The Canadiens won the Cup, but Melrose emerged with a high profile after a successful playoff in his first year with the Kings.
(Denis Brodeur)

The Irvins have been hanging around the Stanley Cup for a long time. *Left*: Dick Sr., with the Stanley Cup, and general manager Frank Selke, with the Wales Trophy, after the Canadiens won both in 1946. *(Mac McDiarmid Collection) Right*: Dick Jr. and Jacques Demers, with the modern version of the Stanley Cup, shortly after the Canadiens won it in 1993. *(Studio Alain)*

Jacques Demers's long-time dream finally comes true. The Canadiens coach lifts the Stanley Cup in triumph moments after his team defeated the Los Angeles Kings at the Montreal Forum, June 9, 1993. *(Denis Brodeur)*

excuses came out after that which were far from the truth. They were so false. To this day the press has been told a half-dozen different excuses about what happened and those are all so erroneous, so far from the facts. Like not being able to handle young players, not being able to handle Europeans, not being able to handle skilled players. Ask Brett Hull, Jeff Brown, Curtis Joseph, and Nelson Emerson. If those guys aren't skilled players then the people that are talking and making those comments aren't very intelligent.

I wasn't shocked at the decision but I was shocked at how it was handled. The people they forgot to ask were the players and people involved. We had a great organization. We were so close-knit and so together. The coaches, the scouts, everybody. It's unfortunate, but coaching jobs, I guess, are all temporary.

When it happened I heard immediately from, like, fifteen organizations in the NHL. Let's put it this way, all the things a few people were critical of when it came to my coaching, the discipline and the hard-work ethic on a day-to-day-basis, people elsewhere in the NHL weren't worried about.

After Brian got all that off his chest we chatted further about coaching and about the ever-present Sutter family, his brothers whom he has played and coached both with and against.

BRIAN SUTTER

When I was playing I never thought about coaching. Never. Not once. It came up all of a sudden. I was asked to think about it at the end of my twelfth year as a player. But as a player I used to look at Scotty Bowman, Al Arbour, Mike Keenan, and wonder why they'd do certain things. As a player I was thinking about what the other team was doing. I never questioned some of the things they did out loud. You always keep it to yourself, but now those things I studied are very beneficial to me as a coach.

People ask me who I try to coach like and I say I try to coach like myself. I look at what Al Arbour's done and I would say I'm very similar to him. I think the most important thing about a coach nowadays is people skills. Everybody says teaching is important, but it's about fourth or fifth down the line in qualities that are of absolute necessity now. You have to communicate with your players, make them understand. If you can do that, then you've got an opportunity to teach them something.

I didn't have a problem coaching the guys I had just been playing with because my attitude towards coaching is very simple: be very honest and be very upfront. If a player's not playing well I'm not going to scold him in front of fifteen thousand people. I'm not going to scold him in the press, unless the player says something in the paper that's detrimental to himself and the hockey club. I do it personally. If a player's not playing well I talk to him like you and I are talking right now and try and find out what's going on. If a player's not playing well the sin isn't in the mistake. The sin is in doing it twice.

I'm honest and upfront and I expect the players to be that way. Their honesty shows on the ice. All you've got to do is look at what we've done this far. During my four years in St. Louis only five coaches won more games than I did. I'm thirty-six years old and feel I have a wealth of experience behind me because of the people I've been with and played for. I played three years for Jacques Demers and he appreciated hard work. Sometimes, when I was injured, Jacques would have me work with him behind the bench. I've been fortunate to know people like Scotty Bowman and Glenn

Hall and to be around Emile Francis, and to learn from those people.

Today you've got players making a million bucks. You've got to make them realize and understand how lucky they are to be where they are, and earning what they're earning. I was fortunate enough to be able to do that in St. Louis. When you take a team that's in the bottom twenty-five per cent and put it in the top twenty-five per cent within a year, you've accomplished something. That's one of the biggest reasons I'm here, in Boston.

In 1991–92, Brian's last season in St. Louis, his twin brothers, Rich and Ron, were playing for him. In Chicago, Darryl Sutter was an assistant coach and Brent Sutter a player. When those teams would meet, and when the three playing brothers were all on the bench, amazingly there would be five Sutter brothers within a few feet of each other. The plot thickened the next season when Darryl became head coach of the Blackhawks and went head to head with Brian when his team played the Bruins.

BRIAN SUTTER

We were brought up with a competitive nature. We had it from the time we were kids. We did everything but boot the shit out of each other all the time growing up. The thing we detested the most, whether it was in a pick-up game of baseball, or hockey, or football, was losing to each other. We absolutely detested losing to each other because you knew you were going to get it, get a good needle, not just after the game but until you played the next game.

When I was a player there was always such a bitter rivalry between St. Louis and Chicago. Then, as a coach, I wanted to win more than ever. When players come to the rink and step on the ice it doesn't matter who's on the other team. It's another colour against you. That's the way it was, and is, when our brothers are on the other team.

I almost got in a fight once with Duane. He's the type of a guy I'd fight with right here, a very competitive individual. He was a big part of that Islanders team. We just went out and played as hard as we could against each other. There's no reason not to expect that.

When I coached the twins there was never any hard feelings amongst the other players. Some members of the press said there was but that's far from the truth. The press criticized the roles I gave them. It's interesting because I was watching a Blues game the other night and Richie Sutter was playing in a position that he played in last year. I wonder if the press is questioning that now. When I coached them their names didn't mean anything to me. One of a coach's biggest responsibilities is putting players in a position to succeed and that's the way I was with my brothers. It was harder on them than it was on me.

I don't mind people saying things about me, or my family, or how I handled my brothers and myself as a coach. But when they're just not on base, when they're totally false, it really pisses me off.

The day I finished putting together this chapter I ran into Duane Sutter at the Montreal Forum. He was there scouting for the Chicago Blackhawks. I asked Duane if he remembered the incident when, as a member of the New York Islanders, he almost got into a fight with his brother Brian. "I remember it very well," he said. "We were playing in St. Louis and I ran one of their players, Jack Brownschidle, into the boards. Brian piled right into me and a real hassle was in the making. But luckily for me Clark Gillies was there too. Clark was bigger than both of us. He jumped between us and said to Brian, "You touch him and I'll eat you for lunch." By that time I was out of there saying to myself, 'Thanks, Clark.' [Laughs] But Brian wanted a piece of his brother that night, no doubt about that."

15

Le Petit Tigre

MICHEL BERGERON

If you want an example of an emotional National Hockey League coach, check out some videotapes of games involving the Quebec Nordiques in the early and mid 1980s. The little guy behind their bench in that era, Michel Bergeron, is your perfect example. The Nordiques became a very good team during that time. They had the Stastny brothers, Michel Goulet, Dale Hunter. Yet the team's dominating personality in the media, and many nights during their games, was Bergeron, who is still known in Quebec as "Le Petit Tigre." He was a picture of elation, frustration, gloom, anger – you name it, Michel would display it sometime between the opening face-off and the final siren. He let it all hang out, every night, especially when his beloved Nordiques were playing the hated Montreal Canadiens.

Michel Bergeron's NHL coaching career started in the Nordiques' second season, 1980–81. He spent seven seasons there, two more seasons (less two games) with the New

York Rangers, then another year back in Quebec when the Nordiques had a terrible team and won only twelve games. Michel became a sportscaster, had a heart attack, and then had his heart broken when Pat Burns left Montreal and he wasn't hired to coach the once-hated Canadiens.

MICHEL BERGERON

When I was a kid I used to stand outside the Montreal Forum getting autographs from the Rocket, Boom-Boom, Dickie Moore, all those guys. I really believed, like all kids, that I would play in the NHL. But one day I said to myself that I didn't have the size or the talent, so if I wanted to stay in this game, I'd better start coaching.

I coached in Montreal the first year they had triple-A midget and my team won the Canadian championship. Then I coached a junior-B team and I won the championship there. The next year, 1974, I went to Three Rivers to coach junior A. They had just fired the coach and he was so popular with the players they went on strike. There I was, a young guy who wanted to coach, but I didn't have any players. It was a hell of a way to start.

After two days they came back and we played in Quebec and lost 7–0. After the game I was all by myself in the bus. The players wouldn't ride with me and the general manager and his people hadn't even come to Quebec. So I had the driver take me to the motel. I called my wife and told her not to start moving right away. I didn't know what I was gonna do or what was going to happen. First no players, then nobody to talk to. But after a month everything was settled. I spent six wonderful years in Three Rivers. We went to the Memorial Cup twice, '77 and '78, and lost in the finals both years.

After the Nordiques' first year in the NHL they demoted

Jacques Demers. Maurice Filion was the general manager and he met with me and asked me to be the assistant coach. I said, "Assistant coach? I'm the best coach in the world. Who's gonna be the head coach?"

Maurice said he couldn't tell me but the guy was one of the best. So, after a couple of hours, and a couple of glasses of wine, I asked Maurice again, who's gonna be the coach? And he said, "Me." So that's how we started the season. After six games Maurice called me to his hotel room. We were in Winnipeg and he says, "Do you still believe you're the best coach in hockey?" I told him yes, and he said, "Okay. You've got the job. I just fired myself."

Every day my first year in Quebec I was real scared of losing my job. Some people with the Canadiens were calling me a junior coach because of things I did behind the bench, and I was real scared, especially after a loss. I had a good captain at the time, Robbie Ftorek, and he was my key leader in the room and a big help to me.

I think I saved my job on a road trip early in the season. We lost a game in Long Island 10–7. Michel Plasse was our goalie and our other goalie, Dan Bouchard, was really mad because he didn't play that night. So on the bus after the game Bouchard was joking and singing. I told him he'd better shut up and he got madder. We had a lot of veterans. I was a young coach who had never played the game and there wasn't much respect for me. But I think they noticed what I did with Bouchard on the bus.

We played in Detroit the next night and after the first period it was 1–0 for us. Wally Weir had speared Danny Gare, so when we came back into the room at the end of the period, I said to him, "Wally, you never do that. You're six-foot-three and if you want to do something you drop your gloves and settle the case. But you don't spear Danny Gare because he's five-foot-seven."

I walked out of the room and I heard one guy say, "Don't worry, Wally. You did the right thing." I'm just outside the door and everybody knows I can hear what the guy said. Now I've got a decision to make. So I went back in and jumped all over the guy who had told Wally he had done the right thing. I told him, "I'm the coach. You're just a player." Everyone was very quiet in the room. I think I saved my job right there.

It didn't take long before we had a good team in Quebec. The Stastny brothers were a big reason. The language was not a problem because they are very intelligent, nice guys. I remember one meeting when I had a puck in my hand. I said, "Boys, we've got a little problem. In this room we've got three Czechs, two Swedes, ten French Canadians, and eight English guys. But there's one thing that's the same for everybody. It's the puck. Take a look at it. It's black for everybody. Now, we've got a rule. When everybody is here we're gonna speak English." I can tell you I never had a problem with language.

I'm from Montreal, but when I started to work for the Nordiques I hated the Canadiens all the time. The rivalry really got going when Jacques Lemaire started to coach in Montreal. He would say things in the paper and I would answer back. There was always a big build-up when we would play. Some of the papers in Quebec would have ten or twelve pages on the games. Maybe it got too big sometimes, but the fans asked for it and they loved it. They still talk about it.

It got to the players too, no question about it. I remember having my meetings before those games and sometimes five or six players would have to get up and go to the bathroom. They were so nervous they were sick. And not only the French Canadians. Dale Hunter and Clint Malarchuk, guys like that too. I never had to give a long speech those nights because I knew they'd be ready.

Dale Hunter was a great guy to coach. He was a leader on

the ice but not off the ice because he was so quiet. He was always rooming with Michel Goulet. They roomed together seven years and Dale would see all the stuff in the French papers and he'd say, "Gou, Gou, translate this for me. What did Bergy say about Lemaire?" It was real funny.

Dale Hunter was the kind of a player who could change a game. He'd make things happen, get everybody going crazy. He broke his leg and then they traded him because they thought his leg wouldn't be any good after that. Now he's thirty-two and has grey hair and he's still doing it for Washington. In Quebec in the '80s Hunter and the Stastnys were my key players. Dale was probably the player I enjoyed coaching most of all.

Some people thought I was too emotional in those days, but I don't think so. I was like that in junior and I was like that in the NHL. I was real vocal behind the bench but I was also close to the players. If they wanted to take a coffee with me, wanted to talk about anything, I was always there.

Right after they traded Dale Hunter to Washington I went to the New York Rangers. It happened at the draft in Detroit in '87. I had been close to Maurice Filion but we had started to have little problems, little fights. I told him that after seven years in Quebec it was maybe time for me to move on. At that time five or six teams were looking for coaches. But Maurice told me that I was his coach. Then in Detroit New York's GM, Phil Esposito, asked Filion if he could talk to me about going to the Rangers and he said it was okay. After the draft Maurice told me I had forty-eight hours to make a deal with the Rangers.

On the way to New York I told my agent, Pierre Lacroix, that no matter what happened I couldn't go back to coach in Quebec. We met with Phil for about five hours and we made the deal. I couldn't believe that the Rangers gave up a first-round pick and $100,000 to get me. I had never won the

Stanley Cup. When I signed my contract with New York it was a sad moment for me in some ways. I felt at the time I had the Nordiques in my heart. It was real tough to leave them.

I really got to love New York. The first few months were tough for my family because the kids didn't speak English. But pretty soon everyone spoke English in the house and it was great. And the atmosphere around the team was so different. Charlie Thiffault was my assistant in Quebec and he went to New York with me. I used to say to him that there was something missing after the practices because there were hardly any reporters around. In Quebec it was a lot different.

I would walk on Broadway and see a sign, "Come see the New York Rangers coached by Michel Bergeron." I would tell my wife, "Hey, I'm just a little guy from Ville St-Michel and now I'm in the Big Apple!"

My second year there we signed Guy Lafleur. He had been retired four years but he called me and said he wanted to try a comeback. I called Phil and we agreed to give him a chance. Our training camp was in Three Rivers and Guy came there, no contract or anything. In the first scrimmage on the first day he scored the first goal. We went to Edmonton for an exhibition and he had a great game. So Phil signed him for a year. It was good for him, and the organization.

I might be the only coach who was fired with two games to go in the season. It happened in my second year in New York and it was a shock. I made the team practice at 7:00 in the morning after a bad game in Detroit. Phil didn't like that. He called me right after and said I should apologize to the players. I said no way, and hung up the phone.

We went from there to Pittsburgh. We were fighting for second place in the Patrick Division and it was the second-last game. Phil called me to his room at 10:00 that morning and said he was going to make a change. I said, "Where? The coach?" And he said yes. I asked him why and he said, "Well, Bergy, there could be one reason, there could be a thousand reasons." So I got up, shook his hand, and wished him luck.

It was April 1st so when I went to say goodbye to the players they thought it was an April Fool's joke. But when I put on my coat and went around the room shaking hands, they knew it was really happening.

I still believe Phil made the wrong call. He's like me, very emotional. I had a great time with him in New York. He's a good hockey man and knows the players in and out of the NHL. That time I think his problem was his emotion. He's like me, he's a very emotional guy.

Quebec called me right after I got fired in New York and I went back there because it was my home. They wanted me back to help sell season tickets. I thought the team could start to win again but in fact it was going down real bad. You just can't accept losing every night. It was a tough year.

Pierre Pagé got hired as general manager by Quebec in the summer. He had a news conference and they asked him about the coach, and Pagé said, "I'm going to think about it." I'm sitting there and this new guy coming from nowhere, he's going to think about me, decide about me? Nothing happened right away. I saw him about a month later and he asked me a lot of questions about the team. So I asked him about the coach. He said he hadn't decided yet.

I knew I was in trouble. I had a six-year contract with the Nordiques. I wasn't afraid then of losing my job. Maybe in my rookie year, yes. But not after nine years. Then one day I was called to a meeting at Pagé's office but he didn't show up because he was in Toronto signing Dave Chambers to coach. I figured I deserved better than that.

Pagé never fired me. He saw that my contract had a clause about me doing TV or radio with the team. So he never said I was fired. He said I would do something different in the organization. I had to decide. I knew I couldn't do radio or TV for the Nordiques because then I would have to be there all the time, travelling with the team, seeing the coach every morning. I went to Marcel Aubut and gave him the contract back. No buy-out, no nothing. I gave him back a five-year contract and I'm telling you, it was tough. It was for good money, real good money.

I came to Montreal and did radio and TV. I had a heart attack but then I was all right and I went back to my broadcasting job. Then, when Pat Burns left, I wanted the job. I wanted to coach the Montreal Canadiens.

Jacques Demers had the first meeting with Serge Savard. Then I met with Serge and told him if he wanted the best coach I was ready to come back. I felt we had a great meeting. When it was over I called my wife and told her I thought I had the job. The same night the Canadiens' team doctor got involved. Maybe it's only an excuse, I don't know and maybe I'll never know, but Serge Savard told Pierre Lacroix, the doctor doesn't recommend we hire Michel.

How come the doctor can decide? I feel great. I want to coach again. Maybe because of what I did in New York when I got into a kind of fight with Phil and said, nobody will hire me again because I'm a dangerous guy. General managers don't want fights and I said maybe it was my last chance to coach.

I was mad at Pagé in Quebec because I felt I was at the best of my career. I don't have anything against the Montreal organization or Jacques Demers. Savard was nice at the meeting. To be honest with you, I was sad, just sad because I didn't get the job.

16

Coach on a Roller Coaster

JACQUES DEMERS

At 7:30 on the morning of March 9, 1993, the coach of the Montreal Canadiens, Jacques Demers, arrived at his office at the Montreal Forum. Shortly afterwards he was joined by his boss, Serge Savard. The two men chatted over coffee, then Savard left for a dental appointment and Demers began making plans for his team's practice later that morning. The Canadiens were scheduled to play the next night at home against the New York Islanders, and the following night in Boston. While at his desk Demers began experiencing chest pains. He contacted the team's athletic trainer, Gaetan Lefebvre, who immediately accompanied Demers to the Montreal General Hospital.

Demers remained in hospital for forty-eight hours, passed all tests, and was released, after receiving a stern warning from the doctors to lose some weight. The Canadiens' assistant general manager, and a former head coach, Jacques Lemaire, replaced Demers for the games against the

Islanders and the Bruins. It was the first time in over fifty-three years that a coach of the Montreal Canadiens had missed a game because of a health problem. That fact is a minor trivia item in the history of the NHL's oldest franchise, but it was another strange happening in the often strange career of Jacques Demers.

Born in Montreal, August 25, 1944, Demers found himself at an early age bearing the responsibility for his poor, working-class family of four brothers and sisters. His mother passed away when he was sixteen. By that time Jacques had left school and was working for Coca-Cola. A few years later his father died in Jacques's arms when he suffered a heart attack while the two of them were driving in the family car. Jacques began taking night-school classes and coaching minor-hockey teams. Hockey began to dominate his thoughts and he found himself dreaming of standing behind the bench of his favourite team, the Canadiens. After twenty years of twisting and turning down a long and sometimes chaotic professional coaching road he finally found his way to the Montreal Forum. In the career of Jacques Demers, what was happening off the ice was often more interesting than what was happening on it.

JACQUES DEMERS

I started out coaching peewee, bantam, midget, and juvenile. The St. Leonard Cougars were in the Montreal Junior League, and when their coach got sick I filled in for the last twenty-five games of the season and it went well. The next year I moved to the Chateauguay Wings, a tier-2 junior team. We won the championship two years in a row. The Laval Saints of the Quebec League offered me $5,000 to coach. I would have had to quit my job at Coca-Cola so I asked for a three-year contract but they would only give me a one-year deal. No way. I had been with Coca-Cola eleven years and was making $6,800.

By then I had made up my mind I wanted to be a hockey coach and I did feel that maybe I gave myself a setback when I said no to Laval. The more I was coaching the more I hoped that maybe someday I could realize a dream and coach in the NHL. But I was prepared to stay in junior B, when, the next thing you know, the WHA came along in 1972. Marcel Pronovost became the coach for the WHA team in Chicago, the Cougars. He called me to be his assistant and I took the job. When I flew to Chicago it was the first time I had ever been on a plane. In fact, it was the first time I had ever been in an airport and I was twenty-seven years old.

It wasn't easy being a French Canadian in a situation like that. I was not totally accepted by the anglophones at first. They were thinking, who is this tier-2 coach coming from nowhere and trying to tell us what to do? He's never played pro hockey. Rosaire Paiement played for the Cougars and he was the toughest guy on the team. One day he stood up in the room and said, "This guy here is trying to do an honest job. If anybody tries to upset him they're going to have to face me." From then on I seemed to be more accepted by the players. It was my first lesson in trying to survive as a pro hockey coach.

Marcel was let go and the guy who really saved my career was Pat Stapleton. He took over as general manager and coach and he was still playing for the team. He decided to retain me and I was his man behind the bench. I ran the bench during the games. We went to the finals the second year in Chicago.

Like a lot of WHA teams we had some funny things happen. One time we were sitting on the plane getting ready to take off for Los Angeles and they announced, "Would the person in charge of the Chicago Cougars please step forward." So Marcel and I went to the front and they told us we all had to get off the plane because the credit card we used to pay for the tickets was no good. By the time we straightened that out that plane had left and we had to take another one. We had times when the meal money wasn't there, salary cheques were late. We were all struggling even though there were some great names playing in the league.

After three years the Chicago Cougars folded and I was fortunate to be hired by the Indianapolis Racers. First I was hired as an assistant to Jerry Moore. The team kept losing and we were in last place and they made me head coach. That job lasted two years and *they* folded. I went to Cincinnati. That lasted a year. After the first year they had a drive for tickets to keep the team going. They set a target of four thousand season tickets. Pete Rose bought four tickets to take it to three thousand because he had just reached three thousand hits. It didn't look like they were going to make their quota. They were going to fold the team and at the time the Quebec Nordiques were looking for a coach. So I went there. I never got fired in the WHA. I did all that moving from team to team because the teams were folding.

I still wanted to be a coach, still wanted to get to the NHL, but it was all very disturbing. Your family pays a tremendous price, buying a house, then moving, buying another house, and moving again. We'd think we were settled and, boom, the team would fold.

When I was hired in Quebec it turned out to be the last year of the WHA. We had ninety-three points and got to the finals. Winnipeg beat us. Then we moved into the NHL and I had finally made it. We won twenty-five games in our first year. That's when I learned a big lesson. I had been talking to a reporter, off the record I thought, when we were having coffee in a restaurant, and told him that as long as a couple of players were kept in Quebec the team would never be a

winner. He printed that and it got me in a lot of trouble. I
learned there are certain people you just can't trust and I
knew from then on I had to be careful how I talked, and who I
talked to. The president, Marcel Aubut, called me into his
office and said, "We're not going to fire you because we like
you as a person. But you're going to have to go down and
coach our minor-league team." The Nordiques were owned
by a brewery and they felt the players could sell more beer
than I could. I understood that.

I went to Saint John, New Brunswick, where they were
setting up a new farm team. I bought a house. They were
going to play in an arena Lord Beaverbrook donated to the
city. Then they discovered he had said pro hockey could
never be played there. So they put the team in Fredericton
and I had to sell the house and move the family again. I was
there two years. In the second year I won Coach of the Year in
the American League. Then Ron Caron was hired as general
manager of the St. Louis Blues and he decided to hire me as
coach. We had to move again, but this time it was the NHL.

When I started in St. Louis there was a very small group of
us running the franchise. Ron Caron, Barclay and Bob Plager,
and I ran the day-to-day operation. Barclay Plager was my
assistant coach. There had been a lot of turmoil there. At one
point the team was going to go to Saskatoon, then one year
they didn't take part in the draft because they thought they
were going out of business. The players didn't know from
one day to another what was going to happen. Harry Ornest
had bought the team and one thing I have to say about Harry
Ornest, he saved the franchise there. He offered me a two-
year contract at $55,000 and $65,000. That was a little low
for coaches. I tried to get more but then agreed with him
because I wanted to get back in the NHL so bad.

One of the great memories I have from my St. Louis
days was what happened when we played Calgary in the

semi-finals in 1986, my last year there. We had beaten Minnesota in the fifth game of a best-of-five, and then beaten Toronto in the seventh game of a best-of-seven. We played Calgary and the winner would go to the finals against Montreal. They had us down 3–2 in the series and in the sixth game, in St. Louis, we were losing 5–1 after two periods.

I came into the room and some players said I gave the best speech they had ever heard. I don't know about that. I just remember talking with my heart. I said, "Boys, no matter what happens here tonight I'm very proud of you. There are eighteen thousand people out there and I'm just going to ask one thing. Let's go out in the third period and do something we've always done. Let's not quit in front of eighteen thousand people. We never have. We've always had a lot of pride in the Blues uniform. We're the team that has come out of our division in the playoffs. Show pride in what you've done and nobody will ever fault you. They'll remember a group of athletes that had a great year."

I could sense something boiling in the room, a lot of character and togetherness. The next thing you know, the third period starts and we make it 5–2, then 5–3, then 5–4. The crowd was going crazy and then we tied it 5–5. I tell you, that was one of the greatest nights for me as a coach behind the bench. We go into overtime and Doug Wickenheiser scored and we won the game. People in the crowd had tears in their eyes. When we got to the dressing room we could still hear them cheering. We lost the seventh game in Calgary 2–1, a real heartbreaker. After Calgary lost to Montreal, a lot of people said we took the Cup away from them that night in St. Louis.

That heartbreaking 2–1 loss in Calgary was the last game Jacques Demers coached for the St. Louis Blues. Before the next season began he had moved again, this time to Detroit, a move that put him in the middle of the biggest controversy of his career.

JACQUES DEMERS

Okay, I'll be totally honest with you. On our last trip to Detroit I ran into Jim Devellano. [Known as "Jimmy D.," Devellano was general manager of the Red Wings.] He was very down. They were having a terrible year. They finished with forty points, dead last. He said, "How are you doing, Coach," and all that. I said, "Jimmy, I don't have a contract for next year and I don't know what I'm going to do." I told him that. Jimmy remembered that.

Now we get into the playoffs. We beat Minnesota. We beat Toronto. While we were in those series Jimmy D. would call. "Hi, Jacques. How are you doing? I hope everything is going well." Never mentioned the Detroit job, but I knew damn well what he was calling for. He came to one of our games against Toronto. Now I'm the one who told him I didn't have a contract. It's been proven. When I saw him I told him to let me finish the playoffs, then I would sit down and talk with him. Meanwhile, down in Florida, Mr. Ilitch [Mike Ilitch, owner of the Red Wings] was at a place owned by Rosaire Paiement. He's watching one of our games on TV and says, "That guy there. I'd like to get him as coach." That's where it all started.

We kept going in the playoffs and after every win Jimmy D. would call me. He'd say, "I'm not gonna talk to you right now. I just want you to know that I'm around." They may have called it tampering but I had told him I did not have a contract. This is the truth. You can write it in the book.

Now we go into the semi-finals against Calgary and my value has tripled. Jimmy kept calling me at my house and I kept telling him I'd talk to him at the end of the playoffs. Meanwhile, after the morning skate on the day of one of the games against Calgary, a Detroit writer, Vartan Kupelian of the *Detroit News,* comes to me and says, "I hear you have signed a five-year contract to coach the Detroit Red Wings." He wasn't asking me about it – not asking if the Red Wings were interested in me. He was saying I had signed a contract. I told him I hadn't signed a contract or done anything with the Detroit Red Wings.

Jimmy D. kept calling me and they found out that I got calls at home. [Reporters obtained phone records proving calls had been made between the two men while Demers was still coaching the Blues.] But now I'm getting some second thoughts. We had gone to the semi-finals with a good group of players. Who knew? Maybe next year the Stanley Cup. And going to Detroit, a team with only forty points. I'm saying to myself, gosh. I mean, I didn't know.

While we were in Calgary a member of the St. Louis Blues organization, whose name I can't say but it wasn't Ron Caron, told me that Harry Ornest had gone out to eat with some of the owners of the Flames. He told me Mr. Ornest had said that night, "I have the best coach in the league. Look what kind of a salary I'm paying him and look where he got my team." I confronted Mr. Ornest on the plane home from Calgary and asked him if he had made fun of me because he wasn't paying me very much. I told him the person who told me was very knowledgeable and knew one of the owners of the Calgary team. He said he didn't say anything like that so I took his word for it.

Three or four days later I went to see Harry Ornest, who didn't know there was a possibility I could sign with the Detroit Red Wings. I was thinking of buying a house in St. Louis but I didn't have any money. I had had a divorce, and my kids and all that cost me a fortune. I asked Mr. Ornest if it was possible for him to loan me $50,000. He answered that he wasn't in the bank business. I said I understood that.

I really loved it in St. Louis. I had Bernie Federko, Brian Sutter, Rob Ramage, Doug Gilmour. I didn't want to leave those guys. They had all been very loyal to me and we had had a great finish to our year. So I decided to buy the house. Jack Quinn, one of the Blues' executives, told me to go ahead. I told him I would but that I wanted to sign a new contract within a week. By that time Mr. Ornest had decided to sign me to a four-year contract starting at approximately $120,000 and going up to $135,000. He was going to give me the loan and I would repay it out of my contract over the next four years.

There was a long weekend, Memorial Day, so it stretched out more than a week. I finally had a meeting with them. Mrs. Ornest, Harry Ornest, and Jack Quinn were there. I said I felt I had been very loyal to them over the past three years and I asked for the contract then. Ron Caron had nothing to do with it and that was totally wrong. So there we were and I asked them, "How many times do I have to ask for a contract?" But I had to wait again.

I went home and my wife Debbie was by that time totally against staying in St. Louis. Debbie has a tremendous influence on me, but I told her we were buying the new house and I wanted to stay in St. Louis. Jimmy D. kept calling and then a few days later the Red Wings threw some figures at me. I compared them to the figures Harry Ornest was offering and said "Wow." We're talking now about three weeks after the Blues were supposed to give me a contract. But by then they were saying that I had bought a house and they were lending me $50,000 and they figured I was staying.

I waited another week, then I called Jimmy D. and said, "Jimmy, I've talked this over with my wife and I'm leaving

St. Louis." God, he was excited. Very excited. But then I told him I had to make sure, I had to give the St. Louis Blues one more chance. He said, "Jacques, they're jerking you around." He was right. They were.

I went to the Blues office and asked to see Mr. Ornest and Mr. Quinn, knowing they were there. The secretary told me they weren't in. So I went back home and told Debbie, "That's it." I phoned an agent, Art Kaminsky. He called Mr. Ilitch and the deal was done. I got $1,100,000 for five years.

I still hadn't signed and I went to my office in St. Louis the same day I was going to fly to Detroit. Ron Caron wanted to show me his list for the draft that year but I wouldn't look at it. I couldn't do that to Ron, a man I loved and respected, because by that same time the next day I was going to be a member of the Detroit Red Wings. If I'm anywhere today it's because of Ron Caron. I went back out to my car and I had tears in my eyes. I had tears, not because I was leaving Harry Ornest, but because I was leaving Ron Caron, Brian Sutter, Bernie Federko, all the guys who had made me feel very special as a coach. I mean, those guys gave me great thrills.

I flew to Detroit and I'm scared stiff someone will see me. I'm walking into the Detroit airport and there's a TV camera crew standing there. I said to myself that it wasn't possible they knew, that someone must have leaked the story in Detroit. As it turned out, some big tennis star was on the same plane and they were there to interview him. But that scared me.

That night, around 1:00, I called Ron Caron and told him I was signing with Detroit the next morning. I told him it was nothing personal between him and me. He was hurt, but not upset, and he wished me luck. Then I called Harry Ornest in Los Angeles. He said he thought Jack Quinn had already signed me in St. Louis. Then he said he was going to give me the $50,000 as a bonus for what I did for his team. I said, "Mr. Ornest, you never told me that. You told me you were lending me the money." I had put down $10,000 on the house and we had to pay it, but as it turned out the Red Wings paid me back for that, so I didn't lose anything. And that was it.

The next morning Art Kaminsky came with the contract and we signed it. It called for the $1.1 million for five years, plus a $100,000 signing bonus. There I was, a little French-Canadian guy who didn't have much money, getting $100,000 right then to coach the Detroit Red Wings. Quite a story, yes. And everything I told you is the honest truth.

Teams hiring Jacques Demers paid an extra price. When he joined St. Louis, Demers had been under contract to the Quebec Nordiques. The Blues and the Nordiques made a trade and received two players, Gord Donnelly and Claude Julien. After Demers signed with Detroit, the Red Wings had to compensate the Blues. In that case Detroit gave St. Louis the proceeds from three exhibition games.

The Red Wings immediately began to prosper under Demers's coaching. In his first season they reduced their goals against by 141, went from forty points and last place to seventy-eight points and second place, reached the Stanley Cup semi-finals, and Demers was voted the 1987 coach of the year. The next season Detroit finished first in the Norris Division with ninety-three points, reached the Stanley Cup semi-finals again, and Demers was coach of the year again.

Demers had helped engineer a dramatic turn-around on the Detroit hockey scene. Steve Yzerman was developing into a superstar, and sellout crowds of twenty thousand were filling the Joe Louis Arena. The only thing missing was the Stanley Cup.

When the Red Wings reached the semi-finals in '87 and

'88 they were beaten both times, in five games, by the
Edmonton Oilers. The biggest crisis Jacques Demers faced
in Detroit happened the night before game five in 1988, in
Edmonton. Several Detroit players broke curfew, got drunk,
and it all became very public. Demers was crushed.

JACQUES DEMERS

I always believed playoffs were a special part of the year. We
had curfews but I never checked them. I relied on the players'
professionalism at a time when everyone is asked to sacrifice. That time in Edmonton, my assistant coach, Colin
Campbell, and Jimmy D. were told late at night that some
Detroit Red Wing players were drinking heavily in the bar.
Colin took care of it, went to the bar and brought them back
to the hotel. The players were pretty drunk, I guess.

Colin and Jimmy D. decided not to tell me because they
felt it would make me mad, get me upset, and maybe change
my way of coaching. But then late the next morning they
decided to brief me so I knew what had happened. Right after
that we were having lunch when two Detroit reporters,
Keith Gave and Mitch Albom, came to me with the story
that some players had broken curfew. Contrary to Glen
Sather, who has given me a shot that I had told the reporters, I
never told the reporters. What had happened was that one of
the players, Brent Ashton, had come into the restaurant at
breakfast and given heck to another of the players, who was
hurt and not playing, for being out drunk the night before
with Bob Probert. The reporters heard that so they were
aware. They knew exactly what happened.

I didn't know what to do. As it turned out, I decided to play
some of the guys who had been drunk, including Bob Probert.
I felt I had a responsibility toward the majority of our team,
players like Yzerman and Gerard Gallant and Brent Ashton,

who had not missed the curfew. I felt I had to put our best line-up on the ice. We were down 3–1 and I wasn't going to have them think I gave up.

It was one of the greatest seasons the Detroit Red Wings had had in twenty years. We were first in our division, fifth overall, and reached the Stanley Cup semi-finals where we were beaten by a better team. That whole season was shattered by one foolish night.

I felt betrayed and cheated. The players apologized to me and, looking back, I don't think it was done to me personally, to offend me or show a lack of respect. I was dealing with a group of players who had personal problems off the ice. Probert got a lot of publicity because of his behaviour. He had been arrested. Klima got publicity. When you're dealing with people who have problems like that you learn very quickly you're not a doctor, not a psychologist. Those are people with deep-rooted problems. So what had been a very magnificent year had a nightmarish ending.

In 1988–89 the Demers roller coaster began going downhill in Detroit. The Wings slipped from ninety-three to eighty points, although that was still good enough for a first-place finish. In the first round of the playoffs they were upset in six games by the Chicago Blackhawks. The downward spiral continued the next season, to seventy points, and the team missed the playoffs. When that part of the roller-coaster ride was over, the Red Wings told Jacques he had to get off.

JACQUES DEMERS

I had been told repeatedly by members of the organization that when my coaching days were over I'd have a job there forever. I had turned them from the Dead Wings into a team the whole city was excited about. After the second year Mr.

Ilitch added two more years to my contract, so they must have been pleased, I had to be doing something right.

Mr. Ilitch called me in on July 13th. There were rumours Jimmy D. was being moved out of the GM job and I felt he was maybe going to ask me to be general manager as well as coach. But I went home empty-handed. He let me go. Okay, financially they took care of me. But I had taken care of them because when I got there the franchise was going nowhere. It was a laughing stock. Forty points.

I have a tremendous amount of respect for Mr. Ilitch for the financial reward, and I chose never to say anything negative about the Detroit organization or the players. But it hurt. When you get fired nobody is there to support you except your wife and kids, your immediate family. It's like you find yourself in a dark room and you don't know which way to go to get out the door.

After I left Detroit there were stories that I didn't get along with Steve Yzerman. Well, I must be the last guy to know about that. I always thought I had a good rapport with Steve Yzerman. I named him captain at the age of twenty-one. He scored sixty goals for me two years in a row and he's never done that since. He's never had as many points as he had with me. I was at the last Canada Cup as a TV commentator and when he was cut from the team we walked back to the hotel together. When I was named coach of the Montreal Canadiens he called and wished me luck. Let's face it, in Detroit I was a very popular person. I think it's just a case of someone trying to pass the buck.

That Demers was popular in Detroit was proven the first time he went back there to coach against the Red Wings, two years after they had fired him. He received the full "media event" treatment: cameras, microphones, and reporters waiting for him when he arrived at the Arena, the

whole works. When he stepped out behind the bench the
fans gave him a great reception. To top off the evening, his
team won the game. But all of that came after another trip
on Jacques' roller coaster, the one that led him to a spot
behind the bench in his home town.

JACQUES DEMERS

For two years after I left Detroit I worked on the radio doing
Quebec Nordiques games. They didn't have good seasons
and there was a poll in Quebec City where eighty-seven or
ninety per cent of the people said I should coach the team. I
felt pressure. I had to face Pierre Pagé every day. I travelled
everywhere with the team. I knew Pierre Pagé wanted to
coach, felt deep down inside he would not hire me. After my
second year the radio station added another year to my contract and my first thought was, that's it, I'll never return to
hockey. I was very happy with what I was doing and with my
new contract.

That was on a Wednesday. On Friday I got a call from my
station that Pat Burns was leaving the Montreal Canadiens
and going to Toronto. Well, my Lord, I held on to that phone
and I froze, maybe for fifteen seconds, maybe thirty seconds.
They wanted me to comment on the radio and for a while I
couldn't say anything. The first thought that came to my
mind was, I could become coach of the Montreal Canadiens.

My phone didn't stop ringing all day. That night I was on a
phone-in show. I refused to throw my name into the hat.
They said Michel Bergeron was promoting himself. I refused
to do that. I had hired an agent, Don Meehan. About two days
later he phoned to tell me Serge Savard was going to call. He
said, "Stay close to the phone." I put some glue on the chair
and sat on it.

Demers unglued himself from the chair, after talking to Savard, and travelled to Montreal to meet with him. There were two prime candidates, Demers and Bergeron. The Canadiens opted for Demers, answering Bergeron's supporters by citing their doctor's opinion that Michel was a health risk because of a heart attack he had suffered the year before.

The whole affair was turned into a circus by the hockey-mad Quebec media. One columnist wrote that the job as the coach of the Canadiens was the biggest in the province. That must have come as a surprise to many, including le premier ministre and his cabinet, the chief of the provincial police, brain surgeons, and those working to find a cure for cancer. The crush of reporters, microphones, cameras, and TV lights at the news conference announcing Demers's appointment made you wonder if World War Three had just been declared.

Demers's first major assignment in his new job showed him how the Quebec media zeros in on the Montreal Canadiens. In early September, the team travelled to London, England, for five days to play two exhibition games against the Chicago Blackhawks. A reporter for the Chicago **Tribune** *was the only media person covering the Blackhawks. There were thirty-three covering the Canadiens.*

JACQUES DEMERS

People think of me as a motivator, a rah-rah kind of guy. After being out of it for two years I told myself that if I ever did come back I was going to take a different approach. I was going to be more patient, work with the kids. This season I didn't get mad at a referee until our thirtieth game. I've worked on keeping my composure. The other day Serge

Savard said, "I didn't know you were this good of a coach."
That's a hell of a compliment.

But I do know this. That two-year sabbatical I took was
two of the best years of my life. And I'm a better coach
because I'm with the Montreal Canadiens. All the emphasis
here is on first place and winning the Stanley Cup. When I
went to St. Louis all they wanted me to do was improve the
team. In Detroit, they had those forty points the year before I
got there, so when we got to sixty it was a big event. Playing
.500 was an achievement. It's a different story in Montreal,
even though they've won the Stanley Cup only once in the
last fourteen years. It's still all they talk about.

*A few days after he became coach of the Canadiens Jacques
Demers was on a radio show along with Serge Savard.
Demers explained his deal with the team and said, "I've got
a three-year contract which means I'll be coaching the
Montreal Canadiens the next three years." Savard then
said, "No, Jacques. That just means we have to pay you for
the next three years."*

*Everyone had a good laugh. But for Jacques Demers, it
was another reminder that for some hockey coaches, the
roller coaster almost never stops.*

17

The Cop and His First Captain

PAT BURNS   BOB GAINEY

A young police officer hunkering down beside his patrol car with his gun drawn, flushing out a robbery suspect, would hardly seem a candidate to one day become a very high-profile, and very good, coach in the National Hockey League. But for sixteen years that scenario was a possibility during every working day in the life of Pat Burns, the one-time cop who has coached both the Montreal Canadiens and the Toronto Maple Leafs. A native of Montreal who grew up not far from the Forum, Burns went through the familiar pattern of coaching in minor hockey before joining the pros, but there were some differences. He struggled with the question of what he wanted to be, a cop or a coach, and when he did make the switch his hockey employer was Wayne Gretzky.

Pat Burns

I guess I was a good student of the game while I was playing junior because I had a lot of bench time. [Laughs] I was the tough guy on the team. I didn't have the skills to become an NHLer. When I was playing junior and senior hockey I listened all the time to what the coaches had to say. One of my friends was coaching a bantam team and he asked me to give him a hand. I said, sure, so I went out. That was in Gatineau. I started helping him and I started liking it. He left and I took over the team. John Chabot was playing for me. We had a real good team in bantam and then in midget. Then I became a scout for the Hull Olympiques junior team.

Through all of this I was on the Gatineau police force. I started being a scout for Hull working for Marcel Pronovost. Then another of my friends, Jean Lachapelle, took over, and I worked a little bit more. I became an assistant coach but I didn't travel with them because I couldn't get the time off. So I just did the home games and the practices. If I had a day off I'd go on a road trip. Then Jean was fired and I took over the team.

In the first year I did both jobs. It was crazy. I was a police officer in the daytime, from 7:00 in the morning until 3:00 in the afternoon. I'd leave at 3:00 and we'd have our hockey practice from 4:00 to 6:00. I was the general manager at the same time so I wouldn't get home until 9:00 or 10:00 at night. Then I was up and on my shift again at 7:00 in the morning. For road trips I took hours off and they were charged against my holidays. So I lost a lot of my holidays that first year. By Christmas-time I thought my eyes were going to fall out of my head.

After that first season Wayne Gretzky bought the team. I thought he would be bringing in his own people to run it. I didn't talk to him when he bought it. One day I was at home cutting the grass and I got a call and this voice says, "Hi, it's Wayne." I said, "Wayne who?" and he said, "Wayne Gretzky." "Oh," I said, "I know you." [Laughs] He starts asking me questions like, "What's our team going to be like? Are we going to have a good team?" and I'm goin', "Whoa, whoa. What do you mean are we going to have a good team?" He said, "You're coming back to coach, aren't you?"

I told him nobody had talked to me yet. I explained to him that I was a police officer and didn't think I could go through another year like the one I'd just had. I told him I had lost all my time off and my bosses were a bit on my ass. He asked me about taking sabbatical leave and I told them they wouldn't give it to me, which they wouldn't. So he said, "Let me talk to them."

Wayne talked to the city and lawyers got involved in it and they gave me a year off. So I coached full-time that year and we went to the Memorial Cup finals. I had some great players like Luc Robitaille. We played Guelph in the final game and it went into overtime. Robitaille had a breakaway and missed. They came back and Gary Roberts scored the winning goal.

The year after that they wanted me to be one of the coaches for Team Canada at the World Junior. Remember that big brawl with Russia? That was the year. I used the Team Canada thing to get another year off. So I had two sabbatical years off and then they said, "Well, what do you want to do? Be a cop or be a coach? Make up your mind." I didn't know what to do.

I flew to Edmonton to see Wayne about it. He said, "Look, you're gonna coach in the NHL one day." I sort of laughed and said, "Yeah, sure. Easy for you to say." He says, "I'm telling you, you're a good coach and someday you'll be in the NHL. So why don't you quit the police force? I'll give you the same salary you're getting as a policeman. Even a bit more if you want. Stay on for three years and I guarantee you some day you'll be in the NHL. You're a good coach." So I resigned from the police force and signed to work full-time for Wayne. This was in May.

There was a clause in my contract that if a pro team approached me I could negotiate with them. Wayne did all of that for me, the whole contract. I didn't have an agent. He told me if I had a chance to coach a pro team our contract would be void. I guess it was about a week after that when I got a call from Serge Savard to say he wanted me to meet him at the Forum. So I get into my car and drive to Montreal and I'm asking myself, "What does he want?"

I go and see Serge and he tells me he wants me to coach the Canadiens' farm team in Sherbrooke. Pierre Creamer had been their coach and he had signed with Pittsburgh. I'm thinkin', geez, and I told Serge I had just signed a three-year contract with Wayne. He asked me if it had a clause about going with a pro team and I said it did. Now I'm feeling bad for Wayne because he's been so good to me. I didn't know what to do.

I called Wayne and he said, "Get back here." So I go back to Edmonton and he said, "You've got a chance to go with one of the best organizations in hockey. Don't even think about it. Go." Then he says, "See, I told you." I reminded him they wanted me to coach in the American League and he said he didn't care because I'd be coaching in Montreal within two years. I told him he could dream and he said, "Just wait. You'll see." So I went back and talked to Serge and they signed me to coach in Sherbrooke. A year later the Canadiens let Jean Perron go and I was in. Wayne was right after all.

My one year in the American League was a great stepping-stone for me because I learned how to handle older players. When I got there everybody tested me, like, who is this guy? Where are the scars on his face? Where's he been? We had a good year in Sherbrooke and the year after I was in the NHL. Six years before that I had bought scalper's tickets to watch the Canadiens play at the Forum. I sat in the blues and watched Bob Gainey and Larry Robinson and Bobby Smith and Mats Naslund. Then, six years later, I'm behind their bench.

So now I'm coaching in Montreal and the first time I walked into the dressing room when the players were there I was shaking. There they are, Gainey, Robinson, Smith, Naslund, all my heroes, and now I'm their coach. They're all looking at me going, you know, who's this guy? I had it tough. The first month was really tough. I was tested by a lot of the players and, if you remember, we were 4–7–1 in our first twelve games. They were saying I wouldn't be coaching when the snow came, I'd be fired before December, this and that. But Serge was really good, very patient. He told me there were problems on the team, a lack of discipline and a lack of team play. He told me that's why I was there, to get it together.

At the start the veterans like Larry and Bob Gainey didn't say too much. They just let me go. I had some problems. I had an incident with John Kordic and problems with Claude Lemieux. I didn't dress Stephane Richer one night because he missed curfew. Then one day they all pranced into my office, Larry, Bob Gainey, Rick Green, Bobby Smith, Naslund, the veterans. They come prancin' into my office and closed the door. I said to myself, oh oh, now what? I guess the mutiny has begun. Bob was my captain and he said, "I know what you're trying to do and I like it. But we need some law and order around here and we want to help." I said, "Geez, that's great." We were flying to Hartford later that day for a game the next night. On the road the coach always gets a suite in the hotel and Bob asked if he could borrow my suite when we got there. He said it would be for just him and the players and he didn't want me there. So I gave them the suite and they had a meeting that lasted about three hours. Then I think we won about eleven straight after that. We just took off from there and never looked back.

The game in Hartford was played November 1, after the Canadiens had lost their previous two games. They beat the Whalers 5–3 and didn't lose two straight again until late January. By then they had lost only five times in their last thirty-seven games. Montreal finished the season with 115 points, two behind the overall-leading Calgary Flames. Those teams met in the Stanley Cup finals with the Flames winning in six games. A few days later Pat Burns was named coach of the year. By then he had pretty well shaken the image of being an "ex-cop," something that bothered him when he started coaching in the NHL.

Pat Burns

It bothered me because they wanted to play up that image all the time. Not that I was ashamed of being a cop. I still respect policemen more than anyone and I'm proud to say that I was a policeman for sixteen years. I retired as a detective sergeant and I was a good cop. But they wanted me to do things, like when *Sports Illustrated* sent a guy to do a story on me. He wanted me to go up on Mount Royal and have my picture taken sitting in a police car with a billystick in my hands. I said, "Whoa, no way. I'm a hockey coach now. I coach one of the most respected teams in professional sports." I didn't want to make the Montreal Canadiens look silly because I had too much respect. I grew up with the Montreal Canadiens, in Saint-Henri, right down the road from the Forum. The Canadiens were like a religion, and I thought a picture like that would have ridiculed their image.

That first year, I remember going into the playoffs saying, geez, this is the playoffs, the big stuff. We played Hartford in the first round and beat them four straight, and then we beat Boston in five. We played Philadelphia and had trouble in that series because we had trouble winning at home. We could win in Philly and that's where we beat them out, in the sixth game. That's when Hextall went crazy, going after Chelios near the end of the last game.

Then there was the Stanley Cup final and I'll always remember that feeling. I got to be pretty close to Larry Robinson, more than with Bob Gainey, who was the captain but a more reserved type of guy. I knew Larry from his junior days in the Ottawa Valley. He came to me before the finals and said, "Burnsy, I want to tell you something. This is the greatest feeling in the world, what you're stepping into, right here. It's the finals. I'll tell you one thing, it's real good to win, but it hurts to lose." I always will remember that because we did lose that series. I remember going into the dressing room and everybody was crying. I went back into my office, closed the door, and I sat there and cried for about fifteen minutes, not knowing why. And then I said, geez, it really does hurt to lose. It was an amazing feeling. I'll never forget that feeling.

After my second year they traded Chris Chelios to Chicago for Denis Savard. [Serge Savard is still being criticized for making that trade.] I knew nothing about it. They had discussed it and I remember saying at the time, "You can't do that." I was at my cottage in Magog and I got a phone call from Serge and he told me that he had made the deal. I asked him, what deal? And he said they had traded Chelios. I asked him who he got and when he told me it was Denis Savard I said, "What did you say?" All he said was that he would call me back. I felt he didn't want to talk about it. I don't think the organization wanted me to know about that.

In Montreal the rap was I couldn't handle superstars, which was not true. I have always been able to handle superstars who want to work, like Doug Gilmour here in Toronto. Patrick Roy always worked and I could handle Patrick. The knocks were about the way I handled players like Claude Lemieux and Stephane Richer. It wasn't that I couldn't handle those guys. It's because they didn't want to work. They didn't want to follow the program.

Sometimes hockey players get into trouble off the ice and because they are who they are the media gets into the act. Pat Burns has had his share of this aspect of coaching. When he was with Montreal three of his players were arrested after a fight outside a club in Winnipeg in the wee small hours. Shayne Corson made news more than once because of incidents on Montreal's downtown scene. There were statements by a Montreal doctor that linked NHL players to an AIDS story. When that happened, the Forum was inundated with reporters who had never been there before and have never been there since. Burns and the Canadiens' captain, Guy Carbonneau, handled the situation very skillfully. Later, in Toronto, one of Burns's players with the Maple Leafs was mugged and robbed in San Francisco. While Pat was in Montreal those of us covering the Canadiens felt his experience as a policeman helped him deal with those kinds of situations.

PAT BURNS

It's tough today because the kids, well, they're richer and I guess they're cockier. It was probably the toughest in Montreal. The thing with Corson was, he'd go out there and have a couple of beers and what-not and trouble always seemed to follow him around. There are guys like that. Shayne's a proud type of individual who would never back down from anybody, on the ice or off the ice. Hey, I heard lots of stories in Montreal about players from their past teams, good players, well-known guys. But in those days you never heard much about it. It wasn't front-page news. There was stuff that went on with my guys before I even got there. There's always mischief.

A coach has to be a protector. At first in Montreal a lot of the players gave me a bit of a rap, saying that I didn't treat them like men. When I was hired in Montreal I was accustomed to following orders. Serge told me the guys had to have discipline, that they couldn't go out drinking and getting into trouble on nights before games. So I became almost obsessed with watching them. I counted the beers because that was supposed to be my job. Then after a while I felt, hey, I shouldn't have to do this. These guys are grown men. What am I doing? This year I haven't checked a curfew once. The thing in San Francisco, the guy got beat up and got his wallet stolen. He said he didn't get into any trouble. The guys jumped him and stole his wallet. So, is the story true? I don't know and I don't care.

When you treat your players like men they know you're behind them. I'm very intense behind the bench and people say I never smile. Geez, there's nothing funny there. I'm very intense. I love being behind the bench because you get so involved in the game. It's not a question of coach against coach. It's just the game.

The temper tantrums and yelling at the referees, that's me. But sometimes it's to get the best out of my players. I've definitely mellowed from my first years, but if the referee isn't calling things they're doing to my players I have to do something to support them. I don't want my players doing it, so I'll do it. Then my players feel that the coach is behind them. I tell them to worry about the game. I'll yell at the referees.

Pat Burns was a very successful coach with the Montreal Canadiens. In his four years the Canadiens finished first in the Adams Division twice, reached the Stanley Cup finals once, and never had fewer than eighty-nine points. Many of us felt the Canadiens, given the talent on the team, had often overachieved under Burns's coaching. Pat was coach of the year once, and runner-up another time. Midway through the 1991–92 season the team held a news conference prior to a Saturday night home game to announce they were rewarding Burns with a new contract. There were rumours it was worth in excess of $325,000 per season. Yet approximately four months later Pat Burns was at another news conference, this one in Toronto, signing another new contract that made him coach of the Maple Leafs. What happened, so quickly, in Montreal?

For one thing, after making it to the finals in Burns's first year, the Canadiens were beaten in the Division finals by the Boston Bruins for the three years after that. In his last playoff year with Montreal, 1992, the Canadiens needed double overtime in game seven to eliminate the Hartford Whalers, a team that had finished twenty-eight points behind Montreal in the regular season. In the next round they were blown out by the Bruins in four straight.

In his four years in Montreal Pat Burns went from the rookie coach who wasn't going to last until December to one of the city's most visible personalities. He appeared in TV commercials, and had his own radio show. Burns's face and words dominated the wall-to-wall media coverage the team received, in both languages. Because of the competition and jealousy existing within the francophone media, the coach

of the Montreal Canadiens must hold a daily news confer-
ence. Pat Burns was a regular, every night, on the early and
late TV news. As the 1991–92 season wound down, the face
on the TV screen wasn't smiling very often. He usually
sounded as sour as he was looking, both on the air and in
print. Callers to the many sports phone-in shows com-
plained that the Canadiens' emphasis on defence was pro-
ducing boring hockey. Burns was fingered as the culprit. The
Canadiens' coach wasn't a happy camper.

Burns's return to Montreal as coach of the Maple Leafs
was a media event and there was a lot of tension in the air
for the two games between his new and old teams. The
Canadiens appeared psyched out by all the hype, especially
when the Leafs defeated them decisively in the first game, in
Montreal. The same thing happened two weeks later in
Toronto.

Late in the 1992–93 season Burns's successor in Montreal,
Jacques Demers, was hospitalized with chest pains. Among
the quotes from the Canadiens' dressing room about the sit-
uation was one from defenceman Eric Desjardins, who, in
wishing Demers a speedy recovery, said that in the space of
two seasons he'd learned the difference between bad coach-
ing and good coaching. About the same time Burns was tell-
ing Toronto newspapers that he was happy coaching for the
first time since he'd been in Sherbrooke. It wasn't exactly an
all-out war of words, but there were a few minor skirmishes.

PAT BURNS

Why did I leave Montreal? Well, I think it was time. The fans
got impatient. I think the media got impatient and I got
impatient with the media. It was time for me to go. It was
getting tough. If I had been behind the bench when the

Canadiens lost against the Ottawa Senators when they opened the season in Ottawa, I probably would have got the boot. I felt it coming and I said, hey, I think it's a parting of the ways now. I'm still young and I didn't want to burn myself. I felt I could move on and help another organization. It hurt when I left. I didn't want to go. I felt the organization wanted me to leave but they didn't want to fire me.

What happened was, I was supposed to go to Los Angeles. That's where I was going. Then my agent, Don Meehan, said "Wait a minute. You're a very marketable guy right now. We're not gonna go for the first team that throws anything at us. We're gonna shop around a bit."

It took about a day. Then he called and told me he thought my best bet would be Toronto. I said, "Toronto?" I thought I was going down to the States. Serge gave me permission to meet with Cliff Fletcher. It didn't take us long.

I find myself very fortunate to coach two of the great franchises in NHL history. The only one who ever did it before me was Dick Irvin. If I ever write a book I'll say that the thing that Irvin did, Pat Burns did. I don't think there will be too many able to coach the Montreal Canadiens and the Toronto Maple Leafs.

The pressure isn't the same in Toronto. I don't care if the Blue Jays win the World Series every year for the next twenty years, Toronto is still a hockey town. No matter how bad the Leafs are, people are still diehard Leaf fans. Now they're coming out of the closet all over Canada. I go to cities and people are thanking me. Even our jersey sales, marketing-wise, went up enormously.

I think after you're four or five years in the same town, even if you have a lot of success, and I had a lot of success in Montreal, I think it's time to move on unless you win the Stanley Cup every year. I'd like to get into management some day. But right now I'm still young and I love coaching. I love being on the ice, working with young players, getting them prepared. Some of the players criticized me when I left Montreal but I look at their games today and they do a lot of the things I talked about.

I think coaching the Montreal Canadiens is the toughest coaching job in hockey. There's no doubt about it, if you're coaching the New York Yankees, the Montreal Canadiens, the Chicago Bears, it wears on a guy. It wears you down and it wears your health down. Last year at the end of the season when we lost four straight to Boston I felt like I was sixty-five years old. Today, I feel like I'm twenty-five again.

After the Canadiens were beaten by the Calgary Flames in the 1989 Stanley Cup finals to conclude Pat Burns's first year as coach in Montreal, the team lost the services of its two most distinguished veterans. Larry Robinson left Montreal to play for the Los Angeles Kings and Bob Gainey retired.

Bob Gainey is one of the few "defensive specialists" in hockey history to have the kind of a career that put him in the Hall of Fame. In 1978, feeling that defensive forwards were being neglected when it came to individual awards, the NHL inaugurated the Frank Selke Trophy for players with that particular skill. Gainey was the winner the first year, and the three years after that. He played on five Stanley Cup winners in his sixteen years with the Canadiens.

The year after he retired Gainey made his coaching debut in an unlikely locale, with a senior team in the small town of Epinal, France. In 1990 he returned to the NHL as the coach of the Minnesota North Stars and led them to the Stanley Cup finals, where they lost to the Pittsburgh Penguins. Two years later he became the general manager as well as the coach, in Minnesota. A few days after I chatted with him in

his office, early in March 1993, Bob learned that his team
would be leaving Minnesota at the end of the season and
moving to Dallas, Texas.

BOB GAINEY

When I was getting near the end of my playing days it seemed
a lot of people had pinpointed me to go on and do some coaching. I wasn't certain that was what I wanted to do so I decided
to step away for a little bit and see the NHL from a different
place. I wanted to find out for myself if I wanted to stay
involved by coaching.

This strange opportunity to go to France came up at the
same time I was really ready to stop playing, so it filled a gap.
I could step away, still keep some sort of touch with the
sport, and get the kind of perspective I wanted to get. Over
there it was like running any team, but much less compli-
cated. But I did find myself in some unusual situations.

They were supposed to have the ice in the arena by the
middle of August. Our first game was the 5th or 6th of September. In France things never work the way they are supposed to work and so the ice wasn't put in until August 31st.
We had five days to get ready and the municipal workers
would only work their certain hours. They flooded the ice
with a hose on a Friday, then went home for the weekend. We
wanted to practise Saturday and Sunday so I went to the
arena between Friday night and Saturday morning, got out
the hose, and flooded the ice a couple of times by myself.

The municipal employees would go home at 5:00 and then
there would be all kinds of hockey teams on the ice after that.
The novices would practise, then the peewees, bantams,
midgets, and our senior team. By the time we'd get on at
10:00 at night there'd have been six teams on and the ice was
completely chopped up. One of our players started to go

there early in the morning and get lessons from the guy on how to drive the Zamboni. So he would drive the Zamboni before our practices, with all his hockey equipment on. The guys would be out there to shovel the extra bits of snow off the ice and put the nets in place. The Zamboni driver would put his skates on, and then we'd practise. We were in what they called Division 1B in the French Ice Hockey Federation. I was a player-coach and I played a lot. I even got on the power play, so you know that was different for me.

Here's one story about coaching over there. We spent the first half of the season in last place or close to last place. Then our team started getting better and we were moving up. I got to know the players. We were playing on the road one night in an important game and I had given the players a long talk, emphasizing that we couldn't take any bad penalties. Sure enough, on the first shift of the game I take a bad penalty. I didn't have anybody on the bench helping me. I changed lines, did everything. I used to skate by the bench and stop for a second and point out the guys I wanted to go on. This game I'm talking about, the penalty box was across the ice from our bench. So there I was, pointing to the players who I wanted on the ice. One guy would point to himself, like "Me?", and I'd shake my head and keep pointing to the guy I wanted. Somebody else pointed to himself, "Me?", and I'm trying to signal, "No, not you, him." It wasn't exactly a great way to coach a hockey team.

I really didn't miss the NHL initially. I was ready for a break from it and I was very serious about what I was doing. It took us two or three months to put the team together. I had different players coming in every night for tryouts. Then around January things started to slow down and I had a couple of calls from North America asking what my plans were and my appetite started to increase. Then the Stanley Cup playoffs started and I felt this incredible urge for the competition. I was sitting up at night trying to get the scores. I really got the NHL bug. The World Championships were going on over in Europe and I went to see some people. Bobby Clarke had left Philadelphia and had become the general manager in Minnesota. Eventually he got into the picture and I came to Minnesota.

When I arrived here from France, Bobby was at the draft meetings. I walked into the building and into an office, not where we're sitting now, but one at the other end. There was a girl there sitting behind a small desk. I asked her, "Where's the hockey office?" She said, "This is the hockey office." I said, "But where are all the people?" and she said, "This is it." I wanted to get a couple of North Stars hats to send to my kids back in France. She said, "We don't have any more. We stopped bringing them in halfway through the season." The Minnesota North Stars were literally closed up and shut down. There was maybe less organization than I had when I started in France. That's where we started from.

The one saving thing I had, well, actually there were two, was that Pierre Pagé spent two years here and did a lot of groundwork as far as building the team was concerned. And Doug Jarvis stayed on as an assistant coach.

So we went to work and it was a tough start to the year. Luckily for me some experienced players were on the team, like Brian Propp and Bobby Smith. I had a general idea of how I wanted our team to play, five-on-five, and team play. But the specifics were a different story, like goaltending. I hadn't spent a lot of time studying goaltenders when I was a player. I figured they either stopped the puck or they didn't. But now I was in a position where the goaltender wanted to know why or how, if or when. Another case was the power play. I'd always thought about it in reverse because I always played in penalty-killing situations. Now I had to think about it from the power-play players' point of view. What to do when you are either up or down by a goal in the last minute of play. Those were the kinds of things I had to get up to speed on, which I didn't realize when I started.

All the good things in my first year here pretty well happened in the last half of the season. When we started there was all this bad karma around the team. There were no people in the building. If you got more than a hundred yards from the Met Center nobody recognized you. There was no emotion attached to the situation at all. Our comeback started slowly, like a small spark, when we started to beat teams like Calgary and Boston. Slowly the players started to feel some pride. They had had such a long string of time where they didn't think they could win. But we never gave up because we could see things in the team that maybe other people didn't see. We had players like Dave Gagne, and like Neal Broten, who is a really good player. And they had to fight through my inexperience as a coach at the beginning of the year. I started to get a little better.

In the playoffs we beat Chicago, who had finished first overall. Once they grabbed that first round I just stepped back out of the way and they went on from there. In the finals against Pittsburgh, I thought we could win. We went in there and beat them in the first game and we played well in the second game but we got beat. We came back here and won game three. Mario Lemieux had been hurt but he came back and in the fourth game we lost 5–3. But we were close. We controlled the third period. In the end, the one force we couldn't beat was Mario.

When I started coaching here there was an adjustment for me in handling the players, the one-on-one situations. I wanted to treat the players in a fashion that I wanted to be treated when I was a player. I wanted to be told what to do. I didn't really want to be ridiculed but I wanted to be told what was right and what was wrong. In Montreal, Claude Ruel worked with me when I first came up. He was an individual coach for me and was able to bring out things in me that helped me develop as a player. I found him very sincere. I feel indebted to people like him in Montreal who allowed me to have such a long run there, such a great career.

That's what I tried to do here, but I had to change my outlook on what makes players go and what makes a team work. Some of the things I wanted to do I found didn't work and some of the things I didn't really enjoy about some of the coaches I was with, I found that I had to do. I guess you could say I have a better appreciation of them now.

I try not to judge the players against myself, the way I played. And I try not to judge the North Stars against the Montreal Canadiens. Very seldom do I talk about the Montreal Canadiens. I don't hammer any comparisons on them.

Coaching allows me to still be part of the game, part of the competition. Players maybe don't realize it but that's what they like most, the competition. Now that I'm in the management part I have to go through a lot of different things before I get to the competition. So there have been more adjustments to make.

Sometimes you ask yourself if you're in the right job, doing the right thing. Some nights I just know that I'm in the right place and I'm so happy I'm still involved. Earlier this year we had a back-to-back series with Chicago. We played here the first night and they beat us, but it was a great game. We went into Chicago the next night and I was sitting in the stands watching the teams warm up. The game was set, the teams were ready, and at that moment I knew there was no other place I'd rather be.

18

New Faces in the '90s

DAVE KING BARRY MELROSE

JOHN PADDOCK

Coaching Stanley Cup winners isn't exactly a young man's game. Since the NHL came into sole possession of the Cup in 1926, only a handful of coaches have been able to win it before reaching their fortieth birthdays. The youngest was Claude Ruel, who succeeded Toe Blake in Montreal. Ruel was only thirty when the Canadiens won in 1969. Before Ruel, only two Cup-winning coaches were under forty. In 1932 Toronto coach Dick Irvin was thirty-nine. In 1941 Boston's Cooney Weiland was thirty-seven.

Ruel's "youngest age" will be tough to better. Since 1969, only four winning coaches have been younger than forty. The Bruins' Harry Sinden was thirty-seven in 1970, and the next year Al MacNeil was thirty-six when he won with the Canadiens. In 1973 Scotty Bowman was thirty-nine when he captured his first, in Montreal. The next coach to win in Montreal was Jean Perron, in 1986. Perron was thirty-nine.

As the NHL moved into the '90s the old guard was hold-
ing fast against the coming generation of younger coaches.
In the first three years of the decade the Stanley Cup-
winning coaches were fifty-six-year-old John Muckler,
sixty-year-old Bob Johnson, and fifty-eight-year-old Scotty
Bowman, who was still outwitting younger opponents
twenty-four years after he first coached in the league.

But there is a new breed slowly taking hold, bringing with
them innovative ideas, a few new words to describe what
they do, and some mod-looking hairstyles. Some have
found interesting new ways to go about the business of
coaching.

George Kingston was fifty-two with close to twenty years
of Canadian college and international coaching experience
on his CV when he became head coach of the fledgling San
Jose Sharks in 1991. Kingston knows the loneliness of the
long-distance runner, which may be useful for someone
experiencing the loneliness of coaching a frequently beaten
expansion team. Kingston competes in ultra-marathons,
which are fifty- to one hundred-mile races run over rugged
terrain. During the hockey season he jogs, and jogs, and
jogs. "There are many coaches who jog," says the scholarly
Kingston. "We do it for mental solitude and to get away
from the stress that builds up during games. There aren't
many places coaches can go. That's why a lot of us jog."

Ken Hitchcock was the coach of the Kamloops Blazers in
the Western Canada Junior League before becoming an
assistant with the Philadelphia Flyers in 1990. Hitchcock is
an American Civil War buff. He holds the rank of second
lieutenant in the "3rd Pennsylvanian Regiment," one of
many such groups whose members don uniforms that are
exact reproductions of those worn by the troops of the
Union and the Confederacy and take part in re-enactments
of Civil War battles on the original battlefields. (Hitchcock

"enlisted" as a private. The general in charge was an avid Flyers fan so Hitchcock received an immediate promotion.)

Ken Hitchcock relates his hobby to coaching this way: *"I became intrigued by the way the Civil War soldiers followed their leaders. A lot that happens in battle is reflected in coaching. What amazed me in the books I read was how these men believed in what their leaders were saying and doing. They followed them anywhere and everywhere. As a coach you would like that kind of respect and admiration from your players for some of the things you stand for and believe in. If they could follow you to a degree that was even close to the way the men followed their leaders in the Civil War, I think a lot of things that were said and done then could really help you in coaching."*

For many years Dave King's name surfaced whenever a coaching vacancy arose in the NHL. A career coach from Saskatoon, King's reputation grew steadily from his start in college and junior hockey through his nine seasons with Canada's national hockey program. Three months after his team won the silver medal at the 1992 Winter Olympics, Dave King signed on as coach of the Calgary Flames, at the age of forty-four.

DAVE KING

I think the first time I ever coached was with a bantam youth hockey team. The guy who was their coach couldn't make it one night so they asked me to fill in. I was still playing college hockey. I learned right away I really enjoyed working with the kids. What I had wanted to do was become a high-school teacher and that was why I was going to University in Saskatoon. I became interested in coaching because of my interest in teaching. It was natural.

When I left university I taught for five years in the high schools in Saskatoon and coached hockey in the community. I went through the system as a coach in minor hockey, junior B, tier-2 junior, and all the time I was still teaching and doing some playing. I got married and my wife was a widow in our first year of marriage. She must have thought, why did I get married? Where is this guy? He's never around.

Then I went into major junior hockey, full-time. I left teaching and spent a year coaching the juniors in Saskatoon and another in Billings, Montana. I looked on it as a short-term thing, figuring that after a couple of years I would probably go back to teaching. I had two successful years and then the coaching job came open at the University of Saskatchewan. I thought, boy, here's a chance to go back to my alma mater as a coach and a teacher, which to me was a great combination. In junior hockey I was only coaching, so the idea of going back to coach and teach was very interesting. I went back and spent four years there teaching recreation classes and coaching the U. of S. Huskies. Then I went full-time with the national team program.

At first, as I got into it, I came to realize that I wanted to be a coach. I coached football, basketball, wrestling, track and field. I loved it. After a few years of coaching hockey I realized I was developing an interest in one sport that meant a lot to me. I made up my mind to try it, so that at least I could say I gave it a try and that's what happened. And I've been there now for seventeen years.

Coaching in the NHL was always in the back of my mind. I knew I'd come here. I just felt there was no rush to get here. I just felt as I watched it that it must be the most difficult place to coach because the turnover rate is very great. Success doesn't guarantee you keep your job. Players have a lot of influence on the coach. In some situations nowadays the owners are friends with the players. So I looked at the way the game was going and said to myself, "Don't rush." I wanted to make sure I really knew coaching well. The more you coach, the more you deal with people. After four or five years I realized that I didn't know it all in terms of the tactics or anything else but I had a pretty good handle on it. So I thought, boy, in the next four or five years I've got to learn how to work with people. I knew that in the NHL that's the biggest factor that either works for you, or against you. It's how you deal with people.

Guys coach for different reasons. There are guys who coach who think that's all they can do. They've played and they have to coach because they want to stay in the game. For me, coaching was something I just felt I would get a lot of satisfaction from. To me, satisfaction is everything. You feel you're accomplishing something when you see your team play a certain way and, hey, you can say, "I was a part of that." I'm not the instrumental person, but when you see your guys execute certain things, a power play or penalty-killing, whatever it might be, when they do some of the things you've set up for them, there's a feeling of creativity, there really is. That's good because you feel like you're part of the group that contributed to making it happen. That's the most important thing, satisfaction.

There are all kinds of individual highs in terms of winning certain games and that kind of thing, but to be honest with you I think the high for me still is watching players develop. I still get a charge out of watching a guy get better, no matter how old he is or what position he plays. That I enjoy.

The lows? Well, when you're making decisions that really affect people, their life, their families, those kinds of things, that's really tough. I don't think anybody enjoys telling some guy that he's toast, he's gone. That's the hardest part. You do it, and you've got to do it, but when you know you're changing a guy's life dramatically it's not easy. You shatter some dreams and, boy, everybody dreams. We all do. No matter what job you've got you dream about something better and when you kill somebody's dream it's no fun at all.

I wish I could have access to books or some form of teaching from the great coaches from the past. We're sitting here in the Montreal Forum and I see all those Stanley Cup banners and I think how great it would be to be able to learn from men like Dick Irvin or Toe Blake. Punch Imlach too. Imagine the things you would have known if you could talk to them about what they thought of, and about the decisions they made. Imagine talking to someone who coached Rocket Richard.

When you're coaching it gets very lonely sometimes. Even if you have assistant coaches, you're still lonely because, as the head coach, it's a totally different world. The players want to talk to assistant coaches instead of the head coach most of the time. I'll tell you, as a head coach it can be very lonely.

The youngest of the new breed of NHL coaches is Barry Melrose. A journeyman defenceman for eleven years with Cincinnati in the WHA and Winnipeg, Toronto, and Detroit in the NHL, Melrose became a successful coach soon after he quit playing. He coached the Medicine Hat Tigers to the Memorial Cup championship in 1988, and the Adirondack Red Wings to the American League's Calder Cup title in 1992. A month later he became head coach of the Los Angeles Kings at the age of thirty-six. Melrose's contract called for a reported $300,000, not bad for someone who, as a kid, had to sell three pigs off the family farm in Kelvington, Saskatchewan, to raise the money to buy his first pair of skates.

BARRY MELROSE

All four of my grandparents came from Scotland. That doesn't happen very often. Basically I'm a purebred Scottish person and I'm very proud of that.

I was an average player, a below-average player, and when I was playing I was always interested in why Montreal was good every year, why the Islanders were good every year. Then it was Edmonton. The winning teams. Also, why did certain teams lose every year. Talent had something to do with it, but obviously there were other reasons, other variables. I came to the conclusion that the coach is very important. I watched what coaches did, my coaches, other coaches. I think when I was about twenty-three or twenty-four I knew that's the line I wanted to get into when I was done playing.

When I was playing, Montreal was the elite organization – and there was Bowman. Sinden always intrigued me, the way he managed the Bruins. One coach I had who was different than everybody else was Jacques Demers. The one thing Jacques, and also Bill Dineen, taught me was that you don't have to be an asshole to be a coach. Players don't have to hate you in order to play hard. A Scotty Bowman can't be a nice guy and a Jacques Demers can't be an asshole. I really learned that you have your own technique to coach and you don't change and become someone else. Everyone has their strengths and weaknesses.

The thing I believe in is getting your team to play hard. That's my goal. If I can get my team to play harder than your team eighty-four times a year, we're gonna win more games on that alone. Then you incorporate your talent and other things. I believe in just getting your team to be prepared mentally and to play very hard physically. That's my whole belief in coaching and it's been very good for me so far. I don't know why but it's just something I've been able to do since I started coaching. Without a doubt that's been the reason for my success as a coach.

When I came to the NHL from the American League the thing I found different was the talent level, the skill of the players. I'm coaching the same way, handling the players the same way. Actually, you can do more things and everything is magnified because of the talent level. But I haven't changed my philosophy. That hasn't been a big adjustment for me.

After I got this job I spent the whole summer preparing myself to handle Wayne Gretzky. Then all of a sudden, bang, Wayne's not with the team. [When I talked with Barry Melrose it was early in the 1992–93 season. Wayne Gretzky had not yet played for Melrose because of the back injury that forced him to miss the Kings' first thirty-nine games.] When it happened we didn't know if he would ever play again. The thing I'm most proud of during my first few months on this job is the way the team handled the situation. The players responded. We never once pitied ourselves, or felt sorry for ourselves, or doubted ourselves. From Day One we knew we were a good club and we were going to succeed without Wayne. We were determined to play well until he came back.

I'm a big believer that X's and O's aren't that important in sports. It's mental preparation, it's mental toughness. That's why I became interested in self-help books. I believe I'm a salesman. I'm selling what I believe in to my players, so I read a lot of books on selling. I read a lot of books about successful people, you know, millionaires. I believe if you're successful in one field you can be successful in another. I really think that's a big part of my success, the people I've met and the things I read about. I've read about group dynamics because, basically, hockey is a group of people working together, just like a sales force in a company.

Anthony Robbins is one guy whose stuff about problem-solving and handling people has grabbed me. His books changed my life. I don't believe in fate but I really believe now that I control my own destiny. We've had some tough things happen to the L.A. Kings, but when you read Tony Robbins and people like him, they teach you how to handle problems. You're finding solutions to your problems rather than dwelling on them.

I think my age is a plus as far as coaching is concerned right now. I have no trouble relating to these players. I have kids the same age as some of my players' kids. I think it's a lot better coming into the NHL at the age I'm at now.

I'm a firm believer in tradition. It means something to a hockey club. I wish the players thought that way too, but I don't think they do any more. There was quite a difference between the Maple Leafs and the Canadiens. Montreal has always made great use of their tradition. I played in Toronto and that team had a lot of tradition. Harold Ballard never made use of it and I always thought that was a big mistake.

You have to win in order to keep your job. That's the bottom line in hockey. But for me, to be coaching against Scotty Bowman or Al Arbour, that's what I love most, that kind of competition. You challenge yourself against those guys. I've watched them on TV my whole life. The most exciting thing about sports is competing against people like that, testing yourself against them.

Television cameras have a tough time getting what are called "reaction shots" when they focus on John Paddock, coach of the Winnipeg Jets. One of the most laid-back of NHL coaches, Paddock signed with the Jets on June 17, 1991, eight days after his thirty-seventh birthday.

A Manitoba native, Paddock had a minor-league playing career interrupted by eighty-seven NHL games spread over five years in Washington, Philadelphia, and Quebec. His coaching career has been somewhat similar to that of Jacques Demers, with Paddock experiencing a few unexpected moves before he made it to the NHL.

JOHN PADDOCK

It started November 22nd or 23rd, 1983. I was playing in Maine. Tommy McVie was coaching and I was the captain. We were a New Jersey farm team and the Devils started out 2–18 that season. They fired Billy McMillan and Tommy went up to coach. They called me in and gave me the opportunity to take over the team. I had to decide in about two minutes. I told them I needed some time to think about it and they said there wasn't any time. They had to know right away. So I said, "I guess so." I went home and told my wife that there was probably going to be a press conference in the morning and I wasn't going to be playing any more, I was going to be coaching. So that was a quick decision. We went on to win the Calder Cup.

The next year Tommy came back to Maine and we were co-coaches. He was really the head coach, as he should have been. But when you've been the head coach . . . I mean, I was happy with being a co-coach for that one year, but it couldn't go on. The next year Philadelphia took over the team in Hershey and I was able to get the head-coaching job. I was there four years and won another Calder Cup.

Bobby Clarke was the general manager in Philadelphia and he offered me the assistant GM job. I took it but to this day I really don't know why. Security, I guess. I figured if there was any general manager in hockey who was secure it was Bobby Clarke in Philadelphia. Nine months later he was fired. Neil

Smith hired me to coach the Rangers' farm team in Binghamton. I spent a year there and then Winnipeg hired me in June of 1991.

I started to think about coaching when I played under Pat Quinn, in Maine. That was his first head-coaching job. I had, and still have, a lot of respect for him. I watched how he handled people. I think he was the first of a different breed of coach. You had to listen to him. He spent a little more time on the technical and tactical sides of things, and he impressed me.

When I started as a head coach, I was walking into the dressing room in that capacity the day after I'd been there as a player. And there was a game that night. It was difficult, coaching the players I'd just been playing with. You've got to come down on the guys and that's always tough. It was tough for me and tough for them. I made Gary Howatt my captain and he took control in the dressing room like a captain should. He wasn't afraid to step on some toes. I think he realized what I was going through and he made the change easier than it might have been.

When you're coaching in a place like the American League, your eye must be on the NHL at all times. If it's not, then you're probably in the wrong business. If you want to be a coach, I think it's important that you spend time in the minors, learning the game. They're not big on assistants in the minors, and I don't know why, because they're developing players down there. As a coach there you have to do everything. You learn about the people because the players don't have anybody to talk to but you. You've got to be able to have some rapport with the players, and I don't mean just your best players. You have to have rapport with guys who are playing only five minutes a game. I still talked with each one after every ten games and we exchanged ideas on why he was or wasn't playing and what his role was. There's nobody else to do it so you're forced to do everything and you basically learn the game that way.

When I came to Winnipeg last year it was easier than it might have been in some other places. The best players on the team were very responsive, Phil Housley, Thomas Steen, guys like them. The year before the team had not done very well so they were wide open to anything. We had a bunch of blue-collar workers so I didn't feel uncomfortable. Troy Murray was another who made it easier.

The biggest adjustment here, with an NHL team, is getting accustomed to the outside things that can affect you and your team – everything from contract hassles to a continuing schedule of play, practice, and travel. You don't get as much practice time as you should have. Like last week, I wanted to meet with our six rookies. We were home for a week and I never got to do it. There was always something on, a team function or something. There are a lot of outside distractions that you have to work around.

You have to respect the players of higher ability. You've got to let them play their game. They've got to respect you, and they have here. But with the best players there's less coaching to do, less teaching. They know how to play. A coach just has to relax and let them play.

But there are some players today who need teaching more than others and that's where you miss the proper amount of practice time. Our Soviet players are accustomed to playing no more than three games a week. They're not used to the travel, play, practice, and travel schedule. They've got to find a way to become mentally tougher. I don't think you can do it with a whip and force them to adjust. They're highly skilled players, they know how to play. But with them there obviously has to be some teaching from a team standpoint on how the game is played in the NHL.

We have a lot of Europeans on the Jets and people are

always asking if there is a language problem. I think it's over-blown a bit. It's not really a problem between the coaches and the players because you can draw something on a board or on a piece of paper, on the bench, to get your point across.

I think the only time language has been a problem is when it comes to split-second decisions on the ice, during the games. Teppo Numminen might be going back for the puck and Sergei Bautin should be yelling at him, like when the goaltender yells, "Look out, somebody's coming!" Until some basic phrases can be worked out and learned, that sort of thing presents a problem. We've done some things to help speed up the process for the Russians. On non-game days in the dressing room they can speak only English to try and get them to learn it.

The toughest day for me is the day of a game, especially in a Canadian city, like Montreal or Edmonton, where there is so much media coverage. Sometimes it takes me half an hour after the practice is over before I can really sit down and start doing my work because of all the interviews and so on we have to do with the press. That makes it a little more difficult than what I had expected when I came to the NHL.

19

Talking About Coaches

Those of us who cover the National Hockey League spend a lot of time talking: in airports and hotel lobbies while we're travelling, in press rooms while we're having our free pre-game meal, and at practices while we wait for them to end so we can do our work. Hockey people have no trouble when it comes to talking and coaches are a favourite topic. While I was interviewing coaches for this book I was also asking others for opinions and stories about coaches and coaching. Their thoughts make up this final chapter.

Red Storey refereed for nine years in the NHL during the 1940s and '50s. Always a colourful character, Red is still ref-ereeing hockey games, for charity, at the ripe young age of seventy-five.

RED STOREY

Phil Watson was a guy I remember. When he was coaching the Rangers in the '50s he would get mad at me and then send out one of his players, Red Sullivan, to take a face-off. Watson would start hollering, "You dumb redheaded bastard! You stupid redhead!" Stuff like that, always with "redhead." But as soon as I'd look at him he'd point at Sullivan and yell, "I wasn't talking to you. I was talking to him."

One of my favourite coaching stories involves your dad. One night in Montreal somebody ran over me right in front of the Canadiens bench. I go down and I'm lyin' there and it's like every bone in my body is broken. I'm thinkin' I'm dead and I'm never gonna get up. Dick leaned over the boards, right above me, and yelled, "I hope it's nothing trivial!"

But to tell you the truth, I never had much to do with coaches. I stayed away from them. One thing I can't figure out today is why so many referees go over to the players' bench to have a discussion with a coach when he's after them about something. I don't think a referee should do that, no way. They're just asking for trouble.

Matt Pavelich had a long career as an NHL linesman. He is currently one of the officiating supervisors for the league.

MATT PAVELICH

I have a lot of memories of Rudy Pilous when he coached in Chicago. He had nicknames for most of the officials. George Hayes was "Beer-eyes." Neil Armstrong, a tall, gangly guy, was "Tanglefoot." I have dark skin so he called me "Sabu." When one of his guys, especially Hull or Mikita, would miss a wide-open net, or not score on a breakaway, when he'd come to the bench Pilous would rush to the stick-rack and get a new stick and make a big show out of giving it to him. In Montreal the fans used to chant "Piloo, Piloo" and he'd doff his hat to them. He was a real character.

A couple of years ago one of our young referees, Richard Trottier, was working a New York Islanders game. He did something early in the game that upset Al Arbour so Arbour got on him right away. Every time Trottier skated by his bench Arbour would yell, "You're the worst referee I've ever seen. You're the worst. You're the worst!" Ron Wicks was a referee who had been in the league a long time and for some reason Arbour hated Wicks, even though they came from the same home town. He'd go nuts if you even mentioned Wicks's name. You could say they had a very poor relationship, and it was like that for years. This night, when Arbour was really giving it to Trottier, one of the linesmen, Ray Scapinello, finally said to him, "You keep saying he's the worst. What about Wicks?" So for the rest of the game, every time Trottier was near Arbour, Al would yell, "You're the second-worst referee I've ever seen! You're the second-worst!"

Max McNab was quoted earlier talking about playing for the Detroit Red Wings when Jack Adams ran the show there. Max played and coached for several years in the old Western Hockey League. One of the game's most respected people, he is now the executive vice-president of the New Jersey Devils.

Max McNab

When I played in New Westminster Babe Pratt was our coach and one year we got off to a poor start. We won two of our first six games and in the first period of our next game we didn't play well and we were down on the scoreboard. In the first intermission Babe came into the room with the team doctor, Dr. Sinclair, and he said, "Fellas, I want you to say goodbye to Dr. Sinclair. He's leaving because we're not going to need him any more. The way you guys are playing nobody's gonna get a bruise, nobody's gonna get his face cut, so we're letting the doctor go. We might call him up on the off-chance we need him, but the way you guys are playing it looks to me you're trying to protect your Hollywood faces. The only way they'd ever use your faces in Hollywood would be in a horror movie."

Later on I was playing for Vancouver and Babe was coaching there too, but they fired him about twenty games into the season. The owner of the team, a fellow named Ken McKenzie, came into the dressing room, told us Pratt was gone, and said we were going to take a vote right then and there because one of us was going to be the playing-coach for the rest of the season. So everybody sat down and wrote a name on a piece of paper. We handed them to McKenzie but instead of going out of the room to count the ballots in private, he sat on the rubbing-table in the middle of the room and announced each one. He'd say, "Here's one for Ullyot" – Ken Ullyot was our captain – "Here's one for McNab – Here's another for Ullyot." I thought Ullyot would win but, as it turned out, I got the most votes. I became the playing-coach and that's how I got my first job as a coach. There was one vote for a defenceman on the team, Pat Coburn. When the vote was over Coburn got up and said, "There's one guy on this team who is too dumb to play on this team. That's the guy who voted for me to be the coach." [Laughs]

If you ask me about coaching today I'd have to say, look at the dynasties. Historically they've been coached by the same men, Arbour, Sather, and Scotty in the modern days. I think basketball and hockey are the worst on coaches, the way they chew them up and spit them out. They've got long seasons. In football they play sixteen games a year and there seems to be more longevity there in the coaching ranks. But lately hockey has become just deadly as far as coaches being let go. I think the teams that were the dynasties indicate that a team has to do it that way. But today it seems nobody who coaches knows for sure just how long he's going to stay around.

The late Fred Shero left a lasting impression and many memories of the time he spent in Philadelphia coaching the Flyers, a.k.a. "The Broad Street Bullies." Shero's strange coaching methods and his distant and aloof personality behind his thick, scholarly-looking glasses earned him the nickname "Freddie the Fog." Whatever his strategy was, it worked, especially in the mid-1970s when he coached the Flyers to two-straight Stanley Cups.

Bobby Taylor was the back-up goaltender behind Bernie Parent during Shero's heyday in Philadelphia. Taylor is now the colour commentator on the radio broadcasts of Flyers games.

BOBBY TAYLOR

Freddie gave the impression of being detached from all the fighting and brawling that went on and the image the team had. He looked like an innocent bystander, but he really did encourage it. His whole thing was us against them. He even had that instilled in us about management as well. It was like we were the group on the firing line, the players and the coaches, while the generals were back there making the decisions. On the road it was the same thing, us against the crowds in the other rinks. So it was a case of "us" having to be together in order to be successful against "them."

He wasn't in a fog. He put on a lot of that. His whole philosophy was to try and take away much of the attention and much of the media hoopla from the players and put it on himself. That way all we'd have to do was play hockey. Our club commanded a tremendous amount of attention because of the way we played. Bernie Parent was on the cover of *Time* magazine. They sent TV tapes of our games to Japan. We were in trouble with the police because of what happened in games in Vancouver and Toronto and that stuff made headlines all over. I was in jail for twenty minutes in Vancouver. In Toronto, when they arrested Joe Watson, one of our defencemen, he said he hoped he'd get the same cell Harold Ballard had been in. Freddie had us play that style and at the same time kept hammering away the fact that we had to stick together.

He did most of his disciplining through his captain, Bobby Clarke, and the veteran players. He'd bring them in and say – and I'll use Ross Lonsberry and Rick MacLeish as examples – he'd say, "Lonsberry hasn't backchecked much the last two or three games. Is something wrong with him? What's with MacLeish lately on the power play? He's not working very hard." So the players would go to these guys and relay the message. In Freddie's mind peer pressure was the best way to discipline. He didn't like yelling at players and he was fortunate he had players who would do that for him. In hockey today if one player told that to another the answer would be, "Screw you. What have you done lately?" We respected our teammates enough to listen to each other.

He didn't say much, but he'd come up with things you'd remember. One day we're on the ice and he starts talking to Bob Kelly – we called him "Hound" – and when Freddie asked him what he had for breakfast that morning Hound told him bacon and eggs. Then Freddie said, "Well, Hound, just remember this. The chicken made a contribution to your breakfast but the pig made a commitment." Nobody knew what the hell he was talking about. He would do that constantly to the players. We'd go away scratching our heads and some of the guys would be howling because they knew Hound didn't know what he'd been talking about.

Freddie was always picking on certain guys to make a point. Joe Watson was a favourite. He'd ask Joe, "Now, Joe, when we're three-on-two and overloaded on one side, what is that off-side defenceman's job supposed to be?" Now everybody is thinking, oh God, what does Joe know about that? And Joe would yell, "Why are you always pickin' on me? Why don't you ask MacLeish or somebody else?" But things like that would get everybody thinking. Freddie was shrewd, very shrewd.

He got a lot of publicity for writing sayings on the blackboard before our games. He did it before every game. He must have read books on quotations. He was an avid reader because his back was so bad he never slept. He'd put those sayings on the board and then ask Hound or Joe to explain what they meant and the guys would laugh like crazy. But if it was an important game it was a bit different. His most famous was, "Win together today and we'll walk together forever." That was for the final game against Boston in '74, and we beat them and won the Cup. I think over the years more of the guys now realize what he said was true. He wanted you to think and grow, not only as a hockey player but as a human being too. He told us that we couldn't keep taking things from the community, that we had to give something back too. I think that's why so many of his players stayed in Philadelphia when they were through playing.

He loved keeping us off balance. One year we were in the playoffs and he said, "I'm getting tired of this game. I think I'll go back to Winnipeg and go to law school." He'd come out with stuff like that and we'd be looking at him, shaking our heads. Then the press would be all over him and they'd be leaving his players alone, and that was part of it. He used to tell us not to believe everything he said in the newspapers.

At the start of every season he'd call everyone in and tell him exactly what his role would be on the team. He'd tell you if you would be playing a lot or not very much. He was always upfront. He wouldn't lie to you. He'd tell you right off the bat.

Freddie liked his beer. One time, in the summer, he called me and he must have talked to me for over an hour. He was telling me I'd play about thirty-five per cent of the games the next season, which didn't make much sense because we had Bernie [Parent]. He said he was going to Russia for a coaching seminar and he wanted me to go with him. He said I'd be going to a goaltender school with Tretiak. He got me all fired up. I never heard from him again so around the middle of August I called him and asked, "When are we leaving for Russia?" He didn't have a clue what the hell I was talking about.

He used to write letters to the players' wives and tell them to leave their husbands alone, quit bugging them so they could concentrate on hockey. At playoff time especially he'd write the wives and explain we were coming to the most important part of the season and he didn't want them messing around with the guys. He'd say he didn't want the players worrying about anything at home, cutting the lawn, taking out the trash, anything like that. And he'd word it so it was clear he didn't want them to be doing anything physical with their husbands, like, no screwing. And our wives would get so pissed off at him. He was funny that way. He was a real piece of work.

After seven years as coach in Philadelphia, Fred Shero left the Flyers to become coach and general manager of the New York Rangers. In his first season in New York, 1978–79, the Rangers reached the Stanley Cup finals, where they lost to the Montreal Canadiens in five games. John Davidson, another ex-goaltender-turned-broadcaster, played for the Rangers at that time.

JOHN DAVIDSON

The year we went to the finals I played about half the games during the regular season and all the games in the playoffs. Freddie never said a word to me the whole time. I liked it that way. I didn't need a coach to tell me that I had to get up for the game because it was a big one. Some people call us strange animals but we know what we have to do.

About three years later Freddie was doing some radio work for the New Jersey Devils. I heard him one night being interviewed about our '79 series against Montreal. We won the first game and then lost four straight. He was saying that after we lost the third game he was thinking about making a change in goal. He said he thought he might take that guy out, that guy who played all the games. You know, what's-his-name. The big guy. What's his name again? Some guys might get upset by that but I thought it was hilarious. That was Freddie, a wonderful guy.

One of the most embarrassing moments I ever saw for one of my coaches was in New York when Jean-Guy Talbot was there. It happened on a day when Don Murdoch and Ron Duguay were late for practice for about the fourteenth time in a row. John Ferguson was the GM and when he saw the shape they were in when they arrived he told Talbot those two guys were gone. He was sending them to the minors and that was it. We go on the ice while they're still getting dressed. They were having a little trouble getting the laces into the eyeholes on their skates. Jean-Guy called us to centre-ice and gave us a big speech about how Murdoch and Duguay were gone. He said they were going to the minors and it would be up to the rest of us to pick up some slack and carry a bigger load. Just as he finished talking we hear a gate slam. We turn around and there they were, Murdoch and Duguay, skating out to join us. Jean-Guy turned beet-red because he's just finished telling us those guys were never going to play for the New York Rangers again. The team never did anything to them and Talbot was very embarrassed.

John D'Amico is another long-time NHL linesman who is now on the league's supervisory staff.

John D'Amico

I was in Montreal doing a game in the '60s when I was fairly new in the league. I had a game there Thursday and another on Saturday. In the first game there was a very close play that was actually offside. I didn't call it and the Detroit player went in and scored on Gump Worsley. I couldn't sleep for two nights thinking about it. Saturday morning I went to the Forum early because I wanted to sort of apologize to Worsley because he was in a close fight for the Vezina Trophy.

As soon as I got into the Forum I bumped into Toe Blake. I was sure he would be mad at me because of the call I missed, so before he said anything I told him why I was there. He took me aside and, to be very frank with you, he sat me down and told me that I was being very honest in doing what I was doing. He said, "If you're honest with the players, if you never lie to them and if you admit you missed an offside, you'll have them with you for your whole career. You're going to have a good career ahead of you and you'll miss some offsides. But I like what you're doing because you're being honest about the whole thing."

It was very good advice from a gentleman I really respected

who won all those Stanley Cups in Montreal. Good advice, and good hockey sense too.

There are plenty of stories about Joe Crozier, one of hockey's true characters, who coached in both the WHA and the NHL. When Crozier coached the Buffalo Sabres in the early 1970s one of his players was Jim Lorentz.

Jim Lorentz

We were going through a bad period. The only player who was doing anything good was Gilbert Perreault and for several games Joe had been accusing the rest of us of just standing around letting Gilbert do all the work. One night we were all dressed and ready to go out for the pre-game skate. Joe walked into the room and started in again about everybody standing around watching Gilbert. Then he says, "All right, Gilbert, you go on the ice." The whole team started to get up and Joe yelled, "No, no, not the rest of you. Just Gilbert. You guys sit down." So Gilbert goes out on the ice by himself. Joe turned on a TV set in the room. He had someone with a camera inside the building following Gilbert as he was skating around. Joe said, "You guys want to watch Gilbert? Now you can just sit there and watch him all you want." So we all sat there for about five minutes watching Gilbert Perreault skate around by himself in the warm-up.

Another time we were in Vancouver and it was the last stop in what had been a terrible road trip. We hadn't won a game and Joe hated to lose in Vancouver because he had spent many successful years there in the minor leagues. We were in the room getting ready and Joe came in and started undressing. He starts putting on an ugly old red sweatsuit he had and we didn't know what was happening. He put on the sweatsuit and he put on his skates, and he never said a word to us. The trainer came in and said it was time to go on the ice for the warm-up. Joe got up and joined in our line and skated out with us. Then he started to put us through some drills, just like it was a practice, and everyone in Vancouver was absolutely in stitches. They had never seen anything like that and neither had we. As far as I know it's the only time a coach ever went out on the ice with his team for the pre-game skate. It didn't do any good because we lost anyway.

But the one I'll never forget was in Montreal during the playoffs in 1973, the year they beat us in six games. In one of the games we lost, Joe thought our defensive work had been pretty shabby, so when we were ready to go out for practice the next morning he said, "I'm gonna show you guys how to block shots. I'll prove to you that a puck doesn't hurt when it hits you." All he had on were his skates and his old sweatsuit and he goes in the net and plays goalie. He had a stick but no pads of any kind, and no gloves. He said to Mike Robitaille, "Okay, shoot a few from the blue line." Mike drifted a couple of soft shots at him and Joe yelled, "Come on, shoot harder!" So Robitaille wired a few, really drilled them, and Crozier actually stopped a couple with his bare hands and a couple with his legs. You never knew what he was going to do and when something like that happens, you never forget it. But I must say I enjoyed playing for him. He got a lot out of his team and he's a real good guy.

Peter McNab, Max's son, had a fourteen-year career in the NHL. During that time he played for Joe Crozier, and for Don Cherry.

Peter McNab

I played my first year in Buffalo when Joe Crozier was the coach and he had a pre-game ritual that put a rookie through absolute mental hell. He'd put all the players' names on the blackboard and then, at various times as you were getting dressed, he'd erase the names of the guys who would be playing that night. At that time in Buffalo we had the French Connection line. Joe would look at the board and sort of laugh, and their names would come off first. Then he'd leave the room. He'd come back and take two or three more names off the board, then leave again. Jim Schoenfeld and Tim Horton were a cinch, so were Craig Ramsay and Don Luce. By the time we were ready for the warm-up there were only four names left and we knew that two of them wouldn't play. My name was usually in the final four. After the warm-up he'd come in kowing that only four guys were looking at the board by then. He'd sort of shield the blackboard with his body, take a quick look around trying to catch us peeking as we were fiddling with our skate laces. Then he'd pull away and two names were left, the guys who weren't playing. I tell you, if your name was still there your heart would sink. But if it wasn't you'd feel you were on top of the world.

One of my favourite stories about playing for Grapes, in Boston, was what happened one night after we had been beaten badly on home ice. We had a very good team and we'd gone ten or twelve games in a row at home without losing. Then we just flat-out blew one, 7–1, or something like that. As we're going off the ice Don says to me, "Thanks a lot," and I thought he was being sarcastic. I look at him kind of funny and he says, "This is great. Blue's here tonight [Cherry's bull terrier] and this is a perfect time for a loss like that. Watch me. I'm gonna take all the pressure off you guys.

You come by my office in fifteen minutes and see what's happening."

Fifteen minutes later I walk into Don's office and all the reporters are there, TV cameras and everything. He's sitting on top of his desk and he's holding Blue, pointing her at one of the reporters, and he's saying, "Look out, she's gonna get you. She's gonna go after you." He was just screaming and I guess the guy was really scared. Then he lets Blue get away but she just took off somewhere else. Don sees me and gives me a little wink and says, "Watch this one on the 6:00 news tomorrow night."

One of Don Cherry's favourites when he was coaching was Wayne Cashman, who was one of his best players during the five years Grapes coached the Bruins. "Cash" is now an assistant coach with the Tampa Bay Lightning.

WAYNE CASHMAN

I have a lot of memories of Grapes. He was a great coach who made the game fun. He made you work hard but he made you work hard for each other. He made you realize it's a team sport. He used to tell us to sit in the dressing room and look at each other because that was who you were playing for, your teammates.

We were flying to Los Angeles to start a three-game trip on the West Coast and he kept telling us how important the games were because we were fighting for first place. On the plane he asked me what we were going to be doing that night, in L.A. I said we'd likely be going out to eat somewhere and then go back to the hotel. He suggested I get the guys together in a bar that was next to the hotel and he'd join us for a beer around 10:00, which normally was our curfew time. So we all go there and just after 10:00, in walks Grapes. He just stands there and doesn't say a word. Then he walks the full length of the bar, turns around, and walks out. The next day he doesn't talk to anybody at the morning skate, not one person, and now he's got twenty-two guys scared. Well, that night we were flying and we beat L.A. easily. After the game we wait for Grapes to come into the room as he always did. No Grapes. Our usual supply of beer wasn't there either. We get on the bus to go back to the hotel. No Grapes.

We go to Oakland to play the next night and it's the same thing. He doesn't speak to a soul, doesn't say a word. Now we've got twenty-two guys more scared than ever. We beat the tar out of Oakland. After the game, same thing, no Grapes and no beer.

We go to Vancouver for the last game on the trip and it's the same thing all over again. We beat them pretty good. By now Donnie Marcotte and I had snuck ourselves a couple of beers. We go around the corner from the dressing room and run smack into Grapes with the beers in our hands. He's sitting there nursing a beer of his own and giggling. He looks at me and says, "Well, it worked, didn't it?" Just then the trainer arrives with a case of beer for the boys. Grapes knew how to use sports psychology long before it was invented.

Coaches don't mind the odd laugh at their own expense. Jacques Demers talks about a pre-game pep talk he gave one of his clubs. "I was emphasizing the word 'man,'" Demers told me. "I was saying things like, 'Hockey is a man's game . . . you've got to go out there and think like a man . . . hit like a man . . . play both ends of the ice like a man. This is a game for men and you're going out there tonight and prove that.' Then," added Jacques, "when I was finished and it was time for the game to start I finished up by saying, 'Okay, let's go, boys!' Did I ever feel stupid."

Gary Leeman played for Demers for part of the 1992–93 season after being traded to Montreal from Calgary. Leeman turned pro with the Toronto Maple Leafs organization. Early in his career there he played for another colourful coach, silver-haired John Brophy.

GARY LEEMAN

Broph was my coach when I was with St. Catharines in the American League. We were playing in Moncton and were ahead 1–0 late in the second period. He made a change to a defensive line because he didn't want them to get the tying goal right at the end of the period. One of the players he put on was Kevin Maguire. Before they faced off Broph called Maguire back to the bench and told him that he didn't want him to carry the puck, but just to keep shooting it out of our zone. So right away one of our defencemen gives Maguire a pass and Kevin carries the puck up the ice and tries to beat one of their defencemen. He gets checked, they throw it back up the ice, go in, and score.

When we got to the dressing room nobody was saying a word. It was the quietest room I'd ever been in. After a couple of minutes Brophy comes in, walks right up to Maguire, and goes nose to nose with him. He says, "What did I tell you?" Kevin says, "You told me not to carry the puck." Broph says, "What did you do?" Kevin says, "I carried the puck." Then Broph says, "You couldn't carry the puck if it was in a pail."

He used to complain that the defence wasn't physical enough in front of our own net. One day in practice Broph said, "I'll show you guys how to handle somebody in front of our net." We had a tough forward, Val James, and Brophy had him stand at the edge of the goal-crease. Broph started to hammer him. I mean, he cross-checked him, bodychecked him, slashed him, tripped him. James would get up and

Brophy would knock him down again. Poor Val couldn't retaliate, of course. After a few minutes of this Broph said, "I'm sixty years old, and *that's* the way you take a guy out in front of the net."

In Toronto one night we had a bad period. Brophy came into the room and shut off all the lights. He said, "You're playing like you're in the dark, so you might as well spend the intermission in the dark too."

They brought up Steve Thomas from St. Catharines where he'd been scoring a lot of goals. The first day he's in the dressing room Brophy says to him, "We've got guys in this room who haven't scored for months . . . for months . . . FOR MONTHS! I brought you up here to score goals. You travelled forty miles to get here, but remember, it's like forty thousand miles if I send you back."

We were losing a lot so the general manager came in and told us John Brophy had been fired and that George Armstrong was going to take his place. Armstrong came in and said, "I know things aren't going well for you guys and they're not going too well for me either. I don't want this job. I don't want to be a coach. But Mr. Ballard is making me do it, so here I am." That wasn't exactly like giving the team a big lift, but as it turned out, it broke the tension.

The late Punch Imlach, who coached the Toronto Maple Leafs to four Stanley Cups in the 1960s, was a controversial character, a man you either liked or didn't like. Reading books that have been written in recent years by some of his former players, it seems that a lot of them were in the "didn't like" category. Jean Béliveau played senior hockey for two years for the Quebec Aces before he signed with the Montreal Canadiens. Imlach was Béliveau's coach in Quebec City.

JEAN BÉLIVEAU

I remember Punch, after practice, he would have a guy chasing me. He'd say, "Jean, you're tall. You can skate fast once you get those long legs going. But you've got to improve your start." He would put me on the spot in the face-off circle, put a guy on the outside rim of the circle, and we'd race. I'd chase the guy back and we'd always start from a standing position. It worked and it did help me improve. I know a lot of people, a lot of his players, especially when he was in Toronto, they hated his guts. I read some of the books, the Sittler book. But me, I had nothing against him. Maybe the situation was different in the Quebec League. We had a good team and the league was good. Punch was quite a character.

One of Don Cherry's stops as a full-time minor-leaguer was in Springfield, in the American League. The controversial Eddie Shore owned the team and the controversial Punch Imlach was the coach.

DON CHERRY

We had a rough team in Springfield. We drank a lot. So Punch started poker games and blackjack games. The night before a game he'd supply the beer and the sandwiches and everythink and he'd be there with us playin' cards until after midnight. When the card game was over there was no place else to go, and with him there with us we couldn't get drunk. He was keepin' an eye on us and we didn't even realize it. He had to motivate a bunch of guys who all knew they were never goin' to the National League, whose hearts had been broken. And being owned by Eddie Shore was like being owned by Darth Vader. I remember one day Shore came down and started talking to the players, trying to coach us, and Punch ripped the shit out of him, told him to stay away from the players because he was the coach. That was like tellin' off Gargantua, but Punch went at him just like a little bantam rooster. He was gone at the end of the year.

He was very tough on you at practice and very vindictive. If he saw you weren't working hard in practice you wouldn't play the next game. I remember he called me a "thingami-bob" one night on the bench and I wouldn't go out on the ice. A "thingamibob." I never played for two games after that.

In Springfield people used to look on us as lepers. Even though we won three championships in a row nobody wanted to play in Springfield. They even had it in their contracts. One year we were still in the playoffs and Imlach had just won the Stanley Cup in Toronto. He came to Springfield to scout and he had a big entourage with him. He was wearing a white suit and he had a white hat tilted back on his head. Remember the white hat? He was the talk of hockey and there I was, the tenth defenceman in a leper colony. He's swaggering along the street and he happened to see me. He walked right over and asked me how I was doing. He even remembered Rose's name. He told me to hang in, and kept on walking. He was the best motivator I ever saw and he was the best coach I ever played for.

John Garrett was a goaltender in both the WHA and the NHL. He is now a commentator for Hockey Night in Canada.

JOHN GARRETT

I played for Bill Laforge in Vancouver. At training camp he was giving us his opening speech and he said, "If you're wondering about my credentials, I have my Ph.D." We're all sitting there wondering about Bill Laforge and a Ph.D. Then he says, "That's for pride, hustle, and desire." He put together three teams for the intersquad games and he called them Pride, Hustle, and Desire. He took the attitude that it would be his way or the highway. A lot of the guys weren't too thrilled. A key player on the Canucks then was a Swede, Tomas Gradin, and the highway would have been all right with him instead of Bill Laforge's way. He was quite willing to have his cheques sent to Stockholm.

If your team lost an intersquad game you would take off your skates but not your pads. The goalies got to take off their pads, but not anyone else. Then you had to run for two miles. We didn't have a very good team so we did a lot of running. He said he didn't want any fights at training camp. Our squad had some tough guys and one day Craig Coxe drops the gloves and starts one and before the game was over there had been three fights. We lost 7–2, so after the game we're taking off our skates and putting on our running shoes. Laforge comes in and says, "What a great game! What a great game! Three fights and you guys won them all. Way to go, guys. No running for you today." That's the way it went with Bill Laforge. He had a great record as a junior coach but he lasted only twenty games with us in the NHL.

I played in Toronto in the WHA for the team that was transferred from there to Birmingham. Gilles Leger was our coach and his philosophy was that the team that scores the most goals wins, so there was very little defence involved. Frank Mahovlich was there and so was Paul Henderson. We were losing most games 7–5, scores like that. After about two months in Birmingham Gilles was kicked upstairs and Pat Kelly was appointed coach. He preached a lot more defence, especially for home games, and we started playing well at home. Gilles had been moved to assistant GM and about a month later he called me into his office and asked me, "John, why did you want to get me fired? I'm serious, why?" He honestly thought that I had played badly in the first couple of months so that he would get fired. I told him I had no intention of getting him fired. That was just the way we played. I think he finally believed me. I hope he believed me.

Pat Kelly left to coach Colorado in the NHL and Glen Sonmor took over. We went from being a passive team to being Glen's Goons. We were officially the Birmingham Bulls, but really the "Birmingham Bullies," as in Broad Street. We had players like Steve Durbano and Gilles "Bad News" Bilodeau and Dave "Killer" Hanson. We played in Cincinnati on Thanksgiving Eve. Jacques Demers was coaching Cincinnati. To give you an idea of our game plan, I didn't start because our other goalie was Wayne Wood who was six-foot-two and weighed over two hundred pounds. He rarely played but Glen said Wood was starting because he was sure there was going to be a big brawl. Just before the game a minister came on the ice and offered a prayer for Thanksgiving and thanked the Lord for the fine group of sportsmen who would be playing that night. He called for a display of true friendship and sportsmanship. About twenty seconds after the minister gives the prayer they drop the puck, and another ten seconds later Robbie Ftorek clobbers Durbano and the gloves are off. Everybody on the ice got into the fight and they were all thrown out of the game. Rick Dudley wasn't on the ice so he wasn't in the fight, but he went to the dressing room and refused to play the rest of the night. It was a classic Glen Sonmor game where we were going to intimidate them.

We made the playoffs and played Winnipeg. They won the Avco Cup that year and lost only one game in the playoffs. That was to us, in the first game. We decided to try to intimidate them in the second game. We must have played half the night two men short. They put about five power-play goals past me and we ended up losing about 9–2. Glen was in his glory behind the bench.

I played for Michel Bergeron in Quebec in 1982 when we went to the Stanley Cup semi-finals. We finished fourth that year, but in the playoffs we beat Montreal and then we beat Boston. We weren't supposed to beat those teams but we did. Then the New York Islanders beat us, but they were the best team in hockey.

From a technical standpoint I didn't think Michel was that great a coach, but we had a good offensive team at the time with the three Stastny brothers. The ethnic thing in Quebec is tough to handle and the media is tough. Michel did a great job with the media. We had some young French guys that were in a little group by themselves, like Dave Pichette and Normand Rochefort. We had older French guys, Real Cloutier, Marc Tardif, and Moose Dupont. Then we had the three Czechs and a few English guys. Michel did a great job keeping the whole team together.

He would come in just before we were going out for the warm-up and convince you that you could beat any team in the league. He wouldn't do it every night but he would before a key game and in the playoffs. He'd go down their whole roster. I remember sitting there when we were playing the Islanders in the playoffs and he's going down their line-up saying, "Look at this Bryan Trottier. He can't skate any more. Mike Bossy has a bad back." He actually convinced us that we should be able to beat the New York Islanders.

Okay, you're supposed to have that attitude, but when you looked at it on paper there really was no comparison between the two teams. But he made it work against Montreal and he made it work against Boston. It ended up that we lost four straight, but I remember, after the series was over, thinking, "How did Bergy come up with those speeches?" But he did. He'd come in with his little book and he would go through the other team, man for man, and he would convince us we were better than any team we were playing against. I really respected him for that.

The New York Islander team Michel Bergeron thought his Quebec Nordiques could beat was coached by Al Arbour. Talk to players from that team today and they are full of praise for the way Arbour coached them while they were winning four-straight Stanley Cups. Ken Morrow was a defenceman who joined the Islanders after playing on the gold medal-winning United States team at the 1980 Winter Olympics. "Al had the ability to keep it interesting for the players," Morrow told me. "That's a big challenge coaches face and Al was up to it. He was able to kick you when you needed it and pat you on the back when you needed it and he'd do it when you were expecting just the opposite. You thought you were going to get kicked, and he'd come up and pat you on the back. He was always full of surprises."

Glen "Chico" Resch was an Islanders goaltender for six years. His last full season with them was 1979–80, when the Islanders won their first Stanley Cup.

CHICO RESCH

You wouldn't think Al was the kind of a coach the players would play jokes on but it happened quite a bit. We would always push a pie in his face on his birthday and we always made a rookie do it. One year it was Bryan Trottier. He waited for Al to come around a corner in the dressing room and he really let him have it. I guess Trots was pretty nervous because he was much too close to Al when he hit him. He knocked him back into the clothes dryer, he knocked his glasses off, and we were scared he might have broken his nose. Al acted like he was real mad. He yelled at Bryan, "I'm going to send you back to Swift Current, only this time you're not going on a plane. You're going on a bus!" Everyone was pretty quiet, then Al started to laugh.

There was another time something like that happened and he didn't laugh. We lost a game in Chicago 8–0. We went home, and at practice the next day everybody found an egg at his place in the dressing room. Al said, "I want you guys to put your egg in your coat pocket, go home, and spend the day like you normally would. If you spend the day the way you played last night there won't be a broken egg in the bunch, you were that delicate about everything in Chicago."

While he was talking Pat Price sneaked up behind him and broke his egg over Al's head. Al wasn't amused at all, what with the egg yolk dripping down over his eyes. He really reamed Price out and you couldn't blame him. Fun is fun, but you have to realize when those times are.

Al Arbour never had the upfront image of other winning coaches like Scotty Bowman and Glen Sather. Those guys had a plan for the media, they played their tunes for them. Al couldn't do that. His approach was very straight, no malarkey, no stunts. He didn't have any ego at all. He just did his job the best way he knew how. That was all he was interested in.

I remember one of the first things he told me was, "Don't let them score on the minor-league side." I said, "Minor-league side?" and he said, "Yeah. That's the short side. If they score on you there you'll be back in the minor leagues."

Tom McVie has inspired a lot of stories with his hard-nosed coaching style. Brent Ashton, who has played for more NHL teams than any other player, had McVie as his coach when he played for the New Jersey Devils. "He skated us to death," Brent told me. "We'd be going up and down the ice forever, and at the same time Tommy would be at centre-ice doing push-ups. He even hired a Marine Corps drill-sergeant to get us in shape. The guy put us through some brutal drills. He'd put his face right up to yours and holler at you. He'd spit all over you, he was so close."

Steve Shutt played for the Scotty Bowman-coached Montreal Canadiens when they were the class of the NHL at the same time the Washington Capitals, coached by Tom McVie, were in the cellar. Steve once told me, "We used to watch the way McVie made them work so hard at practice with all the skating and the push-ups. We figured if they ever beat us Scotty would get the idea we should start practising that way too. So we never let up on those guys. We always tried to beat them as bad as we could."

While most of the men I talked to for this chapter preferred to remember the humorous incidents involving some of their coaches, they gave me some serious comments as well. Bryan Trottier retired in 1992 after earning six Stanley Cup rings, four with the New York Islanders and two with the Pittsburgh Penguins. His Cup-winning coaches were three of the greatest, Al Arbour, the late Bob Johnson, and Scotty Bowman.

BRYAN TROTTIER

I think the best quality a coach can have is to allow his players to have some creativity and individualism. If you get them too regimented I think you're really confining each player's total ability. I think the only time you really need to have discipline is in your own zone. Everyone used to say that Mike Bossy couldn't check his hat and coat, that all he did was score goals. I say he was underrated defensively because he knew what he had to do in our zone, and he did it. Al Arbour allowed guys like Bossy, Clark Gillies, and me to be ourselves. Sometimes we'd come out of a game and he'd ask what I was thinking about on a play where we scored a goal and I had to say I didn't know, couldn't remember. He'd tell me that's what players like Stan Mikita and Jean Béliveau used to say. In certain situations you just do, you don't plan. Al let us be individuals.

Look at Scotty Bowman. He's a very disciplined guy but I'm sure he didn't have a bridle on Guy Lafleur or Steve Shutt. I'm sure he allowed them to have creativity. In Pittsburgh he lets Mario Lemieux be Mario. When Gretzky and Messier and those other guys were flying high in Edmonton, I used to think they had eyes on the sides of their heads, in the backs of their heads, and in their rear-ends. They used to make sideways passes, drop passes, and I'd say to myself, "That's creativity." I'll bet they never practised that. It was just the guys doing their thing.

The mark of a strong coach is a disciplined defence. With your best offensive players, throw them the puck and let them dance. Let their juices flow, and good things will happen.

Bob Johnson was a great coach. Bob had no system. The only thing he required was that you go out there and have some fun. What he wanted more than anything else was for his players to have a great attitude, to come to the rink ready to play. He wanted everyone to be positive, to play with exuberance. We would lose 6–1 and the only thing he'd talk about was how good a play was we made on the one goal we scored. He never worried about the negatives, and he wasn't overly concerned about who we were playing. His practices didn't have any rhyme or reason but, boy, we'd come off the ice dead-tired. Bob Johnson was a unique fellow. He was very pro-Bryan Trottier, and I loved him for that.

Derek Sanderson has led a life inside and outside hockey that makes him unique. Sanderson was rookie of the year

with the Boston Bruins in 1968 and started the play leading
to Bobby Orr's famous overtime Stanley Cup-winning goal
in 1970. Sanderson was a cocky, high-living, free-spirited
kid who jumped to the WHA for a mega-bucks contract.
Then it all collapsed. Instead of looking at his world through
rose-coloured glasses, Derek Sanderson was squinting at it
through a heavy fog of alcohol and drugs. But Derek beat it
and his life is back on track. He is the colour commentator
on Boston Bruins telecasts and plays an active role in drug
and alcohol rehabilitation programs in the New England
area.

DEREK SANDERSON

Coaches today complicate a game that is total ad lib. It's a
sixth-sense game. Can a guy make that play? If you have that
sixth sense you're going to be playing. If you have all the
skills in the world and don't have that sense, you're not going
to be playing. When Tom Johnson was our coach he said,
"Derek, once I open that gate and put you on the ice, you're
on your own. I can tell you a million things but you have to
react. You have to have a feel for what you do."

All the great coaches are students of the game and they
never had superstar status or maybe never even played at the
NHL level. Al Arbour, for example, and Scotty Bowman, and
Harry Sinden. I would have liked playing for Bowman. I don't
care if you like the man or not. We would have had our differences, but I would have worked hard for him. There are too
many players who come out of an organization that tells
them, "Okay, you were a star player and you're a coach now."
But it will work only if he's a student of the game.

Harry Sinden was a coach you'd go through walls for. He
complimented you, or knocked you, in subtle ways. He'd put
the numbers on the blackboard of the players who didn't

have to practice the next day. If you weren't playing well your name was never on the vacation list. On game nights he would have the trainers hang up the sweaters of the guys who would be playing. One night Ken Hodge came in. He was having a good goal-scoring year but he hadn't played well for a while and his number 8 wasn't hanging there. He went to the trainer and the guy told him he wasn't playing. Hodge went snakey, he went berserk. But that was Harry. If you weren't giving the effort you were in trouble. I think the job Sinden did with Team Canada in 1972 was the finest coaching in the history of the game. They tried to force him to use the superstar concept, but in the end he did it his way. I think he saved face for the nation with that one.

It's so different today. You have assistant coaches, and what do they bring to the table? They're sounding boards for disgruntled players. An assistant maybe wants the head job so he tells some players that if he was the head coach they'd be playing a lot more. A head coach has to get loyalty from his assistants, and from management too. Management doesn't give coaches the loyalty they deserve. Players say, "We'll get rid of this guy, no problem." I think Jimmy Roberts said it best when he was in Hartford. He said, "You yell at them today, they laugh at you, and then you're gone." There often isn't too much loyalty in the dressing room.

John Ferguson has been a player, coach, and general manager in the NHL. He is currently the director of player personnel for the Ottawa Senators.

JOHN FERGUSON

Players used to be afraid of their coaches but today they are absolutely not afraid. It's almost a fact that high-price players become partners rather than employees. That's the philosophy of the game today. I can't believe some of the things high-price players say to their coaches today. The coach's philosophy doesn't matter any more. They say, why are we doing this? The high-price players become coaches.

Coaches today seem to decide what players should play in terms of their technical skills. It doesn't work that way. I myself have watched umpteen hundred NHL games and the best players have got to play. All players have to get on the ice, of course, but they've got to play in the right positions. I've heard coaches say of a player that he's got a lot of talent but he can't check. But the game has changed around so much. Now it's a power-play game and a penalty-killing game. That's what coaches today don't realize. Some do. Scotty Bowman, he's going to use two lines most of the night because he's got Mario who is so much more skilled than the others. Toe Blake had that sense too. Toe knew where the players should go to be in their right spots on the team. Coaches are now thinking that technically everybody can play the same way but it doesn't work.

If you're writing a book about coaches you've got to put something in about Claude Ruel. He was a great guy and a terrific coach for young players. [Ruel succeeded Toe Blake in Montreal. In his first year, 1968–69, the Canadiens won the Stanley Cup and John Ferguson scored the Cup-winning goal.]

We used to laugh at the way he would say some things in English. There was the famous one when we'd have a drill and he'd say, "Okay, a two-on-one. Everybody take a man." [Laughs] One time we were checking into our hotel in Los Angeles. Claude wanted a double room so he said, "I'll have a big daily double." I was standing right behind him. I burst out laughing and I said, "I'll have a big exactor."

I was told stories about two NHL coaches who, for obvious reasons, shall remain nameless within the confines of this book. According to impeccable sources, who insist they were there, these stories are true.

A team's charter flight was stacked up over the Toronto airport, unable to land because of dense fog. Finally the coach went into the cockpit with some advice for the pilot. "Why don't you do what we do," he said. "When there's fog in the rink the players skate around in a circle and that gets rid of it. Try flying around in a circle. It might work."

Then there was the coach who was giving his team a rousing pep talk before an important playoff game. He said, "If we lose this one, boys, the season is over. You can get your golf clubs out, and who wants to play golf because it's still cold outside. We've got eighteen shooters in this room and two goalies. You've got to go out and get two shots on goal tonight. There are eighteen shooters in this room and you're all going to get two shots on their goalie which means we'll have forty-seven shots and we'll win this game."

I must point out that neither of these gentlemen has been featured in this book.

Why do hockey coaches get fired so often, and why do they keep wanting to come back to coach another day? I asked that of Jim Devellano, a one-time scout for the New York Islanders who became general manager of the Detroit Red Wings. Jimmy D. is now a senior vice-president with the Red Wings.

JIM DEVELLANO

It's one of the unfortunate aspects of our business that, for some coaches, their time runs out. I hate to give you the usual, simple explanation that you can't fire twenty players.

Often there are circumstances that an owner and a manager can't talk openly about. There are things we feel people don't need to know and sometimes it's those circumstances that create problems.

Coaching is a very precarious job and you do wonder at times why anybody would really want to do it. With the advent of big money the players have really, really changed and they are tougher to handle now. We're dealing with a player union rather than an association and the whole situation is a lot different. I had a much tougher time with the players in my last couple of years as a general manager and it was bothersome because I'm from the old school. I was warned about this by baseball people eight years ago. I have a lot of friends in major-league baseball who told me these things would eventually happen, and they did. We let a lot of coaches go after three or four years on the job. I don't agree with it, but it happens.

Today, players go to the general manager if they don't like their coach. I'm sorry to say that but, yes, they do. They run to the owner too sometimes, because it might not just be the coach they don't like. They may not like the general manager either. We have a big league with twenty-four teams and twenty-four owners. They're all different people and some of them really do listen to the players rather than to the coaches and managers.

There was an exception for many years with the New York Islanders when Bill Torrey was the GM and Al Arbour the coach. Bill Torrey was the boss. He had authority most general managers would love to have. He said that Al Arbour was going to be his coach through thick and thin, and he was. The buck stopped at Bill Torrey and he had tremendous power. I can guarantee you if a GM has that kind of authority the coach, and the manager too, can be around a long time. That's the way it used to be with Lester Patrick and Art Ross and Punch Imlach. They ran the show. But it's changed and the coaches are taking the brunt of it.

The media has changed too. Most cities have great competition amongst the newspapers and broadcast stations, all of them looking for something exciting and sexy to write. There's all kinds of controversy, all kinds of analyzing of the team and the coach. Reporters used to report what happened on the ice, the game. That doesn't happen anymore. Ownership reads it, the fans read it, the players read it. So there is no doubt the game has changed and the life of a coach has changed. I guess there are some of us who haven't changed quite that fast.

Howie Meeker coached the Toronto Maple Leafs for one season, 1956–57. I have never met anyone who loves hockey more than Howie. It was a joy to work with him on Hockey Night in Canada, *and it's a joy to meet him and talk hockey anywhere, anytime. So . . . Hey! Let's stop it right here! for the final words about being behind the bench.*

HOWIE MEEKER

I think that when I coached I knew the game, how it had to be played to win. But I couldn't handle the players. I was thirty-three, thirty-four years old and I got by because I was coaching in the era of $3,500 players in the minors and $7,000 to $10,000 players in the NHL. Normally, when you said jump, they said how high. That doesn't go now. The coach's biggest job is handling each individual. If I had it to do over again I'd have spent another three or four years coaching in the minors, learning more about people. But learning the game itself, what has to be done, hasn't changed a bit. The things we did in our day have to be done today. The better you do them, the more games you win.

I coached at just about every level. I have one regret, that I didn't last longer as a coach in the NHL. I think the personal satisfaction of seeing the individual improve, perform to the extreme, and then win, there's no feeling like it. There's no feeling like seeing a hockey player master a skill and see him grow in a team effort.

I have three daughters and, geez, I've said all my life I'd be most delighted if they married hockey players. They're the finest people in the world. Nobody's as much fun to be around as hockey players and I think that's what keeps coaches coming back. Coaches are a different breed. You and I often wonder why they take the abuse they do. And their families, they take the abuse too. In most cases, with coaches, they're there because it's personal enjoyment. They take the abuse, they get fired, yet the guy goes back. The guy keeps going back! It's a helluva job.

Last Line Change

On the final Saturday night of the 1992–93 NHL season, the Boston Bruins capped a late-season winning streak by clinching first place in the Adams Division with a convincing win over the Canadiens at the Montreal Forum. When the game ended, the Bruins' head coach, Brian Sutter, and his assistant, Tom McVie, walked off the ice arm in arm as they savoured the moment.

For McVie, it was a brand-new experience. The "Professional Rink Rat," as he calls himself, had suffered through years behind the benches of weak, underachieving teams. Now, for the first time in his long NHL coaching career, McVie was with a first-place team. I searched out Tom after the game, congratulated him, and said, "You must feel you've died and gone to heaven." Tom replied, "Yeah. But do you think these guys are setting me up for a big fall?" Sadly for Tom, they had done just that. Two weeks later the Bruins were out of the playoffs, victims of a shocking four-game sweep by John Muckler's Buffalo Sabres, a team that hadn't won a playoff series in ten years.

Other current coaches featured in this book had happier endings to their 1992–93 seasons than Sutter and McVie, notably Jacques Demers, whose roller-coaster ride in his first year as coach of the Montreal Canadiens was the most joyful of his twenty-year coaching career. After a shaky finish to their regular season which saw them fall into third place, the Habs then met their arch-rivals, the Quebec Nordiques, in the first playoff round and promptly lost the first two games in Quebec City. But Demers righted his sinking ship and the Canadiens sailed through to the twenty-fourth Stanley Cup in the team's history, winning sixteen of their next eighteen games, ten of them in overtime.

It's not often a coaching decision is remembered as the turning point in a Stanley Cup final series, but 1993 was an exception. The Los Angeles Kings defeated the Canadiens, in Montreal, in the first game and were leading 2–1 with time running out in game two. At 18:15 of the third period Jacques Demers called for a measurement of the stick that Kings defenceman Marty McSorley was using. It was a gutsy move by the Canadiens coach. If the stick was found to be illegal, McSorley would be penalized and the Canadiens would have a power play. If not, the Canadiens would be penalized and they surely would be heading to Los Angeles down by two games. But Demers's spies had done their work well. McSorley's stick was illegal and the Canadiens went on a power play. Demers immediately pulled goalie Patrick Roy, giving his team six skaters against four. At 18:47 Eric Desjardins scored the game-tying goal. Fifty-one seconds into overtime, Desjardins scored the winning goal and the series was tied. The Canadiens then won two overtime thrillers in Los Angeles, and ended the longest season in NHL history with a 4–1 Cup-clinching victory at the Montreal Forum on the ninth of June. Everyone agreed Demers's call for the stick measurement was the turning point of the series. The local boy had come home, and made good, in the best possible way.

Demers's predecessor in Montreal, Pat Burns, became a hero in Toronto. His team finished just one win short of reaching the Stanley Cup finals, Burns was voted coach of the year, and the Maple Leafs had their fans in a frenzy, just like the good old days.

While Calgary's Dave King and Winnipeg's John Paddock suffered through first-round playoff eliminations, another of our "new breed" in the coaching ranks, Barry Melrose, made it to the Stanley Cup finals with his Los Angeles Kings. After a bitter seven-game conference final between the Kings and the Maple Leafs, which included a media-hyped feud between Melrose and Pat Burns, and the intense media coverage of the Stanley Cup finals, the mod-haired Melrose suddenly had become one of hockey's most visible coaches.

There were the usual comings and goings within the coaching ranks. Mike Keenan and Roger Neilson both came back, as they vowed they would. Mike was hired by the New York Rangers, the team that had fired Roger. Neilson ran his head-coaching record to six teams, this time with the expansion Florida Panthers. Bill Dineen, our "oldest," was shunted back to a scouting job by the Philadelphia Flyers after a late-season rush by his team fell short of a playoff berth. George Kingston, the "marathon man," was fired by the San Jose Sharks.

The most interesting coaching match-up in the 1993 Stanley Cup playoffs occurred when the two men who have coached and won more games than anyone else, Scotty Bowman and Al Arbour, met head-on in the Patrick Division finals. Arbour's underdog New York Islanders eliminated Bowman's defending-champion Pittsburgh Penguins as dramatically as is possible, in overtime in the seventh game.

Scotty Bowman didn't appear to be all that happy coaching Mario Lemieux and the Penguins in the playoffs. Shortly after his team was eliminated, hockey's all-time winning coach parted company with the Pittsburgh organization and signed a two-year contract to coach the Detroit Red Wings. Reports claimed the Red Wings would be paying Scotty over a million dollars a year. When I heard those reports I thought back to 1955 when my father, the man whose records Bowman surpassed, became the highest-paid coach in hockey history. After twenty-five years, four Stanley Cups, and more victories than any coach up to that time, he was signed by the Chicago Blackhawks for $20,000. The boys behind the bench have come a long way.

When he was in the process of leaving the Pittsburgh Penguins and deciding what he would do in the future, Scotty Bowman said, "I have made up my mind. I want to coach." They all do.

Acknowledgements

I wish to sincerely thank the men whose thoughts and remembrances are what this book is all about. Their cooperation and generous giving of their time convinced me once again that hockey people are great people. I am especially grateful to those currently coaching in the NHL who kindly allowed me to interview them a scant few hours before their teams were to play a game.

Harry Neale gave me the idea for this book and was a constant source of encouragement.

Several photos were supplied through the cooperation of the public relations departments of the Boston Bruins, Buffalo Sabres, Calgary Flames, Chicago Blackhawks, Los Angeles Kings, New York Islanders, Vancouver Canucks, and Washington Capitals.

In Montreal, Denis Brodeur and Mac McDiarmid were very generous in supplying photographs. Carole Robertson transcribed the many hours of taped conversations.

329

The chapter on old-timers includes material researched from books written by two good friends, Trent Frayne's *The Mad Men of Hockey* and Scott Young's *Conn Smythe: If You Can't Beat 'Em in the Alley*. *The Patricks: Hockey's Royal Family*, written by Eric Whitehead, was also a helpful source.

A very skilful editor, Lynn Schellenberg, was my head coach. Lynn had help behind the bench from Peter Buck. Once our game began they made all the right decisions and I was very fortunate to work with these two talented people.

I owe a special debt to the publisher of McClelland & Stewart, Douglas Gibson, for his instant enthusiasm and ongoing guidance.

Finally, thanks to Wilma, Doug, Nancy Anne, and Brett, who, as always, gave me their support and understanding from the opening face-off to the final siren.

INDEX